GHOSTS &
HAUNTINGS

GHOSTS & HAUNTINGS

DENNIS BARDENS

SENATE

Ghosts & Hauntings

First published in the UK in 1965 by
The Zeus Press, London, England.

This edition published in 1997 by Senate,
an imprint of Senate Press Limited,
133 High Street, Teddington,
Middlesex TW11 8HH, United Kingdom

3 5 7 9 10 8 6 4

ISBN 1 85958 518 3

Printed and bound in Guernsey by
The Guernsey Press Co Ltd

For MARIE and PETER

ACKNOWLEDGMENTS

In a work of this character research extends over so wide a field that it is not possible to acknowledge one's gratitude to every individual informant. To the many people at home and abroad who have aided me in my task, often going to considerable trouble to supply the answers to my questions, I extend my sincere thanks. I am especially grateful to the many newspapers and magazines which have published my appeal for informants who have had paranormal experiences to come forward, to the editors of the *PLA Monthly* and *Nautical Magazine* for publishing my appeal for nautical ghosts, and to Her Majesty's Stationery Office and Mr. Peter N. Woods for permission to quote from *Soldier* magazine. And I would like to thank Miss Dawn Tindall, Librarian of the Reform Club, for her patient response to my sometimes difficult bibliographical queries; Dr. George Morey, Ll.D. for much useful advice and Mrs. Vivienne Semmence for help with research.

DENNIS BARDENS

PREFACE

On a summer evening in 1993 Sir Michael Layard, the Second Sea Lord, was giving a dinner party to sixteen guests in his home in the Royal Naval College at Greenwich. A steward, Mrs Christine Turner, cleared the table on to a large silver tray and walked out on to the landing by the staircase on her way to the kitchen. Sensing something strange she glanced around and was surprised to see a tall figure in a black ankle-length coat looking into a corner cabinet. The figure turned and briefly their eyes met. Slowly he began to mount the staircase and vanished before her eyes.

Like others before she had met a ghost. The phantasm is believed to be that of Admiral John Byng (1704-57) who was court-martialled and shot in Portsmouth Harbour, England, for mishandling his fleet in the engagement with the French. It was his fate which made Voltaire observe that 'the English like to shoot an admiral now and again to encourage the others'.

However bizarre accounts of ghosts and hauntings may seem to those who have never experienced them, the fact remains that such phenomena are being reported all the time, everywhere, and have been ever since recorded history began. And in endless variety. There are historic ghosts, phantasms attached to particular places, wandering spectres, ghostly sounds, weird and unexplained lights, and the noisy, racketeering ghosts known as poltergeists.

Not long ago a very odd thing happened at the Police Training College at Crewe in Cheshire, England. To quote from the Chief Inspector, from whom I sought information: 'The person who had this experience was, in fact, the eighteen-year-old son of a part-time employee. He apparently went to the snooker room alone early one evening and casually put the balls from the pockets on to the table in a random manner. He turned away briefly and heard a noise behind him. On turning round, all the balls were in their correct places on the table for the start of the game. Apparently he ran from the room to the bar and was as white as a sheet and would not return to the snooker room for the rest of the evening.'

The files of the Society for Psychical Research – the oldest body in the world devoted to objective enquiry into weird and arcane mysteries – and its equally worthy and active counterpart, the American Society for Psychical Research – contain countless examples of authenticated hauntings. Why and how such things happen we cannot be certain, but that they do is beyond question.

One of the most remarkable (and poignant) American cases that came to my notice was that of Mrs Maureen Hayter of Baltimore who, when living in Minnesota with her three children in November 1942, was awakened by a tremendous crash that shook the house. Dashing downstairs to find the cause, she found no break-in, earthquake or gale, and on returning to her bedroom, she encountered the shade of her husband, Commander Hubert Montgomery Hayter, U.S.N., looking affectionate but sad. She touched his cheek. 'It was so cold...' she told me. It was 30 November when her husband, Damage Control Officer on the heavy cruiser USS *New Orleans* was sunk in battle. He died after saving all his men.

It might surprise many to realize that there are more ghosts of living people than the dead. The late Dr Robert Crookall, a scientist who wrote many books on this strange phenomenon, mentions my own case – how my wife, with whom I was sleeping in a lonely Cornish farmhouse, shook me awake, in terror, having awakened to see me standing by the bed looking down on myself! I remarked irritably and sleepily that she had very little to grumble about, having 'got two for the price of one'.

The ASPR has recorded the case of Mrs McCahen who, visiting the Grand Canyon with her husband, saw a lady with whom she had done jury service a year before, walk with her husband and their son up to a cabin. Supposing them to be tired, she decided it would be best not to visit them until the following morning. On doing so, she was astounded to discover that they had only just arrived.

A most remarkable recording I possess is that in which a ghost was seen by four people all at the same time. At 2.30 am on 20 November 1965, my son Peter Bardens was returning from a concert with the rest of the group (The Cheynes) in Portsmouth, England. Peter was driving the van. As they passed through the Surrey village of Cobham, drummer Mick Fleetwood let out a piercing scream. He had seen the shade of a very tall man in a long coat, 'slightly fluorescent'. Peter, glancing backwards, saw it too. The other two members of the group, guitarist Peter Green and bassist David Ambrose also saw it. I recorded all four separately. Their accounts tally. As Mick Fleetwood told me: 'I was petrified...absolutely petrified'.

What lies behind it all? Do these mysteries smack of the impossible? Well, armies of astronomers look out on ghosts day and night. Their telescopes permit them to see in vivid 'reality' not what is but what was. They see what no longer exists. Andromeda, the nearest galaxy, is two million light-years away. They see nothing spooky in that. The further they probe into space, the further they witness the non-existent.

Dennis Bardens
The Savage Club
1 Whitehall Place
London SW1A 2HD
England

CONTENTS

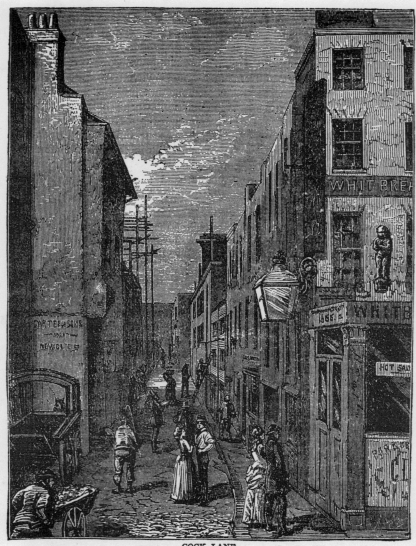

COCK LANE.

Cock Lane, an obscure turning between Newgate Street and West Smithfield, was, in 1762, the scene of one of the most celebrated ghost stories of all time (see page 97).

It has long been in my mind to write a serious book about ghosts and hauntings, but like many human intentions, its performance has been delayed by numberless preoccupations, distractions and the clamour of prosaic priorities.

There is mystery and awe, as well as humour, in the subject. Only the atheist says positively—and perhaps he protests too much—that there is no after-life; that death is death, the end of everything for the individual, the end of hopes and fears, pain and joy, achievement and frustration.

But atheists are in a minority. Even the agnostics, while maintaining that the absence of proof of survival after death precludes its acceptance, qualify that rejection by keeping an open mind on the subject.

For me the fascination of ghosts and apparitions lies in the hint such stories and accounts give of uncharted shores. Steering a middle course between superstitious credulity and dogmatic scepticism, it is possible to approach this subject with objective curiosity touched, let us hope, with humility. For before the great mystery of life and death it will do us no harm to acknowledge that there is much we do not know, still more that remains for us to discover and a great deal which, by reason of our limitations and the short duration of our lives, will for ever remain a mystery.

Although I have a few books to my credit, and have both edited and written hundreds of factual programmes for the radio and television, my basic training is that of a journalist. A journalist is a collector of facts. After long experience he can compare sources, form judgements on the reliability or otherwise of informants and sources of information, and, without losing his humanity, remain to some degree detached from his subject. The search for truth can be satisfying in itself.

But beyond the pleasure of investigating a subject which offers as vast a scope as this, there are more personal reasons for wishing to separate fact and folk-lore, for exploring the dark labyrinths of the arcane and the occult. There have been several times in my own life when I have been conscious of what I can for the moment only describe as contact with or awareness of another dimension, an unknown, indefinable, immeasurable force or manifestation defying appraisal by any known criteria.

My first experience of a 'ghost' (we will come to grips with attempts at definition later) was in very early childhood, when I was living with my brother, sister and foster-parents in a two-storied house in Southsea.

There was something 'not quite right' about that house: a brooding sense of menace would settle, as darkness fell, like an enveloping cloak. The back-garden walls of the houses on the opposite side of the road served also as the boundary of a huge cemetery, and from the windows of the top front rooms of our house we could see, often in the fitful moonlight, a forbidding panorama of greenish-white tombstones, angels holding laurels aloft, and sometimes an ostentatious granite vault half concealed by trees whose branches swayed and sighed in the breeze.

Opposite the front door of this Victorian house was a staircase leading to a landing which gave access to the upstairs bedrooms, and a box-room which was reached by a particularly narrow passage. My brother and I shared a bed near the window of a ground floor back room facing the garden. The window had old-fashioned Venetian blinds of wooden slats, usually left open to admit a good deal of light.

I was lying in bed one morning (the feeble glow of early dawn was just filtering through the slats of the Venetian blinds) when I awakened suddenly from my sleep. I heard a voice say 'put your hands up' and saw, swirling *down* from above me the vague form of a face, dark and shadowy with eyes of near-luminescence. I wanted to call out to my brother, who lay sleeping by my side, but found I could not speak. I seemed to be frozen into immobility, but my arms, with no effort on my part, rose slowly into the air until I could see both my hands above my head. The figure, or presence, hovered for a fraction of a minute, then slowly faded away. As it did so my arms dropped to my sides. Able to move now, I shook my brother awake and told him what I had experienced. 'It was a bad dream,' he said, irritably, and went to sleep again. A bad dream is what I knew everyone would call it, and so the following day I kept the disturbing memory of it to myself. I can offer no explanation for it.

A few years later, when I had graduated to the box-room

upstairs, reached by the staircase and a passageway, I had yet
another strange experience in that house. There was no light
in the hall, and when I went to bed earlier than the rest, some
chink of light was usually allowed through the partly-opened
door of the downstairs room. But on this occasion the door
was closed and both the stairway and passage entirely dark.

On reaching the top of the stairs, the first lap, so to speak,
to the bedroom, I stopped dead in my tracks. In the inky black-
ness, near the skirting, I espied two points of light. For a brief
second I thought that mice might be the cause—although we
never saw mice in that house—until, with a terrible sinking of
the stomach, I realised that the two points were about as evenly
spaced as *human* eyes. In that second something snapped and,
screaming my head off, I jumped, in my terror, the entire
flight of stairs.

Whatever the causes of those two experiences, which were
in due course submerged, as childhood memories are, by other
and happier thoughts and experiences, they have made me, in
retrospect, place them against similar occurrences.

Many years later, when I was a newspaper reporter, and in
my early twenties, I was staying with some friends in Highgate.
In the double bedroom I shared with one of them we both
awoke simultaneously at dead of night. The windows were wide
open and the moonlight was streaming in. But the room seemed
supercharged with *something*, a sense of presence, and in a
particular spot near the door. We both felt the sense of the
uncanny and of terror but, keeping as calm as I might, I got
out of bed, went over to the door and switched on the electric
light.

It didn't go on. In that second, as I pulled the switch down,
a great flash of light came from and *around* the electric bulb,
as though a pile of magnesium powder had been suddenly ig-
nited without the glare disappearing as suddenly as it would
normally do. But the strangest and most unnerving thing is
what followed. The light around the bulb swirled, moved,
changed its outline and form and then floated at great speed
out of the open window!

My friend and I were white and shaken, utterly shattered
by this extraordinary happening. We had both felt and seen
the same thing; *something* had been in that room, and we both
had the feeling that we had been prevented, in some strange
way, from switching the light on. Impatiently I turned the
electric light switch up and down. Nothing happened. 'The
bulb must have gone' I said, without overmuch conviction.

With the coming of dawn, one's nightly fears seemed absurd and cowardly. Of course, I reasoned now, there must have been an electrical fault. I flicked the switch. On went the light, as though nothing had been amiss. I stood upon a chair, detached the electric light bulb and inspected it. The filament was undamaged and firm between its two glass supports (sometimes a filament becomes detached from one point and waves like an antennae; it continues to light so long as it rests correctly on its supporters, but flickers or breaks light when it vibrates; but this was not so in this case).

I then carefully examined the brass end of the bulb, which fits into the socket, as well as the socket itself. There was no fault, no looseness of screws or of the spring plungers which ensure a tight fit. There was nothing wrong with the flex—no bending, kinking, twisting or fraying. There was no tell-tale carbon to indicate a short circuit.

Far from reassuring us, the inspection left us more puzzled than ever.

Next—to the room of a flat in Kensington which was the home of my wife, son and myself for many years. It was an exceptionally large room with steel-framed windows running along one side of it. I slept on a studio couch to avoid disturbing others when I had been working very late into the night.

One night, as I was undressing, the room became pervaded with a strong smell of violets. The scent was so powerful and unmistakable that I was utterly bewildered. What on earth could it be? Nobody in that household used anything remotely suggestive of violet perfume, which I dislike anyway. Neither our talcum powder nor soap was scented with it, while my wife, a sparing user of perfume, doesn't like or use violet perfume at all. As I undressed, the perfume grew stronger and stronger, and as I moved towards the couch it seemed to follow me. I gave it no more thought, and slept soundly.

In that same room, on another occasion, my son, then only four years old, was sleeping on a made up bed in the corner because we had guests staying with us. I was awakened during the night by the most terrible screams from his corner of the room. His terror was so great that, awakened from my sound sleep, I was almost paralysed by the noise, and with difficulty made my way to the electric light switch. My boy had felt something bending over him.

It was only when we had left that flat that my wife said to me: 'Do you realise that you have been sleeping in a haunted room?' She then told me of the experience of a friend of mine, an accountant, to whom I had lent this room when I had been out of town on an assignment. He was a level-headed Yorkshireman never given to excitable displays, or morbid misgivings; a normal, optimistic and extremely shrewd accountant whose work in life was to think and act in exact and tangible terms. He worked with the Ministry of Supply in Sheffield, and always stayed with us on his infrequent visits to London.

It seems that he awoke in this room at night to see, looming over him, a semi-human form, a sort of amorphous, cloud-like form of a substance reminiscent of black smoke. The experience, he told my wife, was uncanny though not unnerving; he hoped to observe it longer but after moving away from the couch it hovered for a few more seconds and then faded away. My wife did not tell me about it at the time. 'After all,' she told my friend, sensibly enough, 'flats are hard to find, and he does sometimes sleep there.'

It was in this same room that the previous occupant, who had been ill a long time, committed suicide by throwing herself through the window on to the courtyard below. I never did get round to discovering whether she used violet perfume. It would have been interesting to know.

It is not irrelevant, perhaps, to mention a strange phenomenom in which I was supposed to have figured, but which I did not myself see. It happened when my wife and I were on holiday in Liskeard, Cornwall. We were sleeping together in the room of a lonely farmhouse, when, in the dead of night, my wife shook me awake. She was in a terrible state of fright. She had, she declared, awoken to see me standing by the bed. She said 'what are you doing out of bed at this time of night?' but the next second realised that I was dressed and appeared, so to speak, to be self-illuminated in an otherwise nearly pitch dark room. Then, in a nasty moment of revelation, she suddenly realised that I was there, sound asleep, beside her. I was looking down upon myself!

Nothing has ever shaken my wife in her conviction that she was wide awake and saw what she saw. Again, I have no explanation to offer.

There was also the very uncanny experience which befell us both when, on the outbreak of war, we helped a party of people to evacuate some German refugee children to a house in Surrey. Built at the beginning of the twentieth century, and standing in well-kept gardens, the rambling red-brick house in neo-Tudor style had been built around an organ. A large central hall, from which the rooms opened, was empty except for the dais on which the organ once stood. There was a running gallery, looking on to this hall, on the first floor, on to which the doors of the bedrooms, opened. Each had heavy double doors.

We were all dog-tired when at last we retired to bed (my wife and I had a small room to ourselves on the first floor) and were asleep in no time. But at about one o'clock in the morning I was rudely awakened by the slow, measured and extremely noisy tread of what I took to be a night watchman immediately above me. The footsteps were heavy and deliberate, such as a well-built man with heavy boots might make tramping on an uncarpeted floor. The noise wakened my wife, too, and we tried unavailingly to ignore it and get to sleep. After a while an unpleasant thought occurred to both of us: a night watchman wouldn't be patrolling that tiny bit of floor all *that* time. And anyway, whose 'night watchman?' There wasn't one. We discovered that the two children in that room, aged six and eight respectively, had slept soundly—and their light shoes couldn't have made the noise we heard. But for obvious reasons we kept this puzzling experience to ourselves.

Another, and immensely more terrifying experience, came my way in 1945, when I was investigating the disappearance of a woman in Prague, who had been murdered by the Nazis. I did not see her but had a distinct feeling that she was in my hotel room one night—and a very unpleasant experience it was. This story I relate at greater length in the course of this book.

Now I am aware that, related in this brief sort of way, the experiences I have outlined might suggest to different readers quite different explanations.

It could be argued that my childhood experiences were occasioned by ill health or the over-imaginativeness to which children are occasionally subject. But this would hardly explain the happenings in the room of my flat, which were noted by *three* different people—myself, my son and my friend—at totally different times.

It is my hope that from the stories, facts and arguments in the chapters that follow, the reader will form his own conclusions and postulate his own alternatives; for in the whole subject of ghosts and hauntings we have something very important, taxing the imagination and offering a challenge to the questing mind. It is a subject in exploring which, rigidity of thinking, fixed ideas, attempts to standardise situations and information, are as unrewarding as they are absurd.

What are ghosts? Do they exist wholly in the mind of the percipient or have they separate existence? Why do some people see ghosts and others never at all? How is it that 'psychic' or paranormal phenomena occur at different times, in the same place, to quite different people having no contact one with the other? How is it that ghosts appear almost invariably to be clothed (only one nude ghost figures in this book)? And why period dress? Common sense dictates that clothes wear out even in—assuming there to be such a place—the 'spirit world'.

And why do ghosts so frequently follow the course of long-vanished tracks? There are innumerable accounts of ghosts walking above or below the existing level of the ground, disappearing through solid walls and doors, descending or climbing stairways which were long since destroyed. The famous ghost of Drury Lane disappears through a wall where a door once stood, while Mr. Bassett-Green, who gave the Godiva statue to the City of Coventry, described to me how he once saw the shadow of a monk walking *above* the level of the road near which an abbey once stood.

Other questions arise. By what criteria do places become haunted? Surely not simply emotional disturbance or fearful tragedy. The soil of Europe is soaked in human blood; there are battlefields where hundreds of thousands of men have perished in every circumstance of agony and hardship, yet these are not 'haunted' in the accepted meaning of the word. In how many cases of hauntings is there an element of corroboration, either from contemporaries or those who have gone before and left authentic, acceptable records? Can such eerie happenings originate in the mind of the beholder—after all, certain illnesses and certain drugs can induce hallucinations? Do inanimate objects, such as furniture and buildings, become imbued with *something* of the emotional charge generated by people who have been there; and is this something, whatever it is, picked up by certain sensitive people, by some process comparable with what we call telepathy?

And what is the definition of a ghost? With what requirements must a shade or phantasm comply to justify the terms? Would it include a ghost heard but not seen, such as the ghostly footsteps I have described? Or the 'ghost' which I merely sensed, but neither saw nor heard, in Prague?

Clearly, we must consider some details of the senses by which such happenings are perceived. How fallible is our eyesight? Can we trust what we 'see?' Or hear? Here, again, we must preserve some measure of humility, for while much is known of the nature of the human brain, and new frontiers are being extended, its workings are still very much a mystery.

The fact remains that ghosts have been seen and described since the dawn of written history. There is no country without them. The Society for Psychical Research, which has collected and investigated unusual phenomena for nearly a century, has found, after painstaking research, that there *is* a positive element of the unexplained and unexplainable concealed among the many stories and reports of ghosts and hauntings.

The humour and ridicule which the mention of ghosts so often incite is an indication of man's deep-rooted fear of them. For, like whistling in the dark, men joke most habitually at those things which worry or puzzle them most. Women are the butt of constant jest because they cannot be understood and their wiles are feared. 'Sick' humour which mocks illness and death can be similarly explained. Madness, which most normal people fear, has an abundance of humorous words to describe it—loony, up the pole, round the bend, daft, barmy and so on.

So too, the innumerable jokes about ghosts tell their own story. Man is frightened of ghosts and the supernatural. Should he be?

Reform Club,   DENNIS BARDENS
*Pall Mall, S.W.*1

Is there 'something in it?'

According to the dictionary a ghost is 'an apparition, wraith, disembodied spirit of the dead, manifesting itself to the senses of the living.' A prosaic description indeed of the manifestation fraught with undertones of past tragedy, of the nameless terror which can grip the observer or the labyrinthine mystery of the unknown.

The definition describes one type of ghost, but has limitations, being based on certain premises not acceptable to everyone; for example, there are some who do not accept the proposition that anything survives death. Furthermore the word 'spirit' is often used as something synonymous with a ghost hence the phrase 'to give up the ghost' (to die) and the references in the New Testament to the 'Holy Ghost' (meaning spirit). To say, therefore, that a ghost is a spirit is tantamount to saying that a ghost is a ghost.

To those who ask about ghosts and ghost stories 'is there something in it?' the answer must be a categorical 'yes'. What ghosts are, in what circumstances or surroundings they are most likely to be seen, whether ghosts have anything in common as ghosts (e.g. bees differ from each other, but all have wings); whether they are benign or malignant, and whether certain types of people are more prone to see ghosts than others—these are separate though legitimate questions which I will explore later.

There has never been a literature of any country, in any period, without numerous mentions of ghosts and hauntings. Plutarch and Pliny, Socrates and Cicero, all the writers of the ancient world took the existence of ghosts for granted. Even today Britain has no less than 150 castles which are reputed to be haunted, while the proceedings of the Society for Psychical Research, covering records of ghosts, hauntings and paranormal phenomena collected and investigated over seventy years, would fill several shelves. Admittedly only the most fervent psychical researcher could ever find enough time to read through

them all, but those records contain enough to defy ordinary
explanation—or even any explanation at all—and bemuse the
sceptic.

And it must be remembered that the SPR was founded, pri-
marily, as a sceptic society. It attempted to define standards, to
measure and assess the imponderable, to make evidence and
information conform as nearly as possible to scientific standards
and controls. It was founded in 1882 by some Cambridge schol-
ars who felt that the subject justified a sober, questing, scientific
approach. The president was Henry Sidgwick, professor of
moral philosophy in the university of Cambridge. His other supporters included Edmund Gurney, F. W. H. Myers, Andrew
Lang, Professor Barrett, Mrs. Sidgwick, F. Podmore, Lord Tenny-
son the poet, Lord Rayleigh and Professor Adams. Many famous
men have been numbered among the society's presidents, including Professor Balfour Stewart, A. J. Balfour, Professor William
James of Harvard and Sir William Crookes.

The scientific status of these men and of such presidents
as Sir Oliver Lodge, Bishop Boyd Carpenter, Professor Henri
Bergson and Professor Gilbert Murray is an indication of the
fascination and interest aroused by the subject in the serious-
minded.

The Society gave itself a clear mandate:

1. An examination of the nature and extent of any influence
which may be exerted by one mind upon another, apart from
any generally recognised mode of perception.

2. The study of hypnotism and the forms of so-called mes-
meric trance, with its alleged insensibility to pain; clairvoyance
and other allied phenomena.

3. A critical revision of Reichenbach's researches with certain persons called 'sensitive', and an inquiry whether such
persons possess any power of perception beyond a highly exalted
sensibility of the recognised sensory organs.

4. A careful investigation of any reports resting on strong
testimony regarding apparitions at the moment of death, or
otherwise, or regarding disturbances in houses reputed to be
haunted.

5. An inquiry into the various physical phenomena commonly called spiritualistic; with an attempt to discover their
causes and general laws.

6. The collection and collation of existing materials bearing
on the history of these subjects.

In effect, this simple yet broad mandate was intended to
separate legend from fact, to discover what remained by the

time allowance was made for crude superstition, the predisposition or mental instability of sick people, and sheer credulity. A big task indeed, for psychic research cannot rigidly be confined to ghosts and hauntings; it impinges inevitably on other related subjects. A phantasm of the living may involve telepathy. The person seen is *en rapport* with the seer, such as in clairvoyance, spiritualism, magic, hypnotism, and so on.

It must not be supposed that psychic research is the monopoly of the moderns. In the ancient world, both Paul and the money-mad Croesus were psychical researchers. Saul effected a disguise before his séance with the witch of Endor; Croesus tested with scepticism the oracles of Greece. Saint Augustine wrote long and learnedly on the whole subject of apparitions and so did numerous sixteenth-century authors, including the philosopher Ludwig Lavater (1527-86). The English mystic poet and artist, William Blake, saw angels sitting on the branches of trees. King Charles sent three officers to Edgehill, following complaints by local inhabitants that the Battle of Edgehill, fought there in 1642 between cavaliers and roundheads, was re-enacted there by ghostly armies with as much noise as was made by the original conflict.

In 1663 a researcher called Glanvill investigated, on the spot, the strange and even droll case of the 'knocking drummer of Tedworth' who haunted the house of a magistrate, Mr. Monpesson, following the confiscation of his drum. Thereafter a ghostly tattoo was beaten, together with a noisy demonstration as might be made by a guard breaking up.

Throughout the centuries, then, the sceptical, the scientific and the credulous have attempted to solve the mystery of ghosts and hauntings. There are theories, but no proofs, as to *why* things happen. But that the incidence of such happenings exceeds the laws of probability, and that their number establishes that there *is* something to investigate, is beyond dispute.

One important landmark in the history of psychical research was the Census of Hallucinations conducted by the Society for Psychical Research in 1889-90. One important question asked was: 'Have you ever, when believing yourself to be completely awake, had a vivid impression of seeing or being touched by a living or inanimate object, or of hearing a voice; which impression, so far as you can discover was not due to any external physical cause?'

The questionnaire was given a very wide circulation, and of 17,000 replies received about ten per cent answered 'yes'. One curious discovery, which emerged from an analysis of the replies, was that hallucinations of living persons were twice as numerous as those of the dead; furthermore, the number of instances in which the ghosts of dead people had appeared elsewhere at the moment of their deaths was no less than 440 times that which could be expected according to the law of probabilities and sound mathematical deduction.

That Census established not only the extraordinary prevalence of ghosts and hauntings in Britain, but the fact that apparently normal people see such things. The obviously neurotic, the sick, mentally disordered or those whose customary objectivity and common sense might have been shaken by some emotional upheaval or shock, were specifically excluded.

I myself had, I remember, quite a surprise when I embarked on a survey of my own, as a basis for a radio documentary on ghosts for the British Broadcasting Corporation. I put a small classified advertisement in *The Times*, asking anyone who had seen a ghost to get in touch with me. Not wishing to be bothered at my place of work or at home by the inevitable practical jokers and crackpots who answer such appeals as well as the more serious-minded, I gave the address and telephone number of a secretarial agency. My instructions to the agency were to take the name and address of any telephone caller and pass it on to me. Letters, of course, were forwarded to me. The advertisement was displayed at the top of the 'Personal' column, and attracted the notice of news agencies, which in turn cabled a story about it and brought me many letters from abroad. To correspondents and telephone callers I sent a letter explaining what my purpose was, and a questionnaire which I invited them to complete and return to me. These questionnaires continued queries which would enable me, in similar cases, to find some common factor; there were also certain questions designed to eliminate practical jokers and those who had recently suffered from bereavement, emotional distress or who were constantly 'seeing things'. I do not say that the testimony of certain ultra-sensitive types, more accustomed to seeing ghosts than others, is without value. But the evidence of self-possessed, phlegmatic people, manifestly in full possession of their normal faculties, was to be preferred—and more especially where some degree of corrobration could be established. Among the questions I asked were: How long did the ghost stay? Did it move? Did it speak? Have you seen anything like it before? Had you heard of any legend or story attaching to the place, which might have made you predisposed to see something? Did anybody with you see it at the same time? And so on.

I was astonished at the flood of replies which reached me. In the course of one day alone over forty telephone calls were received, while the letters ran into hundreds. They ranged from a letter from a rector's wife telling me of two 'resident' ghosts in a rectory near Newbury, Berkshire to another from a housewife at Burton-on-the-water who had bought a chair at an auction sale and found that there was a man to go with it—a genial, pipe-smoking old gentleman whose shade was seen by herself and two of her children. From abroad—Germany, France, Spain, the U.S.A. (for the *New Yorker* had repeated the advertisement)—came an impressive flood. In short, if there were no fires, there was certainly much smoke.

In the field of psychic research, there are some who have given these matters more attention than others, but strictly speaking there are no 'experts' in the accepted sense. The amateur is as likely to reach useful and valid conclusions as the habitual ghost-hunter. Even so, it is interesting to note that those who study such matters under objective and controlled conditions (that is, approaching the subject with an open mind, and with due precautions against self-deception or deception by others) have also reached the conclusion that there is, decidedly, 'something in it'.

Professor Henry Price, Emeritus Professor of Logic at Oxford, believes in haunted houses and apparitions. He told a conference of Modern Churchmen at Oxford a few years ago that 'there really are haunted houses'. There were, he said, apparitions of the dead and of the living. He thought that apparitions of the dead are either the effect of the thought and emotions of a human personality surviving death or are caused by the influence of past thoughts and emotions which somebody had when alive.

Professor Hornell Hart, an American sociologist of Duke University, is equally convinced that superstition, gullibility and mere bad health cannot be accepted as the sole reasons for hallucinations and paranormal experiences. He considers that there is evidence that the human spirit can leave the body during sleep and travel to distant places, where it can be seen by other people before returning to its 'home'. He has in his possession a very large number of cases, and at Newnham College, Cambridge, presented no less than 165 well-attested cases of apparitions of the living and the dead.

Professor Hart has said 'If I saw a ghost in this room, the chances are that you would see it too. This is proof that most apparitions are not just the imaginings of the mind.'

One of the most remarkable cases in his archives is that of an American doctor, asleep on a steamer, who was suddenly assailed by the overpowering sensation of standing in his cabin looking down on his own body. He felt himself transported, then, to the room of a friend in New York who, astonished at his unheralded presence looked up and said 'But doctor, I thought you were a thousand miles away.'

The next day the doctor wrote to his friend describing his eerie experience and the deep and vivid impression it had made upon him. But *before his letter could reach its destination* he received a letter from his friend in New York. The New York man had awakened to see the doctor's ghost standing over him.

The point of that story is that there is two-sided corroboration; it rules out fantasy, indigestion, mental illness and other such causes.

The sort of ghostly experience which rules out any question of subjectivity—that is, that the thing seen emanates entirely from the person who does the seeing, whom psychic investigators would call, in their terminology, 'the percipient'—is the odd case of the Renishaw coffin. Renishaw, the country home of the Sitwell family, dates back to the seventeenth century and has been the scene of many weird happenings. In 1885, after a coming-of-age party for Sir George Sitwell, a guest (Miss Tait, one of the Archbishop of Canterbury's two daughters) complained that she had been terrified in her room, which was near the top of the staircase, by being kissed by a ghost. So adamant was she that she could not even contemplate spending the rest of the night in that room, preferring a made-up bed on a sofa in Miss Sitwell's room.

Sir George, of course, heard about the occurrence before the party dispersed, and in the course of a chat with his agent, Mr. Turnbull, mentioned it to him. Far from laughing about it, Mr. Turnbull, suddenly grave, revealed that on an occasion when the house had been lent to him for his honeymoon, a Miss Crane, sister of a famous artist of the same name and a guest in the house at that time, had had an identical experience in that same room.

Some time later it was decided to do away with the room and incorporate its space into the staircase itself. In the course of the reconstruction involved a strange discovery was made: between the joists of the floor of the room in which the ghostly occurrences had taken place, was found *an empty coffin*, without its lid. It bore traces of having held a body at some time, and from its manner of construction could be traced to the seventeenth century. But whose body it ever contained, or why it should have been placed underneath the floorboards of that bedroom, nobody has explained to this day. What is particularly interesting, however, is that different people at quite different times, not knowing each other and having heard nothing about the room, had an identical ghostly experience. Were the 'inanimate' furnishings of the room, or the substances and materials composing the room itself, imbued with some emotional imprint, or the thoughts of somebody in the past? And had these thoughts by a process of mental telepathy, given the guests the feeling of an actual experience? Or can telepathy be ruled out, and the proposition advanced that some presence or thing, a survival of the dead, visited or inhabited that room to the terror of its occupants? Whatever the answer, nobody could deny that there is 'something in it'.

The greatest number of people on record as having seen the same ghost is, I think, in respect of the ghost of a woman who haunted the house of Captain Paul Blaidsell on the coast of Maine, in 1793. A spectre appeared to him and his family, on the first occasion demanding that somebody fetch her father, David Hooper, as she wished to speak to him. Outlandish though the request seemed, the father was fetched, and declared that from her voice and her manner of expressing herself —and her knowledge of undisclosed family affairs—the phantom was that of his dead daughter.

No less than four members of the family saw and heard her at the same time, and her visits became increasingly frequent. At one time the family, tired and terrified of these activities, fled the house but the same fear that drove them away lured them back, for they feared the revenge and anger of a presence they could neither control nor understand.

These happenings became known to the Reverend Abraham Cummings, whose parish covered much of the coast of Maine, and in a spirit of scepticism, even of derision, he decided to visit the house and reproach its occupants for their flaunting supersititon and fear. But on the way to the house he saw a piece of rock levitate itself from the ground and become in the process a mass of light. Not unnaturally unnerved by this experience, he kept a wary eye on it as he passed and when he had gone a few yards he noted with amazement that the irridescent mass moved over to where he was walking and changed its shape to that of a woman.

For months the spectre of the Blaidsell home manifested

itself, delivering long harangues on local life and how people
should behave, and on one occasion no less than fifty people,
crowded into the cellar, heard and witnessed these phenomena.
The spectre, according to one account, passed through the rows
of spectators like a brigadier on an army inspection visit.

A strange thing about the haunting was that, most unusually,
the spectre spoke so much. She predicted the death of Lydia
Blaidsell in childbirth and once, in answer to an inquiry from
Captain Blaidsell as to his father's health, informed him that he
was dead. The prophecy of Lydia's death came to pass, while
Captain Blaidsell, who had no means of communication with
his father, who lived two hundred miles away, found that he
had, in fact, died.

Most churches and religions have some ritual or service
whose purpose is the pacification, 'laying' or expelling of
spirits from the places they appear to be haunting. So far as
England itself is concerned, such a service, known as 'exorcism'
is by no means uncommon. The ghost of an old lady who
haunted a house in Highworth-road, Bristol, a few years ago,
was exorcised by the Rev. F. Maddock. The reverend Tucker
Harvey, vicar of St. Michael's, Ipswich, prayed in an effort to
exorcise a house where a merchant seaman and his family were
haunted by the shade of a seaman dressed in the manner of
Nelson's day; Penny, one of his three children, wrote down a
description of him. The Rev. John Johnstone, vicar of Ashton
Keynes, Wiltshire, was asked in 1963 to exorcise a poltergeist
(noisy, mischievous type of spirit) from a caravan at Leigh,
near Cricklade, Wiltshire. The caravan shook and 'danced', objects inside it were thrown about and flew through the air.
A family which fled in terror from a poltergeist in a flat in
Peckham Park Road, Peckham, only returned after Mr. Stuart
Lawson, a visiting minister of Camberwell Spiritualist Centre,
had conducted a service of exorcism.

It would seem, too, that no special type of place attracts
ghosts. Places recently reported to be haunted include an aircraft factory, a motor-car factory, a council flat, a textile factory,
a pub, an ex-prisoners' hostel, a garage, a theatre, a churchyard, a barracks and a variety of the more traditional places
such as castles, mansions and historic buildings.

The prevalence of ghosts in Great Britain seems out of proportion to the alleged incidence of belief in them. An 'opinion
poll' a year or so ago revealed that only ten per cent of
people admitted to a positive belief in ghosts, eighty per cent
frankly avowing disbelief and the rest being undecided. I do

not feel, however, that such statistics need be taken very seriously. Most people would be required to give an answer in less time than would permit of serious consideration of the subject or even of accurate definitions; it is not unknown, either, for people approached out of the blue by public opinion poll canvassers to give an answer simply to get rid of the questioner. Perhaps, when giving a negative reply, they may have been echoing the celebrated the Marquise du Deffand who, in the eighteenth century, was also asked if she believed in ghosts. She replied: 'No, but I'm afraid of them.'

2

Reality or illusion?

In considering ghosts, hauntings and what are called 'paranormal' phenomena, it is fair to ask where illusion ends and reality begins. To what extent may we trust our senses? Hallucinations may be real to the beholder; the drunk in the throes of delirium tremens sees monster snakes, pink elephants and all manner of horrors; they are real to him, and his terror will be in simple proportion to that seeming reality. But does that fact give them a separate and tangible existence?

Let us take, as an example, a remarkable 'do-it-yourself' ghost outfit produced in the eighteenth century. It took the form of a large book (so far as I know, the only available copy is in the British Museum Library) called *Spectropia*. The pages consist of bold drawings, in several colours, of the desired 'spooks'. One, say, is a witch borne aloft on the traditional besom. The colours are so chosen that there is an easy complement in the opposite. Let us suppose the witch's malevolent features are coloured *red*, that the broom is *purple* and her trailing robe is coloured *brown*. The art of making your own ghost consists of gazing at one of these illustrations for a few seconds and then looking at some even-coloured surface—say a window, a wall or even the sky. On looking, say, at the sky you will see there, sure enough, the shade of the witch in full flight; her face is *green*, the broom is the correct *brown* and her robe is *purple*.

What happens is that the iris of the eye becomes tired of the colours in that illustration. White is composed of several colours, and if the eye is tired of one of them or a mixture of two, it sees the original outline in the complementary colours. To test this for yourself, take a postcard, draw a bold circle on it, and fill in the circle with green ink—a good, bold drawing ink or a solid matt poster colour. Look fixedly at this card and then at the sky. In the sky you will see a distinct circle of red or deep pink. For white is composed of red, yellow and blue. Green, the colour at which you were gazing, is a mixture of yellow and blue. Your eye, having temporarily tired of this mixture of yellow and blue and being less receptive to them, registered the one remaining constituent of white.

The point of this is that a 'ghost' or phantasm *can* be an illusion—which is not to say that because of it every ghost is an illusion.

Next, hypnotism and the power of suggestion. A person under hypnotism can be told by the operator that a person who *is* in the room is not there at all and the person under hypnotism will fail entirely to see him. Equally, he can be told that somebody who is absent is there, and immediately the flagrant illusion becomes flaunting reality.

In considering hypnotism one should remember the distinct possibilities of *self*-hypnotism. A person does not need to be in a trance to be hypnotised. If you read a book aloud, thereby occupying the conscious mind, and a hypnotist makes suggestions within the periphery of your hearing, you will have been subject to what is called 'waking hypnosis'. If you read a book aloud and play a tape recording in which suggestions of a simple and direct nature are repeated, again your conscious mind will be occupied and the hypnotic suggestion will enter your subconscious mind through the ear, without the 'censorship' normally exercised by the conscious mind.

Can a person, then, 'will' himself into seeing things? Can ritual, with its mystery (some might say mumbo jumbo) and mounting tension, induce hallucinations?

Consider the ghost summoned up by the extraordinary occultist known in Victorian times as Eliphas Levi, friend of Lord Lytton and author, amongst other works, of *Dogme et Rituel de la Haute Magie*. Levi, who was really Alphonse Louis Constant, and had studied both ancient and modern works on magic and the occult in many languages, claimed 'to have discovered the force by which all miracles divine and diabolical have been, and may still be, performed, to possess the key of prophecies ... to have recovered the claviculae of Solomon and opened without difficulty every door of the ancient sanctuaries where absolute truth seemed to slumber ...'

It was in the spring of 1854. Armed with letters of introduction and anxious to escape from the many distractions of Paris, where he was well known, Eliphas Levi came to London. But the occult was an obsession with him. He was sitting in his lodgings studying the Kabbalah when a curious note was delivered to him—the Seal of Solomon cut in half, together with a pencilled note which said: 'Tomorrow, at three o'clock, in

front of Westminster Abbey, the other half of this card will be
given to you.'

At the appointed time he met an elderly but distinguished-
looking grey-haired lady, who was waiting, veiled, in her carriage and displaying the other half of the card she had sent.
As they drove away she asked Levi to conduct a 'complete
evocation'—that is, an evocation of the dead or what we would
commonly call a spirit or ghost. She knew the secrecy with
which those adept in such arts concealed their knowledge from
the profane, and proved to him that she was familiar with
many 'degrees' in the occult sciences—each degree involving a
complicated initiation at the hands of other adepts, in circumstances of complete secrecy.

'She showed me,' says Levi, 'a collection of vestments and
magical instruments, even lending me certain curious books
which I was in want of; in a word, she determined me to
attempt at her house the experience of a complete evocation,
for which I prepared myself during twenty-one days, scrupu-
lously observing the rules laid down in the ritual.'

By July 24th all was prepared to evoke the phantom of
'the divine Apollonius'. And indeed the preparations were
elaborate.

'The cabinet prepared for the evocation was situated in a
turret; four concave mirrors were hung within it, and there
was a kind of altar whose white marble top was surrounded
with a chain of magnetic iron. On the marble the sign of the
Pentagram was engraved and gilded; the same symbol was
drawn on a new white sheep-skin stretched beneath the altar. In
the middle of the marble slab there was a small copper brazier
with charcoal of alder and laurel wood, while a second brazier
was placed before me on a tripod. I was vested in a white robe
very similar to those worn by Catholic priests, but longer and
more ample, and I wore upon my head a chaplet of vervain
leaves entwined about a golden chain. In one hand I held a
new sword and in the other the ritual.

'I set alight the two fires with the requisite and prepared
materials and I began, at first in a low voice, but rising by
degrees, the invocations of the ritual; the flame invested everything with a wavering light, and then went out. I set some more
twigs and perfumes on the brazier, and when the flame started
up again *I distinctly saw before the altar* a human figure,
larger than life, which dissolved and disappeared. I recommenced the evocations, and placed myself in a circle which I
had already traced between the altar and the tripod. I then

saw the depth of the mirror which was in front of me, but behind the altar, grow brighter by degrees, and a pale form grew up there, dilating and seeming to approach gradually. Closing my eyes, I called three times on Apollonius, and when I reopened them, a man stood before me wholly enveloped in a winding sheet which seemed to me more grey than white; his form was lean, melancholy and beardless, which did not quite recall the picture I had formed to myself of Apollonius. I experienced a feeling of intense cold, and when I opened my lips to interrogate the apparition, I found it impossible to utter a sound.'

Eliphas Levi, as the reader will gather, was a man of resource. He directed his magical sword towards the spirit, a hint not to frighten him but obey him. The form disappeared and being commanded to return touched Levi on the arm that held the sword, numbing it immediately as far as the shoulder. He had two questions to ask of the apparition, but for want of speech could only ask them mentally. One concerned a man known to his host, and in answer to his unvoiced question a sort of 'interior echo' answered 'dead!' Wishing, too, to know whether reconciliation and forgiveness were possible between two people in his thoughts, 'the same interior echo impiteously answered "Dead!" '

Levi maintained that he had stated facts as they occurred, and if his account is accurate we can believe him when he declares: 'the effect of this experience on myself was incalculable. I was no more the same man; something from the world beyond had passed into me.'

Levi admits in his account that the elaborate—and theatrical —preparations, the perfumes, the mirrors, the pantacles, could be 'a veritable intoxication of the imagination, which must act strongly on a person already nervous and impressionable.'

But having made this honest admission, he insists that his senses did not deceive him. 'I seek not,' he maintains, 'to explain by what physiological laws I have seen and touched; I assert solely that I have seen and touched, that I saw clearly and distinctly, without dreaming, which is sufficient ground for believing in the absolute efficacy of magical ceremonies.' He sounded a warning to those who might from curiosity or morbid excitement seek to follow his example: 'I look upon the practice ... as dangerous and objectionable ...'

Was the shade of Apollonius, so vividly described by Levi, a figment of his overwrought and overworked imagination or had the spirit of the Greek philosopher, who was born before the

Christian era, and who studied in the temple of Asclepius
(the god of medicine) at Aegae, been brought by mystic means
protesting from his grave? Putting it another way, had the impressionable and distinctly morbid Eliphas Levi succeeded in
hypnotising himself?

This leaves us with another interesting question: can the eye
see what is not there? To this the answer is a categorical 'yes'.
I have already illustrated this point by the references to
'*Spectropia*' and by instances of hypnosis. But what about
balanced, phlegmatic, normal people who have not been hypnotised, who have not been bemused by trick illustrations? Can
they, too, see things that are not there. Once again the answer
is 'yes'.

Mental pictures can be conjured up in the mind of any person of ordinary imagination. Try thinking of somebody you
know, and you will have a good 'inner picture' of them.

Can we, without getting too technical, ask ourselves this simple
question: admitting that the mind can conjure up mental
pictures (as happens, often with startling realism and gro-
tesque drama, in the course of dreams), what is to prevent the
mind *projecting that image forward to the eye*? Will not, then,
the eye see or seem to see what is not there?

Firstly, as to the mechanics of normal sight. Although the
cornea may be likened to the less ambitious sort of camera
lens, the retina, which may be compared to a photographic
plate, is not equally perceptive and sensitive all over. Photographic film is identical in the depth of its emulsion and its
composition and sensitivity, but whereas the centre of the retina
can transmit what it sees in immense detail, its millions of cells
sending their individual messages back to the brain, along individual nerve fibres, the surrounding patches are nothing like
as precise. One might compare the centre of the iris and the
surrounding areas in terms of telephone lines; the lines (nerve
fibres) in the centre are individual lines, while the rest are
'party lines' used by more than one subscriber, serving a whole
bunch of light-sensitive cells.

There is an analogy to be drawn between the television
camera and the human eye. The television camera, through
its photo-electric cells, transmits individual impulses, the 'vision'
or scene, back to the camera; these individual messages co-
ordinated into complete pictures but consisting really of
thousands of constantly-changing pieces in a moving mosaic,
can be seen in the small monitoring screen at the back of the
camera. The camera can't think up images and project them

forward ... but the mind can, as it does in the case of hallucinations.

The images we see—which are transmitted backwards by the optic nerves—and a type of valve, for which the medical term is synapse, ensures that these nerve impulses will travel only in the right direction and not backwards and forwards. Each nerve fibre has its own valves, set at intervals along the nerve. But it can happen, particularly under the influence of such drugs as mescal and opium, that the action of these valves or synapses is inhibited. The mind's conjecturings are transmitted forward to the retina, and then, like any other image in the retina, backwards again to the brain, where they are indistinguishable from reality.

I remember a remarkable experiment carried out by an artist, Basil Beaumont, before the war. A London hospital was experimenting with the effects of mescal, a drug used by the Aztecs to produce religious ecstasy and made from the roots of a cactus plant; it is in fact one of the few 'divine' plants known today; the soma of India which had amazing legendary properties, cannot now be identified; nor can the nooma of Persia.

Beaumont asked permission to be experimented upon, and it was granted. Rather optimistically, he took along with him brushes and paints, hoping to capture in graphic form whatever he might see while still under the influence of the drug. He entered the experimental room, lay on the couch provided, and doctors gathered round as a dose of mescal was injected into his left arm. I have before me a verbatim account of his experiences as he described them to me at the time:

'The experience was not a pleasant one. I felt myself slipping into a world which changed, gradually, its tone, colour and tempo. The change was gradual, and only when it had gone several stages did I experience a slight feeling of panic. The walls of the room, which were a neutral colour, were now tinged with red and were almost luminous, as though lit from behind by electric light. Then they seemed to recede, to move slightly, now changed to a greenish hue and to be exuding sound.

'Suddenly, all around me, the air became filled with the sinister beat of tom-toms, while above rose the concerted voices of invisible choirs singing the most wonderful music. I entered a world of madness and hallucination, but these hallucinations seemed at the time to be very real. The spectres and visions had a terrifying reality.

'I could hear the voices of the doctors, but they seemed to

take on a different tone, and, looking at them, I was shocked
to see them change form, becoming horrible monsters with
talons and hair and distorted limbs . . .'

Beaumont tried to scream, but was unable to do so. Told by
the doctor to put out his hand and look at it, he did so and
recoiled in horror; it withered before his eyes, becoming transformed into a monkey's paw! A curious feature of his hallucinations was that all the colours seemed to have sounds of their
own, sounds peculiar to each colour. Thus on hearing a type of
sound he was predisposed to see the colour associated with it.
All sense of time vanished. Incidents which seemed to him to
have happened in the flash of a second took, he found afterwards, over an hour, whereas experiences which seemed to
stretch into eternity lasted in reality only a matter of seconds.

The innocent garden into which the doctors led him appeared
to be a type of tropical jungle infested with the creeping,
crawling monstrosities of Bosch. There were buildings too, in
the Mexican style, juxtaposed, absurdly enough, with the tower
of a Salvation Army building. He remembered wondering at
the time how such a structure came to be in a jungle. The doctors accompanying him suddenly assumed the appearance and
role of priests, leading him firmly but with ceremonial precision
towards a sacrificial altar . . .

Enough of mescal. The brilliant play of colours which it
induced could equally have been brought about by another
drug, Indian hemp. Opium can induce hallucinations. Starvation sometimes has the same effect. I have simply given the
effects of mescal on *his* vision; others, notably Aldous Huxley,
have tried similar experiments. The point I am making is that
what a person sees is sometimes reality, at other times illusion
and on some occasions a mixture of both.

As there are something like a million nerve fibres from the
retina to the cortex, each with several synapses or valves, it
will be obvious to the most amateur engineer that there is ample
scope for things to go wrong. There is no equivalent in the
brain to the flat cinema screen receiving its projected image.
There are, indeed, an equivalent number of visual units in the
cortex, but there are ten thousand million cells in the brain,
with only some of which contact is made through the eye. In
face of a mechanism so immensely complex we must maintain a
certain humility. So much of its functioning remains a mystery even to those who have spent a lifetime in specialised study
of it.

Therefore, to the question 'are ghosts reality or illusion?'

my answer must be: there is scope for illusion in human observations, but even accepting this premise, it neither disposes of nor explains an immense number of strange, abnormal or weird occurrences.

3

Some varieties of hauntings

Before we explore particular types of haunting, it might be as well to establish at the outset how numerous the different categories are. Obviously, there are many stories which cannot be typed, nor am I concerned to create arbitrary classifications.

Nevertheless, there are groups of stories having something in common. There are poltergeists, for example; a distinctive and highly inconvenient and unnerving type of ghost, given to violent disturbances such as the lifting of tables and the smashing of crockery. There are the harbingers of death who, with pale minatory fingers and sightless eyes, beckon one to doom or bring their gloomy presage of the death of others. An example of this is provided by the late Mr. W. Bassett-Green, a wealthy quarry owner who gave to the City of Coventry its bronze statue of Lady Godiva.

Mr. Bassett-Green was staying at a house near Winchcombe. On coming from Winchcombe Station, and walking on his way home one November night, when it was fairly dark, he reached the hollow near the cemetery. Then as he told me: 'I had an uncomfortable feeling that someone was following me, but I couldn't see or hear anything. Suddenly, a tall, dark figure came along the middle of the road and overtook me, *walking about two feet above the ground.* I was so interested, thinking, well, I wonder what sort of boots the man's got to walk in the air like this. I was on the point of saying to him "for goodness sake come off the road, come on to the footpath before you're killed" (it was a main road) when he suddenly vanished into thin air.' Mr. Bassett-Green realised he had seen a ghost. He had been to see a cousin who was gravely ill, and hardly connected the two incidents until he got home. There he was given the news that his cousin had died a few hours after he had left him—at the time, in fact, of the strange visitation.

Mr. Green was a newcomer to the district, and knew nothing of previous reports of this same ghost having been seen. Old inhabitants were astonished that *he* should have been surprised.

'What!' they said, 'you've lived here nearly six years and you've never heard of the Winchcombe Ghost?' No, he said, he hadn't. He asked them to describe to him what they'd seen, and in each instance their description was the same as his experience: a tall figure, rather like a monk, walking above the level of the roadway.

Winchcombe is rich in history; it was a place of note even four thousand years ago. The skeletons of a chieftain and his family were found a few years ago in a barrow on Belas Knap, one of the highest points of the Cotswolds, near by. Here, too, King or Saint Kenelm was supposed to have been murdered by his ambitious sister or mother. Queen Catherine Parr, the last wife of Henry VIII, came to live at Winchcombe and married Lord Seymour the Lord High Admiral; her death gave rise to sinister surmises and only a few years ago her tomb was desecrated and the Queen's remains thrown into the fields near by. These were, of course, decently reinterred.

A magnificent abbey once graced the town and there have been many tales of music coming at midnight from the Abbey Church, and the sound of monks chanting.

I visited with Mr. Green the stretch of road where he had his strange experience. He told me that, knowing that dogs are sensitive to such things, he had thought of taking his own with him to the spot to notice her reaction. A neighbour strongly counselled him against such a foolish course, for another neighbour had once had the same idea and taken his dog. On reaching the spot the dog began to howl and growl at something it appeared to see but which was invisible to its master; then, losing its head completely, it raced off in terror and was never seen again.

Not long afterwards a husband and wife were walking along this road with their little daughter whose behaviour seemed rather strange. They asked the little girl what she was about, and she explained that she had bent down to stroke the head of a dog which was accompanying them, only to find that there was no dog there at all!

One former resident of Winchcombe contributed this interesting piece of corroboration of Mr. Bassett-Green's experience in a letter he wrote to him: 'At that time I was residing at Isbourne House, Winchcombe. I was walking home after visiting some friends at Postlip Villas on the Cheltenham Road. It was a clear, frosty night in the winter of 1929-30. I was a little way down the Pyke Bank when something caused me to look around. To my surprise I saw what appeared to be a

monk. I spoke to him but could get no answer. We were now
walking side by side on the left-hand side of the road going
towards Winchcombe. We rounded the bend at the foot of Pyke
Bank, still walking side by side.

'About fifty yards along the road the monk turned left and
walked into Mr. Forty's field and disappeared. Later, when I
spoke about my weird experience, I was told that that particular stretch of road was known as "the monk's walk". I only
wish my father were alive to tell you this himself, but I
can assure you that he was not the type of man to imagine
things.'

Mr. Bassett-Green made further inquiries among local residents and found plenty of corroboration for the story of the
Winchcombe Ghost. One story he related to me concerned two
local men who resolved to rob an orchard near by. It was a
moonlight night, and the conspirators arrived on the scene
just before midnight. The Winchcombe man was up one tree,
busy 'scrumping' and his mate was up another about twenty
yards away, when a tall, dark figure hove into view and made
for the very trees in which they were hiding. Quickly the elder
warned the other: 'Look out. There's a bobby coming.' But as
they cowered, still as death, behind the thickest of the foliage,
both were appalled to see the spectre of a monk, through
whose transparent body and garments the trees behind him
could clearly be discerned. When the ghost disappeared, the
older man scrambled down to look for his mate, who had,
however, fallen from the tree in his fright, taken to his heels
and ran. His terror was so great that he swore his hair stood
on end to such an extent that his cloth cap was lifted by it!

It is related of a cyclist that, when approaching that part
known as Margrett's Hollow, he was mystified by the fact that
his bicycle would not respond to the routine foot pressure on
the pedals. There seemed no mechanical explanation for it.
With a strange shivering down his spine, the cyclist dismounted
and inspected his machine; the chain had not disengaged, the
tyres were as fully inflated and sound as ever, but the wheels
turned reluctantly and only by force on their axles, and would
simply not respond to pressure on the pedals. Now thoroughly
frightened, and oppressed by an inexplicable sense of menace
verging on panic, the man mounted the machine and tried
again. It was hopeless, as though some invisible force were determined that he should not proceed on his way. He had no
choice but to *drag* the machine for a distance—and by the time
he got to the other side of the decline the restraint or obstruc-

tion ended, the wheels moved smoothly and normally, everything was as before.

The Winchcombe Ghost fits two categories. Appearing as it did at the moment of the death of Mr. Bassett-Green's friend, it may be classed in this instance as a death visitant. But it is also a 'local, resident' ghost—meaning that over the years it has appeared sporadically and to different people.

A more spectacular example of a death visitant may lie behind a strange, almost incredible story told to me in the spring of 1964. It concerns the death of Marilyn Monroe.

I was convalescing in a country home after a severe illness, and noticed a young man who had been admitted after taking an overdose of sleeping pills. He looked thin, rather withdrawn and sad. I found him wandering, quiet and aloof as ever, in a lonely country lane, and as we walked along together I told him I was writing a book about ghosts. Suddenly he seemed more alert and interested.

'I have a story I could tell you—one that happened only recently to me,' he said, 'but the trouble is, I don't suppose you would believe me. You'd say I was crackers.'

'I wouldn't say any such thing,' I assured him, 'tell me about it.'

His experiences first started when he was working as a switchboard operator with two other men in a London hospital.

'Suddenly I felt terribly ill and began vomiting for no reason at all, exclaiming to my friend at the same time: "My God! Marilyn!" He tended me sympathetically, and as I recovered from the oppression and nausea, I remarked to him: "That was a strange thing for me to say. Why on earth should I say that?" "I was wondering that, too," he replied.'

The following day, when he read his morning paper, my informant made an extraordinary discovery. At the time he had been taken violently ill and uttered her name, Marilyn Monroe, the lovely film star, had taken the poison from which she died.

My informant had never seen Marilyn Monroe on the cinema; he was in no sense a fan of hers or particularly interested in her. There was no reason why she should have been in his mind at all.

'After that,' he told me, 'I dreamed about her every night; a blonde lady in cycling shorts, of extraordinary charm and beauty. I mentioned this odd circumstance to a friend, who suggested that I go to a spiritualist meeting at John Street, Bloomsbury. I did so, and ever since, although this will sound very strange to you, I have missed her; I've had a sense of being cut off from somebody to whom I was very close. Of course, I had a good deal of ribbing from workmates to whom I told my story; after all, Marilyn was an internationally-famous star, a famous beauty, and I don't pretend to good looks.

'Well, at another spiritualist meeting, a clairvoyant picked me out. She didn't know me, and I'd never met her before. She told me that I was missing somebody who had passed over, and I said that was true. She saw me cycling with somebody (very strange that, for I had dreamed continually of cycling with Marilyn). Curious to see what others without a clue about myself could tell me, I attended another meeting. This time the clairvoyant said: "Somebody has jumped over you. You haven't long to wait now. Did your clock stop?" When I got home, I discovered an amazing thing, and remarked upon it to my wife: *both our clocks had stopped at twenty minutes to twelve.* My wife was scared, and so was I. For that was the time at which the clairvoyant had asked about our clocks. My wife hadn't been out—nobody could have slipped in to alter the hands or stop the clocks, in order to create an impression and, of course, it wouldn't have paid anyone to do it even if they wished.

'One night at home I heard a voice in my room saying "Eddie, I want you in my ward. I'm doing a film here." I don't know why I used these particular words, but I was impelled to say "Will you take me in my dream?" At this she seemed upset. "You big stiff!" she said "I'll take you tomorrow morning."

'A few weeks later I was sitting in an armchair when I felt a tension, a strangeness, as though something was in the room; I became paralysed, unable to move, and heard a voice, loud and clear, within my head—a woman's voice, musical and pleasant and with an American accent. I got the words: "Words can't express . . ." and then it faded progressively, sounding like "one who goes to another . . ." And during the time she was speaking there seemed to be an orchestra playing in the background.

'Three or four weeks later I was sitting by the fire at home, recovering from a slight attack of pneumonia. I wasn't asleep but just lying back, when suddenly I had that "paralytic" sensation again, being unable to move my head or arms. Dimly, I could see the shadows of people coming into the room. A woman stood over me, but I couldn't see her face clearly. As I looked up she stooped and kissed me. She put her hands on my chest, and I felt an icy cold. I said "Oh, my God, your hands are cold!" She seemed to say "Let's have a look at you." I must have dozed off. I dreamed I walked into the other room and there, in the dark, was Marilyn, sitting down where the toys are usually kept. Her face was brilliant white. I said "Are you Marilyn Monroe?" and she replied "I *was*." I pointed to her cheek and said "Where is that beauty spot, if you're Marilyn Monroe?" and she said "I've had it removed." '

The man often saw Marilyn Monroe in his dreams, and on one occasion when he was awake. He made a tour of Fleet Street photographic agencies, collecting actual photographs of her in order to check on similarities between the person he saw, and assumed to be Marilyn Monroe, and the person in the pictures. At a séance he attended in Doughty Street, London, with the photographs in his pocket, he was told that a spirit alleged to be present "wishes you to know that she knows you have her photograph in your pocket."

The story had a strange and what might have proved a tragic sequel. For no reason he could think of, the man one day secured a quantity of sleeping tablets and made his way to a square in Victoria in which Marilyn Monroe had stayed during one of her last visits to London. There he swallowed the pills, went into a coma, was found lying unconscious in the pouring rain by a policeman, was rushed to hospital and rescued in the nick of time.

Hallucinations? Mental illness? Telepathy? Whatever the explanation the man told his story rationally and with conviction.

So much for that category—on the subject of telepathy and the part it plays in the appearance of apparitions, we shall treat at greater length later on.

Britain (though not only Britain) abounds in haunted houses and castles. Glamis Castle, the ancestral home of the Earl of Strathmore and the birthplace of Princess Margaret, is a particular and typical example. There is a tradition that if you count the windows of Glamis from inside and out the numbers never tally. There is, despite the almost mystical beauty with which sunshine and spring flowers can invest its ancient stones, a brooding melancholy about this vast, rambling castle. It has two ghosts, seen over the centuries by many different people whose accounts in fundamental detail have not differed: the wraith of the tormented Jane Douglas, burnt at the stake in the sixteenth century for allegedly conspiring with others to murder King James V; and the spirit (sometimes seen) of the profligate Earl Baerdie who is said to have staked his soul in a game with the devil and enacts his frightful penance, so the story says, by playing an endless game in a secret room which is said to exist but has never been discovered.

One of the children of King Henry VIII is said to haunt Windsor Castle, one of the castles which William the Conqueror built as a western bastion against the invader—although, of course, it has had many additions and alterations to it in the centuries which have followed. If there is anything in the theory that inanimate things can become imbued with the atmosphere of things past, Windsor should indeed be haunted. A few of the monarchs who have lived there—or, one should say, resided, as most of them had other palaces to live in—were William the Conqueror, Henry II, King John, Edward III (who started the legend of King Arthur and the Round Table by inviting knights to feast with him at a Round Table), Henry VIII, Queen Elizabeth, Charles I and James I.

Windsor's ghosts include the ghost of Queen Elizabeth, seen in the library of Windsor Castle. Other 'historic' ghosts include the shade of the wretched Catherine Howard, still said to run screaming along the haunted gallery to the Chapel at Hampton Court, banging on the chapel door in a panic-stricken effort to convince the King that she had not been unfaithful to him, in a hopeless attempt to prevent the execution that followed. The Cambridge Mansion, Sawston Hall, is said to be haunted by yet another royal ghost—of Queen Mary I, sister of Queen Elizabeth. When Queen Mary's brother, Edward VI died and widespread unrest and insurrection followed, Mary fled to Sawston Hall for the refuge willingly given by the Huddleston family, where she stayed until news reached her that her retreat had been discovered. Her ghost has been seen in the room in which she slept, and the interesting thing is that all who have reported it over the years have been able to agree on the fact that she was wearing the dress in which she appears in the portrait of her in Sawston Hall, and that she was holding her prayer book in such a way that her hands, which were particularly beautiful and graceful, showed to best advantage. All of them, too, describe her as smiling—a fact of especial interest, for Mary's life comprised so much fear, controversy and intrigue that only at Sawston, where she was welcome, secure and among friends, was she really happy and at ease.

But if ancient and historic buildings have the reputation of being haunted, it should not be supposed that places of prosaic and commonplace atmosphere are immune. In 1936 David Belshaw, a machinist at a textile factory at Standish, near

Wigan, collapsed at work on seeing a ghost. He had looked up from his machine to see a man in a long coat, breeches and something white, suggesting a collar, round his neck. His description identified a former rector of Standish, the Rev. Charles Hutton. The mill was built on land formerly belonging to the rectory, and the Rector had a financial interest in the mill, which he sometimes visited. His spectre, when seen, was floating at a height of above two feet from the floor.

At a factory in Bracknell New Town, Berkshire, there has been a whole succession of night watchmen because of the 'ghost' of a former watchman, now dead. The dead man had a dog, Gyp, which was his constant companion, and men have declared they have heard it barking at night. On one occasion a watchman heard the checking-machine being operated. On investigating, he found a workman's card had been stamped at midnight, although there was nobody about at all!

Nor are factories the only unhistoric places to be haunted. Many a council house has been reported to have its ghost.

Yet another type of ghost, which happens to be quite numerous and yet somehow is thought less about by people interested in the subject, is a phantasm of a living person. Extraordinary stories exist of people being seen at vast distances away, at a time when they were alive.

One of the best-known cases of the appearance of the ghost of a living person concerns the wife of John Donne, the poet, Dean of St. Paul's Cathedral.

Donne was a devout preacher, a writer of sensitive prose and poetry, and a man in whom sweetness and ardent vigour harmonised. At the time of this happening, Donne and his wife were living in a house in Drury Lane with a friend, Sir Robert Drewry. King James decided to send a mission by Lord Hay to the court of the French King, Henry IV, and Sir Robert, who also had to go, asked Donne to go with him.

Mrs. Donne was expecting a child, and when her husband told her of the plan she expressed the gravest misgivings. She begged him not to go, and he agreed to stay at home—but on Sir Robert's repeated insistence he changed his mind, and his wife, reluctantly, let him go.

Sir Robert and John Donne took about twenty days to reach Paris safely. Two days afterwards Sir Robert left Donne alone in a room where they had dined with some friends, and returned to find him in a kind of coma. 'I have seen a dreadful vision' Donne told him, 'since I saw you; I have seen my dear wife pass twice through this room, with her hair hanging about her shoulders and a dead child in her arms; this I have seen since I saw you.'

Sir Robert tried to reassure Donne. 'Here Sir, you have slept since I saw you, and this is the result of some melancholy dream, which I desire you to forget, for you are now awake.' But Donne was adamant. 'I cannot be surer that I now live, than that I have not slept since I saw you; and I am as sure that, at her second appearing, she stopped and looked me in the face and vanished.'

The following day Donne's anxiety had not abated, nor his conviction as to what he had seen. Sir Robert, convinced now that his friend *had* seen something, despatched a special messenger to Drury House to discover how Mrs. Donne was and what had been happening, if anything. In due course the messenger returned. Mrs. Donne lay very ill at Drury House. After a long and dangerous labour she had delivered a stillborn child —at the very hour of the very day that her husband had seen the distressing vision.

This is a good example of a 'ghost' or vision of a living person, the interesting point being that the information collected afterwards, and which John Donne would have had no other means of knowing at the time, confirmed his 'hallucination'. But there are many other phantasms of the living which have been witnessed simultaneously by more than one person. There was the extraordinary case of Mr. East, of New Street, Aberavon, who, in 1935, *with two other companions* saw a friend of his, Sam Bowden, vault over the railing of an allotment, come towards them—and then disappear. Utterly bewildered, they went to Sam's house, to learn that he was not there, but had gone to his mother's house at Taibach, a village two and a half miles away.

Another distinct—and disturbing—category of haunting is that by the poltergeist. This appears to be some force or spirit, sometimes mischievous, often malignant and usually frightening, which delights in throwing things, lifting things and smashing them. Stone-throwing in particular is a common phenomena, of which examples could be quoted from all over the world. Such stories persist from the most ancient to modern times. In A.D. 355, according to Jacob Grimm in a work, *Deutsche Mythologie* (Gottingen, 1835), a poltergeist drove the people in one household in Bingen-am-Rhein to distraction —stones were thrown about, they were pulled out of bed and subjected to violent buffeting. In modern times we have the spectacular happenings at Borley Rectory, and a story of a poltergeist at a seaside hotel in England, which was told to me and has never hitherto been published. Two brothers, whom I know, were waiters at the time and, as was then the custom—for this was just before the Second World War, before the onset of the Catering and Wages Act—had come to work 'the season' during the summer months. Having handed their cards to the hotel manager and been given their instructions, they took their fibre cases containing their belongings to the bedroom which the two were to share with two other waiters. As the room was quite full, with its four beds, the cases had to be stacked on top of the wardrobes; only essentials such as the dark waiters' suits, being hung up.

One of the waiters—a burly, phlegmatic and fearless man who fought his way with the British Army through to Berlin —put it this way:

'We had gone to bed one evening, after a hard days' work, and after chatting for a bit, we all fell asleep. Then, all of a sudden, all hell was let loose. There was a loud crash in the room, making us jump out of our skins, and something heavy flew through the air, just missing my head, crashing against the wall and falling with a loud thump on the floor. Soon, objects were flying all over the room. When we turned the light on, we found the objects were heavy brass knobs. None of the beds had these knobs. The door was closed and so were the windows —they couldn't have come that way. We were all terrified and shaking like leaves; it was absolutely uncanny.

'This sort of thing kept happening, and we were scared to mention it to the manager for fear he should think we were off our heads. But something happened one day which clinched the matter for me once and for all. I'd left the room to go to the toilet, which was almost next door. I'd no sooner closed the bedroom door when there was the most terrific crash inside, the noise continuing for several seconds. I dashed inside to find that my fibre travelling case, which had been firmly on top of the flat wardrobe, was lying upside down on the floor, the top unfastened and everything scattered all over the floor. So, too, was another case, *which had been standing by a bed.*

'We went to the manager and asked for our cards, saying we wanted to leave immediately. Instead of being aggressive as we fully expected—for it's hard luck when waiters walk out on the job in the middle of the season—he didn't seem so surprised, but was obviously uneasy. He asked us what was the matter, and when we told him, made no attempt to deny it, saying the

same thing had happened before, and begging us not to let the
guests or anybody else know about it.

'We heard later that the room in which we slept was one
in which Marconi once carried out experiments. There was
absolutely no explanation for these things that I can see. Practical joking was out of the question.'

I have omitted the name of the hotel, because, unfortunately, such reports can be damaging to custom. But the case
is a clear example of a poltergeist haunting—hallucination can
be ruled out. A curious feature of things thrown, especially
stones, is that they come, even when the phenomenon occurs
indoors, on a trajectory and not in a direct line as if thrown
by human hands, furthermore, they are frequently hot
when handled. Some weird manifestations come within this
category: in a school near Richardton, Canada, in April, 1944,
lumps of coal jumped out of a pail like Mexican jumping
beans; in July, 1935, a servant girl in Prague was astounded to
find that as she walked towards a door it would automatically
open before she reached it, and that potatoes in a cellar rolled
towards her; in South Africa (Cape Town) in 1932 a house in
Maitland, a suburb, was haunted by a poltergeist able to cause
spontaneous conflagration. Papers allowed to flutter to the
ground would burst into flames. So, too, did clothing locked
safely away in cupboards. Seemingly, such happenings are normally impossible but the implications can be considered later.
For the moment it will be enough to say that the behaviour and
doings of poltergeists constitute a distinct 'branch' of haunting.
It is true that in a few cases fraud has accounted for the
phenomena—but in none of those I have mentioned, nor in
hundreds of others.

There are military ghosts—a considerable galaxy of them,
witnessed and attested by logical men who could plan complicated campaigns, and could face and witness wholesale death
and wounding unmoved; men of keen perception, habits of
realism and undoubted courage.

In 1816, a guard at the Tower of London saw what he described afterwards as 'a shadowy bear walking up the stairs in
the twilight'. He lunged at it with his bayonet, which shattered
against the wall. The ghostly presence walked on unaffected and
the guard, having told his unlikely story to others, died of shock
a few days later.

A former Constable of the Tower of London, Colonel E. H.
Carkeet James, has related a story which he claimed was vouched
for by two senior officers of the King's Royal Rifle Corps. It

happened just over a century ago, in the winter of 1864. A soldier of that regiment was on sentry-go at the entrance to what is now called the Queen's, and was then called the King's House. Found insensible at his post—a most grave offence and not less at the Tower of London—he was tried by court martial.

Military tribunals are not noted for their credulity, but the story related by the unhappy soldier was so explicit and direct that none of them, with their long knowledge of men, could doubt him. He had seen a ghostly figure approaching him, challenged it three times, and as the figure came on lunged at it with his bayonet and fainted with horror as he saw it go through the figure with no effect at all. Two independent witnesses supported the sentry's story, and he was acquitted. There is an interesting coincidence in these two widely-separated happenings.

But military ghosts are not always to be found in military environments. A director of a publishing company, motoring down to the country from London, heard whispering and voices, and saw soldiers sitting round a fire, its flames reflecting against their plumed helmets, breastplates and spears. It was only when he had driven past them that he had a sense of the uncanny. He seemed, in a nasty flash of revelation, to remember that he had seen the outline of a tree *through* a man resting against it. He consoled himself with the thought that this must have been an illusion, that he must be tired, that perhaps a film company was camping out there to avoid reassembling for the shooting of further scenes the following day. Yet he was still uneasy when he arrived at his inn. And he was scarcely to be comforted by the greeting accorded to him when it was noticed how pale and harassed he seemed: *'Ah, so you've seen them too?'*

And there are examples of battles being re-fought by ghostly warriors—one on what is now known as the Central Ammunition Depot at Kineton, Warwickshire, where the Battle of Edgehill was fought in 1642. Months later, local residents were awakened by all the din and noise of a fresh battle, and were astounded to see, on the moors, the Roundheads and Royalists fighting again. The stories were so general that King Charles sent three officers to investigate. The investigators confirmed the truth of the stories and even claimed to have recognised some of the cavaliers killed at Edgehill!

Then there are animal ghosts. Such phantasms, whatever may be the explanation of why certain people see them, can be immensely terrifying; often more so than certain other types. Spectral dogs form part of the ghost-lore of every county in Britain. A dog ghost was said to haunt a lane leading from Mousiad to Lisworney Crossways in Wales for years. The 'shucks' of Norfolk: spectral horses, cats and other animals, are to be heard of everywhere. There was, for instance, the Mauthe Dog which haunted the guard-room and vicinity of Peel Castle, which it would reach *via* the churchyard. In delivering up the keys to the captain every night, the sentry had to make his way through the churchyard and as all the men knew about the 'dog' and most had seen it, by common consent, this duty was performed by two guards. One night, however, a sentinel who was the worse for drink swore he would go alone, and boasted in a loud voice that he would strike the dog if he met it, cursing it the while. Within an hour he was back again, eyes staring, white as a ghost, paralysed with horror, even unable to talk and describe what he had seen. He died soon afterwards.

The range of phenomena covered by the generalised but convenient word 'ghosts' is indeed endless. There is ghostly music. It is extraordinary how many reports there have been of this over the centuries, including the ringing of bells both large and small. There are ghostly sounds, some so noisy that they could be heard a street away. There are some very strange reports indeed of haunted furniture and objects which bring in their wake disturbance or misfortune.

Many crimes have been revealed, it is said, by the intervention of ghosts. In a lecture given in 1922, a Harley-street specialist, Dr. Abraham Wallace, quoted the case of how the victim of the Merstham Tunnel crime in 1905, Mary Money, appeared as a ghost, and how a medium, on boarding a London bus, heard a voice telling her to follow a particular man because he was Jack the Ripper and intended to commit another murder. 'Jack the Ripper' was a fanciful name given to the unknown perpetrator of a whole series of particularly brutal murders of East End prostitutes, involving mutilation suggesting an obsessive sexual aberration. The medium, convinced that the man was a sinister character, told the police; the man was kept under surveillance and from that time the murders ceased. Then, said Dr. Wallace, the authorities certified the man as a homicidal maniac, and removed him to an asylum, where he died some years later. Whose was the voice that 'spoke' to the medium as she boarded the bus?

There are ghosts of the sea, of mines, of mountains, of

rivers and lakes. There are trees believed to be imbued with or inhabited by ghosts.

Once again, one asks with a mixture of curiosity and awe: are these things 'thought impressions' registered as a kind of photograph on places and things? Or does *something* comparable to the human intelligence survive death? The answer to the latter is evident in the quite authenticated stories, which I propose to give later, where crimes have been exposed and the actual siting of treasure revealed, by wraiths. And it must be remembered that the hauntings which occur are not simply of things *seen* but often of things felt. There is too much mystery for mirth, even though there is so much beyond explanation.

4

Murder will out

The evil that men do lives after them,
The good is oft interred with their bones.

Shakespeare's words are appropriate when considering the many
well-authenticated cases of the phantasms of murdered people
appearing on or near the scene of their crimes and in some
instances exposing the culprits. Some of these stories are so
extraordinary that they not only presuppose some form of telepathy but appear to support the idea that—whatever the reasons and causes may be—*something* of human intelligence and
personality, capable of manifesting itself visually and sometimes
auditorally, survives death.

Cicero, in ancient times, described how two Arcadians jour-
neyed to Megara together, one staying at a friend's house and
the other at an inn. During the night the ghost of the latter
appeared at the bedside of his friend, his features eloquent of
fear and distress. At first much frightened, the friend dismissed the vision as an illusion caused by travel weariness and
tired nerves, and fell asleep again. But yet again he was
awakened by a vision of his friend, this time appealing to him
that, although his first appeal had gone unheeded and he was
now dead, his murder should be avenged. His body, he revealed
was hidden in a dung-cart, which in the early hours of the
morning would pass through the city gates.

By now convinced of the validity of his vision, the friend
awaited the arrival of the dung-cart at the city gates with
trepidation. As the cart rumbled through he threw himself at
it and found, sure enough, the body of his murdered friend
concealed there. The innkeeper was tried for murder and
executed.

There are many examples of such cases throughout the
centuries. Consider the strange story of Eric Toombe whose
father, the Reverend Gordon Toombe, was once the incumbent
of Little Tew, Enstone, Oxfordshire.

Eric Toombe, who was nearly thirty years of age, was partner with an evil character called Ernest Dyer, in a farm known ironically as The Welcomes, at Hayes Lane, Kenley, Surrey. Toombe mysteriously disappeared and although the police were suspicious of Dyer they could establish no real link between him and Toombe's disappearance. In 1921, however, the farmhouse was destroyed by fire. The police entertained the strongest suspicions that it had been an act of arson by Dyer himself; yet probe as they did, the police could pin nothing on the suspect. True to habit, the police kept an eye on the man whom instinct told them was a bad character. On November 16, 1922, they decided to pounce on him, convinced that they could now bring a specific charge of fraud against him and arrested him at a Scarborough hotel. In the course of a fierce struggle Dyer, who had pulled a revolver on the police, shot himself and died.

In 1923, Eric Toombe's mother had a vivid dream during which she saw her son lying at the bottom of a cesspool at the farm. The vision was so terrifying that she told her husband about it and he, in turn, informed the police who dragged the cesspool and found the injured and decomposing body of the murdered youth, precisely as his mother had dreamed. He had been shot through the head, and was easily identified by his wristlet watch and other belongings, which Dyer had been too crafty to retain, well knowing that their possession would have been incriminating. Dyer, using Toombe's passport, had gone to Paris and drawn £1,350 from Toombe's account by forging his signature.

Another murder revealed by the victim's ghost is that of Mrs. Barwick, wife of William Barwick. While walking through the countryside near Cawood Castle on Monday, April 14, 1690, he resolved to murder her—why, subsequent accounts never made clear—and having done so, threw her into a near-by pond.

A contemporary account says that his brother-in-law, Thomas Lofthouse, was watering quickwood at about half past twelve the following day, when the shade of a woman appeared to him, whose features he identified as being just like those of the murdered woman's. She sat down against the pond on a small hill, and as Lofthouse walked by her on his way to the pond, and again on returning from it, he noticed her dangling 'something like a white bag' on her lap, vaguely reminiscent of an unborn baby. His suspicions thoroughly aroused, more especially as Barwick had made conflicting and inaccurate state-

ments as to his wife's whereabouts, Lofthouse went to the
authorities, and Thomas Barwick was arrested. He confessed to
his crime and, the pond being dragged on the basis of his information, the murdered woman was found to be wearing
clothes corresponding with those seen in the 'vision'. Barwick
was tried and hanged.

Aubrey, in his famous book *Miscellanies*, says that in the year
1647, the son and heir of Lord Mohun, who was a brave and
dashing dandy, a master of fencing and a superb horseman,
had a quarrel with Prince Griffin, as a result of which he
accepted a challenge to a duel on horseback in Chelsea Fields
in the morning.

The young buck went on his appointed mission on that
fateful morning in good spirits. But when he reached Ebury
Farm (nearly 500 acres of meadow and pasture, near what is
now known as Chelsea) he was attacked by some hooligans who
shot him dead.

Mohun was murdered at ten o'clock in the morning. At that
very moment—for he glanced at the clock and noted the time
—his phantasm appeared by the bedside of his pretty if vulgar
mistress, who lived in St. James's Street. He came to the edge
of the bed, drew the curtain, looked down on her, and made
to go away. She called after him, but he took no notice. Puzzled,
she rang for her maid and asked her where Mr. Mohun had
gone; but the maid told her, much astonished, that nobody
could have come in as she had the key to the chamber.

Another case of the ghost of a murdered man appearing to
others at the time of decease occurred when Mr. Brown,
brother-in-law to Lord Coningsby, appeared to his sister and
her maid in Fleet Street, just at the time when he was being
murdered in Hertfordshire, in 1693.

Surtees's *History of Durham* tells of a strange event in 1631:
'One Walker, a yeoman of good estate, a widower, living at
Chester-le-Street, had in his service a young female relative
named Anne Walker. The result of an amour which took
place between them caused Walker to send away the girl under
the care of one Mark Sharp, a collier, professedly that she
might be taken care of as befitted her condition, but in reality
that she might no more be troublesome to her lover. Nothing
was heard of her until, one night in the ensuing winter, one
James Graham, coming down from the upper to the lower floor
of his mill, found a woman standing there with her hair hanging about her head, in which were five bloody wounds. According to the man's evidence, she gave account of her fate; having

been killed by Sharp on the moor in their journey, and thrown into a coal pit close by, while the instrument of her death, a pick, had been hid under a bank along with her clothes, which were stained with her blood. She demanded of Graham that he should expose her murder, which he hesitated to do, until she had twice reappeared to him the last time with a threatening aspect.

'The body, the pick and the clothes having been found as Graham had described, Walter and Sharp were tried at Durham before Judge Davenport in August, 1631. The men were found guilty, condemned, and executed.'

This grim story, which seems beyond rational explanation, is comparable with the murder of an itinerant pedlar in New York State in the middle of the last century.

The house in which this long-forgotten drama was enacted—an abundance of written statements and sworn affidavits is available, by the way—is still preserved as a curiosity in Lily Dale, New York State; but it stood originally in Hydesville. As a building it is commonplace and dowdy but for spiritualists it ranks almost as a shrine since for them it is held that, in a strikingly evidential manner, the survival of human personality beyond the grave was proven there.

The facts, easily confirmed from historical records, are these:

Between 1843 and 1844 a Mr. and Mrs. Bell occupied the house, and for the last few months of their stay there the household chores were carried out by a girl called Lucretia Pulver.

Mr. and Mrs. Bell were well known in the village. One day, in the manner of the times, a young pedlar called. He was a personable young man, aged perhaps about thirty, and he carried his box of merchandise.

Subsequently, the maid recalled that Mrs. Bell behaved as though she must have met the talleyman before, but the nature of their relationship, if indeed there had ever been one, was never established. The pedlar stayed with them.

What is certain is that the maid found herself summarily dismissed by Mrs. Bell and before leaving, chose a piece of material from the pedlar's selection, with the injunction that he should leave it at her father's house. This he undertook to do, but it was never subsequently received.

Mrs. Bell offered to give Lucretia a lift when she left, and the two men were left in the house. Hardly a week had passed when Lucretia was surprised to find her services asked for again. Returning, she found Mrs. Bell in possession of many of the articles she remembered seeing in the pedlar's box; but this did not seem suspicious to her at the time, as she might well have bought them.

From the day of her return, Lucretia noticed something creepy about the house. Unaccountable noises, such as rappings and bangings, came from the room the pedlar had once occupied, while at other times footsteps were distinctly heard, starting from that room and going downstairs to the cellar. It is hardly surprising that Lucretia, when left alone in the house, was nervous and afraid, yet on one occasion, when she sent for a friend and a brother to stay with her for company, the phenomena continued and scared them all.

One day, looking for something in the cellar, Lucretia fell into a hole of freshly-dug soil. Her scream brought Mr. Bell racing down and when she asked, mightily puzzled, why the cellar was dug up, he dismissed it by saying they were 'rat holes'.

Shortly afterwards, the Bells left. A Mr. and Mrs. Weekman and a Mrs. Lafe then moved in—but not for long, for Mrs. Lafe, one day entering the kitchen and closing the door behind her, saw the shade of a young man in a black frock coat, fancy waistcoat and pantaloons—the garb of the pedlar as described by Lucretia. The three tenants also heard the noisy rappings and ghostly footsteps. This was too much for them, and they left in a hurry.

Then along came Mr. John Fox, his wife and two little girls, Margaretta and Catherine aged about twelve and eight respectively. It was a purely temporary expedient, for he was a farmer from Canada settling on a farm near by, and until his new home was built they decided to make do with the adequate if uninspiring house, so similar to many others in the vicinity.

Within days of the Fox's tenancy the ghostly disturbances recommenced—banging, rattlings, and most unnerving of all, mysterious footsteps. But while these might be dismissed as imagination, Catherine's terrified complaint that she had felt an icy hand touching her face at the dead of night, and bedclothes pulled from the bed by unseen hands, could not be dismissed lightly.

One day, when Mr. Fox was testing the windows and doors to see if their vibrations might account for the sounds, although innumerable tests had proved that they did not, one of the girls noticed that there was a 'response' in sound. That is, if in testing the doors Mr. Fox made two knocks there were two 'ghostly' knocks to follow. Finding her nerve, the girl challenged the 'presence' or whatever it was, to copy her. She clapped her hands—and the answering echo was always of the same number, but in *knocks*. She made the gesture only of clicking her fingers, emitting no sound; the precise number of knocks followed. Mrs. Fox tried asking questions of fact, such as the age of her daughters, the age of her dead child. Neighbours were called in, and arriving in a mood of derision and scepticism, were astounded to find their ages correctly given in response to their questions.

A Mr. William Duesler, however, a former tenant of the house, decided to tackle these strange happenings in a more scientific way. By dint of repeated questioning, and by stating what number of knocks would be interpreted as 'yes' or 'no'— all this, by the way, not in private but before an assembly— he managed to elicit that the 'subject' of these disturbances had been murdered, robbed of his goods, and buried in the cellar.

Scarcely able to believe his ears, Duesler sensibly called in two other witnesses who could attest to the strange information now being imparted to him.

At this point the former maid, Lucretia, came forward. Her story about finding the soil in the cellar disturbed had a sinister ring. Mr. Fox dug in the cellar and found there an empty hole and scraps of hair and bone, which a doctor declared to be part of a human skull.

Things now took another dramatic turn. The two girls were alleged to have mediumistic powers and began to enjoy a sensational vogue as spiritualists, leading not unnaturally to rumours that all was not well and that the integrity of the Fox family was open to question. At best, the Foxes were thought to be credulous; at worst, they were either tricksters or in league with the devil. Both the sisters, their childhood ruined by the morbid home environment and disturbing publicity, had subsequently unhappy lives. Margaretta in a fit of exhibitionism 'confessed' to having faked manifestations but she had become such a drunkard that half the time she did not know what she was saying or writing. She later retracted the 'confession' which had been made for money.

The climax came long after, in 1904 when the haunted house was deserted and some children were playing in its ruins. The east wall of the cellar collapsed, burying and nearly killing one of them. A man who raced to the rescue could see the reason for it, for the 'wall' was a false one, hastily and inexpertly constructed long ago. Between this partition and the genuine wall of the old cellar were found the mouldering bones of a man—minus the skull—and a tin box of the type used by pedlars in those days.

The remains were at last decently interred. The knocking ceased.

5

Spirits without rest

I have long entertained the suspicion that emotion and thought are not transient things, but actual sources of energy whose impact on places and things, subject to conditions of which we at present know too little, can be permanent. This suspicion is to some extent sustained by the haunting of places which have been the scene of great tragedy.

We must not be misled, however, into the over-confident assumption that, inevitably, tragedy leaves its imprint on a place in the form of a haunting or spectre. Were this so, few parts of the world would be fit to live in. The millions and millions of people who have perished in battle over the centuries would render almost every woodland, mountain range, field and city psychically suffocating with its atmosphere of terror and suffering. Is Alexandria haunted? In parts, certainly, but the greater part is not although a million people were once put to the sword there.

Yet I remember a strange story told to me by a young pilot with the Royal Air Force when I stayed with his unit in Western Germany two years ago. He was a healthy, matter-of-fact, high-spirited youngster who, in the course of a flight by helicopter over Celle, had noticed two squat buildings belching forth smoke. But to his bewilderment, as he flew even lower, the buildings disappeared. Instead, there were silent fields, two solitary men edging mass graves—graves holding more than 5,000 people—with blocks of stone to give those melancholy acres some semblance of dignity and peace. For this was the site of Belsen concentration camp, where hundreds of thousands of civilians from all over Europe had suffered torture, indignities and death; where the crematoria had belched forth the smoke of burning bodies day and night. I visited this place with Peter O'Brien, the staff photographer of *Soldier* magazine. Even as we approached this camp, now a cemetery, we felt the chill and miasma of concentrated evil. No flowers bloomed. An unearthly silence hung over the place. 'Notice something?' said Peter, 'There's not a bird singing.' We read an inscription on a simple monument which tried vainly to combine love for the departed with sorrow for their fate and anger at their oppressors: EARTH, CONCEAL NOT THE BLOOD SHED ON THEE! Perhaps, I thought, the invocation had some force. I remembered what the pilot had told me: 'I have never seen anything so real and definite in my life as those chimneys belching smoke. My eyesight's perfect, and I'm used to observation. Both Austers and helicopters are used, as you know, for reconnaissance.'

His experience, however, could be attributed to the powerful and painful ideas associated with that place. Yet this visit to Celle was made in 1960—fifteen years after the war had ended. But there are innumerable places where the hark-back to past tragedy is more real and tangible and even more terrifying.

If one presupposes a soul, this being a metaphysical argument which can be argued indefinitely, then one may assume that it can know sorrow and joy, and that the extremes of suffering and horror may disorder it. Perhaps the *intensity* of horror, terror and pain has some permanent effect upon localities or buildings.

The records of hauntings suggest this. Although death in itself can hardly be deemed a cause of haunting, certain violent ends such as suicide and murder, seem to be a more likely cause. The spectre of Lady Hamilton of Bothwellhaugh has haunted her ancestral countryside for years. For while her husband was away from home, 'a favourite of the Regent Murray seized his house, turned his wife on a cold night naked into the open fields, where, before morning, she was found raving mad, her infant perishing either by cold or murder'. For years, the ruins of the mansion of Woodhouslee were troubled by the distraught phantom of a woman in white, bearing in her arms her murdered child. And some time after a new mansion had been built, incorporating some of the materials salvaged from the older building, she appeared again.

After Stalin's death in 1953, his secret police chief, Lavrentyi Beria, fell into disfavour. A power so absolute, sustained by the secret and all-embracing machinery of a nation-wide force, tends to make a cruel man even more cruel by providing scope for his evil appetites. It was so with Hitler, Eichman and Himmler; it was equally true of Beria, once described in the large Soviet Encyclopaedia as 'The faithful comrade-in-arms and pupil of Stalin ... one of the outstanding leaders of the Soviet Communist Party and Government'. The new Soviet

Government lost no time in arresting Beria and trying him and shooting him in secret.

At the height of his power Beria, like Himmler, had personal control of the vast prison camps and forced labour camps in Siberia and elsewhere. Apart from sending men, women and children to their doom, Beria took a sadistic delight in torturing prisoners himself as well as both authorising and organising their torture. His personal residence in Moscow, a huge luxurious mansion guarded by heavy gates, had rows of cubicles or prison cells in the cellar. Often Beria would go out at night in his bullet-proof car and summarily arrest any pretty woman who happened to be passing; there did not have to be any legal pretext. She and any other victims similarly collected would be whisked back to the mansion where, with the active connivance of his evil partner and deputy, Abakumov, they would engage in drunken orgies culminating in rape and sadism. The absolute power of the ex-gangster Stalin and his ruthless extermination of all who stood in his way set the standard for his temporary favourites. So long after the event, truth sounds like the crudest melodrama; but the sombre tragedy enacted in Beria's house was real enough.

If there is anything in the idea that inanimate objects can be affected by emotion, it should come as no surprise to hear that Beria's home thereafter had the reputation of being haunted. For a long time it stood deserted. Despite the fact that religion and superstition are both discouraged and ridiculed, and that talk of ghosts should have been dismissed by the Communist faithful as superstitious nonsense, there were no immediate takers for the house. The authorities, maintaining a polite silence as to the previous reputation of the house, made it available to the Tunisian diplomatic mission as an embassy. Apart from the offices usual to an embassy, for clerical and routine diplomatic duties, there was living accommodation for the Tunisian Ambassador, Ahmed Mestiri, and for Mrs. Mestiri and their two children. Before long the night air in the mansion was rent by fearful shrieks, groans, maniacal laughter and shouts of derision. One night Madame Mestiri awoke to see a shadowy figure by her bed, warning her to leave, as tragedy hung over the house. And in early 1961 tragedy did indeed strike—at the two-year-old son of M. Ahmed Arfa, a Counsellor at the Embassy, who fell from a window on the sixth floor and was killed. Not long afterwards M. Chadli Charouche, the Tunisian Consul, skidded near Moscow River while driving home, was flung into the river and drowned.

The Mestiris were glad to be recalled and replaced by others.

A particularly malevolent ghost, of whose appearances innumerable accounts exist at different periods, is that of 'Terrible William' otherwise Lord Soulis, who practised black magic at Hermitage Castle in Roxburghshire, Scotland. In pursuance of his evil rites, so local tradition goes, he would kidnap local children, incarcerate them in his castle dungeons, murder them and use their blood in appalling rituals. When at last news of his misdeeds became common knowledge in the village, the people took him prisoner, bound him in chains and threw him into a cauldron of boiling lead. Often his shade has been seen in the environs of the castle, re-enacting his crimes.

The ghost supposed to haunt Littlecote mansion owned by Major George Wills, son of the tobacco magnate of that name, is a fairly typical example of what we may call 'a past tragedy' spectre. Tragedy certainly did occur in that rambling fifteenth-century mansion set in its 6,000 acres estate. Built between 1490 and 1520, it lies about half-way between Hungerford, Berkshire, and Ramsbury, Wiltshire. An earlier house, dating back to the thirteenth century, stood near by and remains of it have been uncovered by excavations. In the thirteenth century it belonged to Roger de Calston, but in 1415 it passed into the Darrell family, remaining in their possession until 1589, when 'Wicked' Will Darrell, who certainly seemed to have deserved his name, was killed on October 1st while hunting in the park. In front of the entrance gates, where once the old Gate House stood, is an ancient elm. Legend has it that it will flourish with the fortunes of the house's owners, but it is known as Darrell's Tree, and if it is anything to do with him its decay is symbolic.

It is a magnificent mansion, with its huge panelled Great Hall and stained glass windows, its helmets and armour and bandoliers, its superb drawing-room with its lovely hand-painted Chinese wallpaper and Aubusson carpet once in the Palace of Versailles. There is a charming library, a Dutch parlour, a brick hall containing a secret passage for eavesdroppers, a Cromwellian chapel, and leading from the chapel gallery . . . a haunted landing.

The fireplace on this landing is associated with the murder of a child, whose wraith is supposed to have appeared and caused 'Wicked' Will's horse to shy and kill him.

On a dark and stormy night, says the legend, in the year 1575, Darrell sent his servants to Mother Barnes, a midwife living at Shefford in Berkshire, with a promise of high reward

if she would attend a lady who was about to have a child. She
allowed herself to be blindfolded and after a rough ride on
horseback behind one of the messengers ... but here, in Mother
Barnes' own words, paraphrased only to avoid the archaic spell-
ing, is her terrible story:

Towards dawn, she arrived at a splendid mansion, and was
set down near a door; a messenger gave a prearranged signal
by knocking or ringing, and a tall, slender man came to the
door, wearing a long gown of black velvet and carrying a light.
She had no sooner entered the door than he made it fast,
shutting out those who had brought her. He led her upstairs
to a great chamber in which there was a chimneyed fireplace
in which a great fire burned fiercely. She passed through yet
another chamber into a third, richly furnished, in which there
was a four-poster bed with the curtains drawn.

The man in the black velvet gown whispered in her ear:
'In yonder bed lyeth the gentle woman that you are sent for
to come unto; go unto her and see that you do your utmost
endeavour towards her, and if she be safely delivered, you shall
not fail of great reward, but if she miscarry in her labour, you
shall die.'

Amazed—and probably terrified as well—the midwife made
her way to the richly-laid bed. In it, in the last pangs of labour,
lay a young woman, her face concealed by a vizor or some
such armour. Shortly afterwards she gave birth to a male child,
which the midwife, lacking the barest necessities of her craft,
wrapped in her midwives' apron. As she made her way from
the bedchamber she met the man (Will Darrell) who asked
whether the lady had given birth to a child or not. Replying
that the lady had been delivered of a male child, she un-
swathed the baby, asking for the proper clothes in which to
wrap him.

Darrell forced her to the fireside and demanded that she
throw the newly-born infant into it, alive. Desperate with grief,
the midwife went down on her knees and entreated him to
spare the baby's life, offering to care for it herself as her own.
But Darrell would not agree and, seizing the child, threw it into
the flames, commanding the midwife to go back to the woman
in the bed, where she stayed until, in the morning, she was
allowed to return home in the company of the messengers who
had brought her.

This terrible crime, according to local legend, is sometimes
re-enacted by the ghost of the distracted midwife with the
child in her arms. Both the bed in which the wretched woman

was delivered of her child, and the fireplace in which it perished, are there still.

The present owner of the mansion has not lived there since
his father's death although it is open to visitors. Death duties
make it impossible nowadays to live in so vast a house. He
himself, he tells me, has never seen the ghost. But from his
brother, Sir Edward Wills, I have this first-hand account of his
encounter with a ghost in that house:

'Whilst on weekend leave from the army at Netheravon I
was with my wife in my room at Littlecote on the Friday,
Saturday or Sunday night *preceding* December 5, 1927 (on
which day my first daughter was born). Sunny, my wife's Pekin-
ese, slept in a basket in the room.

'My room was the first up a few steps from the Long Gallery
(now the 'Regency' Room). Next was my father's dressing-
room in which my brother (now Major George Wills) was asleep.
(He was ill at the time and had gone to bed early). This room
leads in through a bathroom to the first bedroom where my
father and mother were sleeping.

'The weather was extremely cold, and there was not much
heating in the passages in those days.

'On the first two nights we were disturbed (as well as the
dog, who barked) by the noise of somebody coming up the
creaking stairs from the Long Gallery. But I thought little of it
as there was a bathroom near.

'The same disturbance occurred again on the Sunday night.
This time I leapt out of bed and opened my door, where I saw
a lady with a light in her hand and the shadow of her head on
the ceiling of the passage. She seemed to have fairish hair, not
very tall, and was in a pink garment. Then, without extending
a hand, she entered the dressing-room where my brother was
fast asleep. I followed her in with a torch in my hand. The
door was wide open, but there was nobody there except my
sleeping brother (who is seven years younger than I).

'The next morning, when I told my parents, my father said
"For the last three nights George has asked me to be more
careful to close my door when undressed for bed, as he found
it open all three mornings and it's cold with it open!"

'Incidentally, the late Colonel Beech was seen *here* (e.g. in
Meggernie Castle, Glenlyon, Perthshire) during the time of his
death—three times over a few days; first by my mother and her
maid, then by a sister of mine and thirdly, by myself.'

This story is particularly interesting because of the corroboration by Sir Edward's father of the fact of the door being

unaccountably open. There is also the interesting fact that the
ghost was seen to enter the room in which Sir Edward's sick
brother, George, was sleeping.

The fearful tragedy enacted at Littlecote, attested in detail by
the midwife in a statement dictated to Anthony Bridges, may
well have left its indelible and psychic imprint upon the house.

One of the difficulties, I suppose, in dealing with a subject
as amorphous as that of ghosts is that another dimension—or
several—seems to be involved. The experiences challenge reason; they leave one with a feeling of inadequacy, and for
reasons of pride as much as of logic, we refuse to believe. *'I've
never seen a ghost'* the sceptic says, often with satisfaction, as
though that establishes the fact that there can be nothing
worth while to discuss, nothing further to learn.

Such scepticism is understandable. A disordered mind can
conjure up many things: fear and apprehension exercise a
morbid influence on the imagination. There is a type of roman-
tic whose belief, self-induced, in his own fantasies and pre-
suppositions becomes a kind of self-hypnotism. To illustrate
my point, if once you become suspicious of somebody, almost
everything they do will appear suspicious to you. Innocently
somebody reads a letter; it may be from a young nephew
thanking the reader for a birthday present of half a crown, but
to the prejudiced observer the thing will look far more sinister. To the person, therefore, who has never experienced anything paranormal, the subjective experiences of others make
little sense.

Yet I shall not easily forget my own encounter with a ghost
in January, 1946. It was a ghost which I neither saw nor heard,
but it remained a terrifying experience.

It was in Prague, and the war had been over only a month
or so. The streets were scarred by battle, and the sidewalks
decked with patriotic ribbons and a treasured photograph, in
memory of some freedom fighter who had fallen there. There
was a scarcity of everything; sugar and butter and meat were
unheard-of luxuries.

I was sitting in my room at the Esplanade Hotel, working
out what my day's routine was to be. As special correspondent
of the *Sunday Dispatch* and *Illustrated*—then a thriving illustrated weekly—and a 'stringer' for a national daily newspaper,
life was interesting enough. Czechoslovakia was gradually returning to normal, although no constitutionally elected government yet existed and the provisional government, with its mixture of Communists, Catholics, Social Democrats and exiles re-

turned from London, had no real mandate from anybody. A
quarter of a million Russian soldiers were in the country, and
strategic places such as the uranium mines at Yachimov, Ruzin
Airport at Prague, and the National Bank, were under Russian
control.

The morning's post, as I sipped my ersatz coffee, had little
of interest. A few dreary, badly-stencilled handouts combining
the jargon of the civil service with the clichés of propaganda—
and one postcard, from a friend in Sevenoaks:

> '. . . don't go to inordinate trouble in the matter, but as
> you happen to be in Prague, could you find out what's
> happening to Mrs. Lillian H? The last address I have is
> c/o Mrs. X., number . . . Husinecka, Prague . . .'

It seemed little to ask, so I consulted my street map and
found that Husinecka was quite near. Even so, the name of
both Mrs. H. and Mrs X had a Jewish—and therefore an ominous—ring. In the holocaust and contagion of organised hate
unleashed by the Nazis, only a pitiful remnant of Europe's Jewish population remained. Men, women and children, irrespective of age or infirmity, had been subject to every imaginable
and unimaginable cruelty and indignity before being granted
the protracted release of death.

The address proved to be a box-like block of flats starved of
paint and void of character. There was no life, and the stairs
were unlit and crowded with prams, garbage cans and empty
bottles. I had to strike a match to find the number of the flat I
sought, and only after incessant ringing was the door opened
—by only a few inches. In the half-light I could see an elderly
woman, I don't know why, but her face seemed familiar to
me. Yes, she said, she was a friend of Mrs. H. But the joyless
way in which she said this, and her general nervousness, terror
almost, made me fear the worst. She asked me into a dingy
sitting-room and broke out into such an uncontrolled volley of
talk that I wondered if she were mad. On second thoughts I
realised that her general demeanour was understandable when
one considered the effects of cumulative nervous strain. After
all, she was a German Jewess. Somehow, she had escaped the
gas ovens, but she must have lived in fear through those long
years, concealing her Jewishness, terrified lest it should leak out;
and now, with feeling running so high against Germans, Nazi
or non-Nazi, even Germans who had been settled in Czechoslovakia for more than 200 years, she was likely to be the
victim of violence because of her origins.

I let the stream of talk spend itself, then in answer to my questions, the story of her friend, Mrs. H. emerged. She was a humble sewing-woman, sixty-two years old and a widow, living alone in a bed-sitting room in Prague when the Germans invaded. She eked out a bare living by odd scraps of sewing and mending. A few family photographs, one or two threadbare dresses of poor quality, and some treasured books were her only possessions. But with the Germans came the reign of terror. Her passport was stamped with the letter 'J' and she was not allowed to work, nor to draw rations. Every Jew knew that the process of attrition was only a half-way house to terror.

In despair, she decided to go underground, to pretend to disappear in such a way that it would be inferred by the authorities that she had committed suicide. Accordingly, she left her passport, identity papers and a few odds and ends, together with a suicide note in her room. She filled a humble fibre suitcase with a few garments and left it with her friend in Husinecka. Then, under an assumed name, she joined a convent on the outskirts of Prague. I felt pretty certain that the nuns must have known she was not a Catholic, but had shielded her for humanitarian reasons.

Mrs. X, as she told me all this, also said that she made a practice of visiting Mrs. H. regularly at the convent. This was well meant, but was almost certainly a mistake. Nuns do not receive regular visitors, and the fact may well have been noticed. At any rate, Mrs. H. enjoyed immunity until 1944 when, for some reason, the convent was raided by the Gestapo. All the sisters were arrested and never heard of again. And Mrs. H's true identity was detected. Two pitiful postcards told the remainder of the story: one, from Terezin in Czechoslovakia asked for a dress and some spectacles; the other, from Oswiciem in Poland, said simply 'I am well'. This would be all she would have been allowed to say, and even this meagre concession by the Germans was unusual. But Mrs. X knew what it meant; it meant 'goodbye', for Oswiciem was an extermination camp where hundreds of thousands of Jews went to the gas chambers, besides meeting death by hanging and ill-treatment. And Terezin had an evil enough reputation as it was a transit camp, where prisoners were sorted, by a mere glance, into two classes—those who were to live, and those condemned to slave labour.

While reading the postcard I had a curious feeling of being watched, and a 'tingly' feeling in the spine. I gave it no more thought, however. Nor did I tell Mrs. X that she might have, unwittingly, encompassed the death of her friend by her visits. She had had troubles enough. I thanked her for her help, and made arrangements to visit Terezin to see what evidence I could find of Mrs H. having been there in transit to Oswiciem.

It all seems unreal now—that grim red-brick fortress built by the Empress Maria Theresa as a munitions dump. Even at Terezin, the cremation ovens had been busy, and when the American Red Cross had neared the premises sacks of human ash had been dumped into the stream. Over sixty thousand Jews were done to death there, and thousands of cardboard boxes each containing the calcified remains of a human being, abandoned—the Germans had retreated so fast that there had been no time to jettison them. They had kept these remains as a kind of grim 'tally' in support of the returns of slaughter made to Berlin.

Typhus had been raging there when the Russians arrived. The sleeping sheds, void of blankets or linen, mere wooden slats or racks on which human beings were crammed in conditions worse than that of cattle, were separated only by a brick wall from the swimming pool constructed by Czech students, who were afterwards murdered, as an execution yard with gallows and three machine-gun emplacements. The wall opposite was pitted by bullet-holes.

Certain inmates were conceded a temporary immunity by keeping a card-index of the prisoners. It was in no sense a complete record. Mrs H. was probably there no more than a day or so, and nobody had bothered to record her fate. I was certain she was dead, because her few pitiful belongings had been returned to the Jewish community in Prague—a procedure occasionally utilised in order further to demoralise and terrorise such Jews as remained.

I returned to the hotel in Prague and retired to bed. My third-floor room was large and comfortable, with a hall and bathroom attached. The furnishings were modern—a large wardrobe, dressing-table and double bed with satinwood headboard. There was a bedside table with a reading lamp on it, and there was a large, handsome chandelier, too bright for general use.

At two o'clock in the morning I was awakened *instantly* by what I can only describe as a noise like a pistol shot in my head. In that instant my attention was directed to a particular part of that room, just near the door, in the hall or alcove that led to the door of the apartment. I could see nothing, yet *knew* with every instinct I possessed that something was there. I could even tell its height. Further, I knew—how I don't know—that it was Mrs. H. She was trying to tell me something. The room seemed flooded, pervaded by an overpowering atmosphere of sadness charged with menace.

In a sweat of fear, and only by a considerable effort of will, for I felt almost paralysed, I reached for the reading lamp switch. The room, centrally-heated, was inordinately cold. The light seemed to dispel the supercharged tension and gradually, the fear and horror lifted. I could feel the presence becoming weaker and weaker, until at last the room, except for myself, was empty—a sad, desolate sort of emptiness, a vestigial remnant of the sadness which had flooded the room in that strange way.

It will be said, I suppose, that my sad mission to Terezin had made some impression on my imagination. I can only say that the experience was very real—a sense of something indescribable but tangible. That incredible, almost electrical tension in the air; that all-pervading sadness tinged with menace ... I do not think this was a synthetic product of strained nerves. The experience of visiting Terezin, sad as it was with its reminders of mass slaughter, and of crude and needless inhumanity, was not at that time unusual. In one night's air raid on London over six hundred people were killed and many thousands of men, women and children injured, but I have never heard of a place haunted by the spectre of an air-raid victim. Violence in itself, as I have said before, does not produce these phenomena. There are other factors, perhaps some concatenation of circumstances favouring the 'registration' of strong emotion. But even if one accepts that vague hypothesis, there remains a greater puzzle. It might explain ghosts which hark back to the past, treading their old familiar paths and making an endless ritual of once transient acts, but how would it explain an active manifestation of some kind of intelligence *after* death?

'Something indescribable but tangible ...' This often sums up the nature of ghosts sensed but not necessarily either seen or heard. Consider the experience of Mr. Philip Cohn, a Newton Abbot estate agent. He writes to me:

'I can give you an occasion which happened to me personally, although I am not in any way prone to the supernatural. Some twenty years ago my wife and I visited the famous Compton Castle at Compton, near Torquay, and we took our pet greyhound with us. When we entered the dungeons the dog,

who was not normally of nervous disposition, was rooted to the
spot, literally petrified. His hair stood up on end, he was shivering as if in a rigor, and his eyes protruded like organ stops.
We ourselves felt that some other presence was there and had
a great job in pacifying the dog. It is an experience we will
remember to this day . . .'

There is reason to think that animals and children are more
receptive or sensitive than many adults. In this case the dog
was 'petrified'—terror-stricken at what seemed to it a real and
paralysing cause of terror; it was something it saw—yet neither
Mr. nor Mrs. Cohn *saw* anything. They just had a feeling that
something was there.

6

Harbingers of death

In Chapter 3, in the course of enumerating a few of the many varieties of ghosts, I mentioned the Winchcombe Ghost, which has often been reported in that locality, and which appeared to Mr. Bassett-Green just at the time that a relative whom he had just visited, had died. I mentioned, too, the strange case of a London hospital worker being taken violently ill and crying 'Oh Marilyn!' at the time that Marilyn Monroe committed suicide.

The harbingers of death, or death visitants, are those spectres whose coming presages doom or disaster, either immediate or imminent. There is a strong supposition that on occasion, tele-pathy—contact between two minds separated by distance, but habitually in sympathy—plays a part. The following is a statement made to me by Mrs. Maureen Hayter of 133c Dumbarton Road, Baltimore, Maryland, U.S.A.:

'In November, 1942, I was living in Minnesota with my three children while my husband, Lieutenant Commander Hubert Montgomery Hayter, U.S.N., was far away in the Pacific. (He was forty-one on October 17th, and was First Lieutenant and Damage Control Officer in the heavy cruiser U.S.S *New Orleans*). One night I was awakened by a terrific jar, so violent that I got up and went downstairs to investigate. I found nothing amiss, and again retired. Suddenly my husband was beside me, and we were bathed in a heavy mist. But his arms were protectively about me. We had been months apart, and now I had such a sense of that protection and of being re-united. I looked up into his face. There was a look of ineffable longing and of sadness. I touched his cheek and it was so cold. Next morning I decided that it had been a comforting dream, for I had not heard from him for some days. I was strengthened and buoyed up by it. Days passed, then I recalled his expression and the cold I'd felt with foreboding. Thus, when I received the fateful telegram announcing that he had been killed in action, I felt that I had been forewarned and given the needed courage to meet the disaster. Checking back, it had all occurred on November 30th, when the Battle of Tassafaronga took place, and when he perished courageously after saving all his men. I am not a dreamer, and I firmly believe that his heroic spirit and presence was transmitted across those many miles to reassure and sustain me. It was truly a final farewell.'

A sad and poignant experience. There was the closest of bonds between man and wife; they had married on April 8, 1926 and had three children, two daughters aged fourteen and fifteen and one son aged four, none of which experienced anything unusual. Mrs. Hayter was living at the time of the ghostly visitation at 312 Grove Avenue, Albert Lea, Minnesota. Lieutenant Commander Hayter directed the damage control operations until overcome by the poisonous fumes, and Mrs. Hayter is convinced that as he sat at his desk his last thoughts were of his family. He received the Navy Cross posthumously, and a destroyer was christened in his name by Mrs. Hayter.

That is a fairly typical example of a death visitant, or apparition at the moment of death. From earliest times many examples of these have been recorded.

An experience, equally tragic, befell the wife of the engine-room Artificer Charles Matthews, a Portsmouth man, who was one of the crew of the submarine L24, sunk during manouevres in 1924, off the South Coast of England. Charlie Matthews had a strong premonition that the submarine's voyage was doomed to disaster, and told his wife so. He knew he would not come back. 'I know what will happen,' he told his wife, 'the boat will come up, take her distance, go down, and when we come up again we shall be struck by something.' So miserable did he feel that on the night before he was to embark he was utterly unable to sleep, and in his distress of mind wandered about in the rain. He was quite ill when he left at seven o'clock the following morning.

One afternoon shortly afterwards, Mrs. Matthews heard her husband calling her in their home. She turned round exclaiming, 'Is that you, Charlie?' At the same time Mrs. Dicks, who stayed in the same house, heard Charlie Matthews's voice saying, 'Look after her.' At that time the submarine had met disaster—in circumstances, according to experts who considered the evidence afterwards, identical with those foreseen by the sailor. Sailors as a class are not given to gloomy predictions before they sail but his prediction was all too true. Here, premonition was followed by a death visitant. His ghost was not seen, but *heard* at the time of the disaster.

The death of Napoleon was attended by two strange circumstances. A few days before his death Napoleon told Montholon, one of his entourage, 'I have just seen my dear Josephine, but she would not embrace me; she tore herself away when I tried to take her in my arms.' And at the moment Napoleon died his apparition appeared before his mother at her house in Rome. So real did he appear, so solid and living, that his mother thought that by some wholly unexpected twist of fate he had been able to come home. But he told her that he was 'at this moment delivered from his suffering'. Three other people saw him.

In folk-lore there are innumerable stories of death visitants. Some of these stories are based on facts, others no doubt have become garbled in the process of re-telling over the centuries. Such visitants, however, can sometimes be in animal form.

There was a remarkable occurrence in 1924 in connection with the death of Mr. Lionel Monckton, the popular composer. A close friend, Mr. Donald Calthorp, who was an actor-manager, was with several other actors in the Green Room Club, Leicester Square, which Monckton himself frequently used (he, too, was a member).

The actors suddenly noticed that Donald Calthorp stiffened, looking sad and concerned. He brought the conversation to an abrupt end, saying 'I believe something has happened to Lallie Monckton.' A few minutes afterwards Calthorp looked excitedly in a particular direction, and the eyes of the others followed his, wondering what could have caught his eye. 'Why, look!' said Calthorp, excitedly, 'there is his dog!' The two actors, Paul Arthur and Huntley Wright, could see nothing, and thought Calthorp was joking. A few hours later news reached the club that Monckton had died—at about the time that his friend had seen his dog, which he had often brought with him when he visited the club.

Lord Byron once related the story of a captain at sea who was sound asleep in his berth when he felt a weight upon his bed. Upon opening his eyes, he saw his brother, slouched across the bed, looking so real that he concluded he must be dreaming, and closed his eyes. But on opening them again, the vision was still there. He reached out a hand to touch his brother's coat (his brother was also a ship's officer) and found it dripping wet. In his terror, Captain Kidd, as his name was, called out in alarm. His brother officers came running to his cabin, but as they pushed open the door, the apparition vanished. A few months afterwards Captain Kidd received the tragic news that at the time he had seen the vision, his brother (who was in the same service in the East Indies) had been drowned in the Indian Ocean. To the end of his days Captain Kidd, a stolid, fearless and phlegmatic man not given to fanciful imaginings or morbid misgivings, maintained that the vision as he saw and later described it, was a fact.

The question of whether ghosts do or do not exist has always fascinated people. Sometimes it has led to compacts being made between friends. In two specific cases these arrangements, often made in a mood of light-hearted scepticism, have led to strange and terrifying results.

The first story is told, in his autobiography, by the famous lawyer and statesman Lord Brougham (1778-1868), Lord Chancellor of England. Lord Brougham was a man given to the sober assessment of facts. He had the lawyer's dislike of superficiality, empty showmanship and sloppy thinking. His wit, gaiety, deep knowledge of life and of people, coupled with his tremendous success and his prodigious memory, add extra weight to his story. He writes that as a youth he had discussed questions of immortality and survival with a close friend. Their questing curiosity determined them, if ever they should have the opportunity, to put the facts of the existence or non-existence of immortality to the test. They promised that if one should predecease the other, he or his wraith would appear to the survivor, as proof of his ability to do so.

Like most compacts of lifelong friendship, so common to school days, the somewhat melodramatic pact was forgotten in so far as their respective lives led them in different directions and they saw nothing of each other for years. One day Lord Brougham, who was at home, decided to have a bath. He placed his clothes on a chair, and going to retrieve them after having had his bath, he was astounded to see the phantom of his old friend sitting there. The experience was so unnerving that he fainted. Shortly afterwards, by what Lord Brougham called 'a singular coincidence' he received a letter telling him of the death of his friend.

A similar promise was made by two men at Oxford in 1850. The Reverend Theodore Alois Buckley a chaplain of Christ's College, and his close friend, R. H. MacKenzie, were arguing the merits and demerits of various theories of immortality and survival after death. Buckley, as a convinced Christian, would not concede any doubt about the soul's survival, so the two friends made a compact: Whoever died first would appear as a ghost to the other, in such a way that there could be no doubt about it.

Buckley, tragically, died young—at the age of thirty—on January 30, 1856. That night, between midnight and 1.30 a.m., MacKenzie was lying in bed. The candle which was the room's only illumination was guttering, being almost spent. At ease with the world and ready to doze off—and certainly with no thought at all of his friend—he suddenly felt a cold, damp hand placed over one eye. Looking up, he saw Buckley in his usual clothes with his document wallet under his arm in characteristic style, standing by his bedside. Torn between fear and curiosity, and remembering, with deepest misgivings, their mutual arrangement, MacKenzie kept his eyes on the ghost of his friend. The figure, seeming to realise that it had been recognised, moved backwards towards the window, stayed for about a minute, and then faded away. Buckley had appeared at the very moment of his death, or very shortly afterwards.

There was an even stranger sequel. A few nights afterwards the spectre again appeared to MacKenzie, this time holding in his hand the exact image of a letter which, only that day, MacKenzie had picked up from a box of correspondence. It was a letter written by Buckley when he was alive.

Scotland abounds with stories of death visitants. The family of Grant Rothiemurcus had the 'Bodach au Dun' or Ghost of the Hill whose appearance was said to be a warning of certain death. The Kinchardines were forewarned of their death by a singularly unpleasant and menacing spectre, the 'Lham-dearg' or Spectre of the Bloody Hand. Tulloch Gorms had their 'girl with the hairy left hand' (mentioned by Sir Walter Scott) while members of Lord Byron's family would learn of their impending doom by the appearance of The Black Friar, who,

'arrayed in cowl, and beads, and dusky garb'

haunted the cloisters and other parts of Newstead Abbey.

In Burke's *Anecdotes of the Aristocracy* (Volume 1, page 329) there is an extraordinary story concerning the Rev. James Crawford, rector of the parish of Killina, County Leitrim, Ireland. In 1777 he was crossing, on horseback, the estuary known as 'The Rosses' on the coast of Donegal with his sister-in-law, Miss Hannah Wilson, sitting on a pillion behind him. She, seeing that the water had already reached up to the saddle-straps, implored him to turn back before they were all drowned.

'I do not think there can be any danger,' Crawford told her, 'for I see a horseman crossing the ford not twenty yards before us.' His sister-in-law looked in the direction indicated and saw the horseman distinctly. Crawford drew rein and shouted to the other horseman that he wished to speak to him. The horseman stopped, turned round and displayed to the terrified couple a ghostly and ghastly countenance alive with malevolence and dynamic hate. Quickly Crawford turned round and raced home as fast as his horse could take him, telling his wife of the spectre they had seen. She told him that according to local legend, a drowning in the estuary was always foreshadowed by the spectre's appearance.

Crawford had been badly scared. But as a clergyman he felt he ought not to yield supinely to fear of evil, sustained as he hoped and believed he was by the purer forces of light. And so, attempting to cross the ford of the Rosses on September 27, 1777, he was drowned.

Many of the old castles in Germany have legends attached to them concerning the appearance of an apparition at the moment of, or before, a death in the family. The Elector of Brandenburg's house in Berlin was, it was said, always visited by an apparition in white which roamed restlessly about during the critical phases of sickness, and at death. Italy has similar legends. One concerns the family Donati in Venice, one of great wealth and lineage. Jacobo Donati, while sleeping, was awakened by the door of his chamber being opened and the head of a man being thrust in. Other servants in the house testified to a similar experience. Shouting with rage and alarm, Donati sprang out of bed, drew his sword and explored the palace—but without effect. The next day his son and heir, who lay dangerously ill, died.

There is the interesting, and carefully attested, story of the appearance of a death visitant to Captain Frederick Marryatt, commanding officer of a ship during the first Burmese war. One night he observed a stranger enter his cabin and, taking it for granted that anyone entering by stealth and without permission must be a robber, he sprang from his bed to attack him. There was a full moon, and in the bright light he clearly recognised his brother, who came to the side of his berth and was heard to say distinctly, 'Fred, I have come to tell you that I am dead!' and then vanished. Capain Marryatt, true to the punctillious traditions of his service, recorded this strange occurrence in his log book. When he returned to England, he discovered that his brother had died at the time his ghost had appeared.

An extraordinary case of a 'death visitant', a spectre which had, seemingly, some prescience of the future, is related by Sir Ernest Bennett in *Apparitions and Haunted Houses*.

On December 3, 1908, a Roman Catholic priest, called for the sake of anonymity 'Father C', was living in the official residence of the Bishop of Southwark in St. George's Road, South London. It is a large, rambling house and although on my last visit it looked cheerful enough, there is still an air of gothic gloom in its long passages and stone floors.

'One other priest was living in the house,' Father C recalled, 'but at this time he was away from home, so that the Bishop and I were alone except for the servants, whose quarters were in the semi-basement ... On the evening of the 2nd, the Bishop and I dined together and after dinner he went to his room and I to mine on the third floor.

'At about 6.30 a.m. on December 3rd I got up and proceeded downstairs to the bathroom. As I turned the corner of the stairs from my room on the third floor and was proceeding down the flight of steps which led to the landing on the second floor, I saw an elderly man standing at the foot of the stairs. He was a stranger to me and wore a cassock and white cotta or short surplice. The man, who had grey hair and a very long straight upper lip, stood with his hands joined and his head on one side, looking at me in an inquiring sort of way. I thought he was some priest who had come after dinner overnight and that he was looking for the Bishop's oratory, and was about to speak to him when he vanished completely. I still thought he had gone into one or other of the passages and looked for him in both. Until I failed to find him, I had no idea but that he was a living man ... after breakfast I asked the Bishop if anybody had stayed in the house overnight and he said "no". I then went about my usual work and at luncheon the bishop told me that Father F of Bromley, Kent, had died that morning at 6.30 a.m. As I did not know him even by sight this information did not affect me at all.

'About five or six weeks later I was appointed to take the place of this Father F at Bromley. When I got settled in and began to visit my parishioners I went into a house and in the parlour saw a large framed photograph of an elderly priest— without a shadow of a doubt the man I had seen on the stairs on December 3rd. When the owner of the house came in I asked "Whose portrait is that?" She replied "Why, don't you know? That was dear Father F."

The curious aspect of this case, as to the authenticity of

which there is not the slightest question, is that the ghost seemed to know that Father C was to succeed him.

We like to think that time mitigates tragedy—that if something happened long ago, it can be a subject of jest. It is, by this reasoning, normal to joke about the execution of Anne Boleyn, but inhuman to laugh at the recent execution of a criminal, although the former was innocent and the latter was not. Yet, although the example of a 'death visitant' which I now propose to describe happened a century ago, it remains a moving story.

We must imagine ourselves back in the days so vividly described (and certainly not exaggerated) by Charles Dickens, when the streets of London were crowded with homeless and starving children—the days of ill-lit streets, freezing workhouses, Bumbledom and patronising charity. Children often slept in rags in the gutters. Chimney-boys were stripped naked and forced to climb inside soot-encrusted chimneys where they often became jammed or even suffocated by fumes from the straw lit in the fireplace to spur them to renewed effort. The thieves' kitchens were, for many, their only refuge from the cold. Such charitable institutions as did exist for abandoned or orphaned children were pitifully few.

Against this social background a good priest could do much to mitigate a child's harsh lot. Indeed, before the advent of the welfare state the priest or parson would be almost the only man the distressed would feel entitled to approach. Such a man was Dr. Todd, who ran a Roman Catholic orphanage in Greenwich. Amongst his charges was an intelligent, quick-witted and somewhat undisciplined boy called Tom Potter.

Tom had no home except the orphanage, but was devoted to his harassed and hard-worked mother, who was employed as a maid in the comfortable home of a Lloyd's underwriter who lived on Croom's Hill, Greenwich.

Launching Tom in life was no easy matter. His independence and high spirits were against him in a period still excessively class-conscious; when 'to try to get above oneself' was *lese majestie* and where some degree of guilt was expected to accompany poverty. However, Dr. Todd managed to place Tom Potter, in 1863-4, in a trading house in Manchester, but he was eventually deemed unsuitable and dismissed. He was next put on a ship at Woolwich, and was drafted after a time to one of Her Majesty's men-o'-war.

One day, the doorbell at the house in Croom's Hill rang. Mrs. Potter answered it. There was Tom Potter, pale, ragged, starving and exhausted; with a number of others, he had deserted.

Mrs. Potter took him round to see the patient and persevering Dr. Todd at the orphanage. 'You're here again, Tom, are you?' he said, and led the boy and his tearful mother into his study. There he impressed upon the boy the serious consequences of his action. He could be arrested and severely punished if he let things drift and was subsequently caught; and caught he almost certainly would be, as he was without work and would have to get some employment and support. He was now too old for the orphanage, and anyway they could not condone a breach of the law. But Dr. Todd promised to get in touch with the captain himself, tell him of his high opinion of Tom's character, ascribing the boy's impetuous desertion to being easily led, and the insecurity deriving from his unsatisfactory home life. The captain consented to take Tom Potter back 'with only nominal punishment'—a phrase whose meaning after all this time we can only guess at. And Tom was shipped off on board the frigate *Doris,* bound for the West Indies.

Mrs. Potter left the house at Croom's Hill and married again, becoming Mrs. Cooper. She was replaced as housemaid by a girl called Mary, who had never met her predecessor, nor heard of the boy.

On the night of September 8, 1866, a storm howled and swept through Greenwich and torrential rain poured down. The doorbell at Croom's Hill rang insistently and Mary, quickly smoothing her apron and running her fingers through her hair, went to answer the front door.

There, huddled under the portico, was a young boy, barefooted, shivering with cold, pale and distraught. Mary, disgusted and possibly frightened—homeless urchins were all too numerous, and many were thieves—asked him what he wanted, told him to be on his way, and closed the door with a thankful bang.

Mrs. Hubbard, the lady of the house, was ill at the time, but her bedroom commanded a view of the hall and put her just within earshot of the front door. She thought she recognised the voice of Tom Potter. 'Who was that, Mary?' she called out from her bed. 'Oh ma'am,' said Mary, 'it was a little sailor boy. He wanted his mother. I told him I knew nothing of his mother and sent him about his business.'

'What was the boy like?'

'Well, ma'am, he was a good-looking boy in sailor's clothes and his feet were naked. He looked pale and in great distress,

and when I told him his mother wasn't here he put his hand
to his forehead and said "Oh dear, what shall I do?" '

Mrs. Hubbard was immediately stricken with conscience.
Tom, for all his waywardness, was a likeable boy and in her
own heart she would have liked to have adopted him. Now she
felt he had been turned away from the door in foul weather,
homeless and hungry and probably too scared or contrite to go
near the kindly priest again. She talked it over with her husband. She was sure the boy had run away again and anything
could happen to him in London. He might take to crime, or
die of starvation, or commit suicide—a common enough occurrence. She sent for the boy's mother, but Mrs. Cooper had
neither heard nor seen anything of the boy, although greatly
worried by the news, so it was decided that they should go
and see the priest, taking Mary, the new housemaid who had
answered the door, with them.

At the orphanage, Dr. Todd listened to their story. On a
table he had arranged numerous photographs of boys who
had been or were staying at the orphanage. He pointed to one
lad—not Tom Potter—and said to Mary 'Is that the lad?' 'No,'
said Mary, 'that was *not* the one I saw; *this is the one.*' And
she pointed to a photograph of Tom Potter.

In October, a letter arrived at the orphanage from the Admiralty, giving the news that Tom Potter had died, following
a tragic accident on board the *Doris*, on September 6th just
two days before the boy appeared at the doorway of the house
where his mother once worked, and which he had visited
before. On July 28th he had fallen from the masthead and,
after lingering in agony for a few weeks, had died raving and
calling for his mother.

A strange example of a woman being seen walking about
shortly after her death was reported in the *Psychic News* of
January 2, 1939. Her ghost was seen by *two* people simultaneously. The circumstances were these:

On Monday, December 8, 1938, near the market town of
Great Dunmow, a woman shot her husband and then committed suicide by the same method. The discovery was not
made until 7.45 the following morning, for the couple had been
alone in the house. The servant who discovered the tragedy
fetched the police who arrived and found the couple dead at
8.30 a.m. At whatever hour, therefore, the couple had died, it
is absolutely certain that the doctor summoned to the scene
certified them dead at 8.30 a.m.

That morning a married couple were motoring to the station

to catch the 9.30 train. As usual, they allowed themselves just
sufficient time to do it comfortably, and passed the house of
tragedy at 9.20 a.m.—forty minutes after the man and woman
inside had been examined by a doctor and found to be dead.
But as they neared the house they saw the woman walking towards them on the pavement. The husband, who was driving,
said 'Oh, there is Mrs.—— She gives me the creeps.' His wife
looked in the direction indicated and saw the woman. 'So it
is,' she said. When they later read of the tragedy, and the
alleged discovery of the bodies at 8.30 a.m., they went to the
police and said that the facts as stated must be wrong, because
they had definitely seen the woman at 9.20 a.m. and had
continued direct to the station, where they caught their 9.30
train with just a few minutes to spare. The police, however,
are habitually fussy about times, and all the records, both of
the servant's report and the officers and doctors who went to
the house, were in complete agreement about it. So there it
was; whatever the explanation, the dead woman *was* seen at
the very least forty minutes, and probably much longer, after
her death.

The late Edmund Gurney, M.A., whose famous work *Phantasms of the Living* is a unique classic of its kind and the
product of the most painstaking and objective research,
quotes a remarkable case of a 'death visitant' which occurred
in 1883.

The Rev. Robert Bee, then living at 12, Whitworth Road,
Grangetown, near Southbank, Yorkshire described to Gurney an
experience which he had had ten years earlier. His statement
reads:

'On December 18, 1873, I left my house in Lincolnshire to
visit my wife's parents, then and now residing in Lord Street,
Southport. Both my parents were, to all appearances, in good
health when I left them. The day after my arrival in Southport was spent in leisurely observation of the manifold attrac-
tions of this fashionable seaside resort. I spent the evening in
company with my wife in the bay-windowed drawing room upstairs, which fronts the main street of the town. I proposed a
game of chess, and we got out the board and began to play.
Perhaps half an hour had been thus occupied by us, during
which I had made several foolish mistakes. A deep melancholy
was oppressing me and at length I remarked: 'It's no use
trying to play; I cannot for the life of me think about what I
am doing. Shall we shut up and resume our talk? I feel utterly
wretched.''

' "Just as you like," said my wife, and the board was at once put aside.

'This was about half past seven o'clock, and after a few minutes' desultory conversation, my wife suddenly remarked: "*I* feel very dull tonight. I think I will go downstairs to Mama for a few minutes."

'Soon after my wife's departure, I rose from my chair, and walked in the direction of the drawing-room door. Here I paused for a moment, and then passed through to the landing of the stairs.

'It was then exactly ten minutes to eight o'clock. I stood for a moment upon the landing, when a lady, dressed as if she were going on a business errand, came out, apparently, from an adjoining bedroom, and passed close to me. I did not see her features distinctly, nor do I remember what it was I said to her.

'She passed down the narrow, winding stairs, and at the same instant my wife came up again, so that she must have passed close to the stranger—in fact, to all appearances, brushed against her.

'I exclaimed, almost immediately, "Who is the lady, Polly, that you passed just now, when you were coming up?"

'Never can I forget, or account for, my wife's answer. "I did not pass anybody," she said.

' "Nonsense," I replied, "You met a lady just now, dressed for a walk. She came out of the little bedroom. I spoke to her. She must be a visitor staying with your mother. She has left no doubt, by the front door."

' "That is impossible," said my wife, "There are no guests in the house. They all left nearly a week ago. In fact, there is no one at all indoors, apart from ourselves and Mama."

' "Strange," I said, "I am certain I saw and spoke to a lady just before you came upstairs, and I distinctly saw her pass you. It seems incredible that you did not perceive her." '

(In his account to Edward Gurney, Bee insisted that he saw both women *simultaneously*.)

'My wife positively asserted that she had not seen anyone coming down the stairs. We went downstairs together and I related the story to my wife's mother who was busy with her household duties. She confirmed her daughter's previous statement.

'Early next morning, a telegram reached me from Lincolnshire. It was from my eldest sister, Julia (Mrs. T. W. Bowman of Prospect House, Stechford, Birmingham) and announced the afflicting intelligence that our dear mother had passed away the night before, and that we (i.e. myself and wife) were to return home to Gainsborough by the next train. The doctor said it was heart disease which, in a few minutes, had caused her death.'

When all was over, Mr. Bee asked his brother the exact moment of his mother's death. The answer was *ten minutes to eight o'clock*. Being taken ill in the street, she had died in her dress and boots. Although he had not seen her features clearly, and would not have done so had she been a real person, for the hall light was very dim, the apparition he had seen represented his mother exactly in size, dress and general appearance.

Mr. Bee was asked if he had ever had any previous experience of the kind. He had not.

This story is a striking one because the most careful investigation confirmed the facts as stated. There is no doubt that the apparition *did* appear at the moment of death and it could not have been a real person, because it was not possible for Mrs. Bee to have failed to notice anyone passing her on the same staircase.

An uncanny story was related to Gurney by a man who, although asking for his name to be withheld, submitted all the names and addresses necessary for verification. In 1876 he was living in a small agricultural parish in Eastern England, and occasionally met—but did not attempt to know well—a young man who occupied a large farm on his estate. While his house was being altered the young farmer lodged with his groom. He appeared to be a straightforward, if not particularly interesting type, knowledgeable about farming and fond of field sports and country life. Dr. Gurney's informant felt no interest in the man beyond that of a landlord to his tenant.

One afternoon in March, 1876, when he was walking home from the railway station with his wife, he was accosted by the young man who attached himself like a limpet and talked solidly to them all the way up the sixty yards' drive to their very front door. But he was not invited in. About half an hour later they met him again and the young man made the same attempt to strike up a warmer friendship. He appeared to be depressed and cast down at the bad times and the low prices of farming produce. He asked to borrow some wire rope, which was agreed upon, and as they parted the young man said, to the other's surprise: 'Come and smoke a cigar with me tonight.' 'I cannot very well,' was the reply, 'as I am engaged this evening.' 'Do come,' the man persisted. 'No,' was the reply, 'I will look in another evening.' With that they parted. But about forty yards away the young farmer turned, faced the other man, and said, 'Then if you will not come, good-bye.'

The rest of this striking narrative I give in the informant's own words:

'I spent the evening in my dining-room in writing, and for some hours I may say that no thought of young Mr. B passed through my mind. The night was bright and clear, with full or nearly full moon, and without wind. Since I had come in, slight snow had fallen—just sufficient to make the ground snow white. At about five minutes to ten o'clock I got up and left the room, taking up a lamp from the hall table and replacing it on a small table standing in a recess of the window in the breakfast-room. The curtains were not drawn across the window. I had just taken down from the nearest bookcase a volume of Macgillivray's *British Birds* for reference, and was in the act of reading the passage, the book held close to the lamp, and my shoulder touching the window shutter, and in a position in which almost the slightest sound outside would be heard, when I distinctly heard the front gate opened and shut with a clap, and footsteps advancing at a run up the drive. When opposite the window the steps changed from sharp and distinct on gravel to dull and less clear on the grass slip below the window, and at the same time I was conscious that someone or something stood close to me outside, only the thin shutter and a sheet of glass dividing us. I could hear the quick, panting, laboured breathing of the messenger, or whatever it was, as if trying to recover breath before speaking. Had he been attracted by the light through the shutter? Suddenly, like gunshot, inside, outside, all around, there broke out the most appalling shriek—a prolonged wail of horror, which seemed to freeze the blood. It was not a single shriek, but more prolonged, commencing in a high key, and then less and less, wailing away towards the north, and becoming weaker and weaker as it receded in sobbing pulsations of intense agony. Of my fright and horror I can say nothing—increased tenfold when I walked into the dining-room and found my wife sitting quietly at her work close to the window, in the same line and distant only ten or twelve feet from the corresponding window in the breakfast-room. *She had heard nothing.* I could see that at once; and from the position in which she was sitting, I knew she could not have failed to hear any noise outside and any footstep on the gravel. Perceiving that I was alarmed about something, she asked "What is the matter?" "Only someone outside," I replied. "Then why do you not go out and see?" I said: "There is something so queer and dreadful about the noise. I dare not face it. It must have been the banshee shrieking." '

That occurrence was on Thursday night, March 9, 1876 at ten p.m. At that moment the young man who had said 'good-bye' had swallowed prussic acid and, shrieking with pain, had died in the groom's house—the groom and his wife had gone to bed. This was by no means near the house where the piercing, prolonged scream had been heard. Indeed, as the informant put it: 'It is utterly impossible that anything short of a cannon ball could have reached me from B's lodgings, through closed windows and closed doors, and the many intervening obstacles of houses and gardens, farmsteads and plantations, etc.' Very early that following morning, he examined the ground beneath the window, and the grass, and the gravel drive but there were no footprints whatsoever; just the untroubled covering of snow which had fallen the previous evening. That slight snow had fallen at 8 p.m., no later. After that, the night was bright and fine and very still. There was also a rather sharp frost. The young man, it is thought, had committed suicide because of an unhappy love affair, but the mystery was never finally resolved. As for the extraordinary (and unnerving) experience of the landlord, telepathy scarcely explains the matter; it is one thing to assume that by virtue of certain unknown natural laws or propensities, he was 'tuned in' to the young man who had just taken his life. But the footsteps on the gravel path? The unlatching and closing of the gate? The panting heard on the other side of the shutter? How account for those?

Then there is the well-authenticated case of a death visitant in Cambridgeshire in 1850. Timothy Cooper was one of a very large family. His father was a Baptist minister living in Soham, and between the son and his mother there was a very deep and close bond of affection. Cooper was working in London and hearing that his mother was very ill, got leave of absence from work to come home and be with her. On the night before he was to leave her and return to work, as it was known to the mother and all around her that she was dying, he said, in his distress at having to leave her at such a time: 'Mother, if it is possible, when you pass away will you come and tell me?' She said 'I will if I possibly can.'

'On the morning of October 7th,' Cooper reported, 'I awoke

and felt like a soft hand touch me and heard the well-known voice say "I am gone", and something seemed to glide away from my side. I awoke the young man who was sleeping with me and said "My mother has gone. She has just been here and told me so," and just as I said it the clock standing on the stairs struck three. The news came to hand that my mother had died at five minutes to three.'

A striking example of a death visitant (and again the result of a compact between friends) is related by Frederic W. H. Myers in *Human Personality*. The Rev. Arthur Bellamy of Bristol related how his wife, as a schoolgirl, had made a pact with a school friend that whichever died first would appear to the other. When, therefore, she heard of her friend's death in 1874, she told her husband about the promise that had been made. Mr. Bellamy had never seen this friend, or even a photograph of her.

About two nights later Mr. Bellamy, in bed with his wife, woke up suddenly. His wife slept on soundly. In the light of the fire, and of a candle which had been left burning, he could see a strange woman seated beside the bed. Her costume and expression, and most of all her beautiful hair, meticulously dressed, impressed him, although this impression was mixed with surprise and bewilderment. He looked at her for several minutes, then she vanished. There was no natural explanation—no obstruction which sleepy eyes might have 'translated' into something approximating in outline and colour. And when he described the woman to his wife, who had seen and heard nothing and was not even dreaming, she revealed that it exactly described her dead friend. 'At school,' she added, 'we always used to tease her about her hair, which she always arranged with special care.'

In *The Gentleman's Magazine* is an interesting account of a ghost which, appearing to the Rev. Jeffrey Shaw, Rector of Souldern, Oxfordshire, informed him that he would die soon and suddenly. Shortly afterwards he was seized with an apoplectic fit while reading the service in church, and died within minutes. This occurrence is recorded in the register of Brisley Church, Norfolk, under the entry for December 12, 1706, with the observation: 'I, Robert Withers, M.A., Vicar of Gatley, do insert here a story I had from undoubted hands, for I have all the moral certainty of the truth of it possible.' And the Rev. Jeffrey Shaw's tombstone in the chancel of Souldern church bears an inscription which the present Rector has kindly copied for me:

> HERE LYES THE BODY OF
> JEFFRY SHAW, B.D.
> RECTOR OF THIS CHURCH
> WHO FELL DOWN DEAD WHILE HE WAS
> READING DIVINE SERVICE THEREIN
> ON SUNDAY NOV XVII MDCCCVI
> BLESSED IS THAT SERVANT WHOM HIS LORD
> WHEN HE COMETH SHALL FIND SO DOING.

The rectory in which Mr. Shaw lived was completely de-molished because it was very damp and rebuilt in 1896. Since then, so the Rector, the Rev. Maurice G. Sheldon informs me, there has been no haunting.

Apparitions which warn of death, or announce it, or appear soon afterwards have been recorded ever since history began. One day perhaps, when more is known of the dimensions of time and space, some explanation may be found of these strange phenomena. Telepathy seems to play some part in these occur-rences and may even be a factor in those cases where the phantom appears *after* death. The emanations of the mind, as the encephalograph used in hospitals proves, are—however faintly—electrical. It is possible even to measure the voltage of mind-impulses.

We must be chary however of quasi-scientific explanations. As J. W. Dunne reminded us during his lifetime, and tried so hard to explain in such works of his as *Experiment with Time*, the past, present and future are not so neatly separated as we like to imagine. Thought impulses generated or transmitted from the brain may travel and, under certain conditions yet to be satisfactorily defined, be 'received' by the percipient. But what justification or proof have we that such thoughts travel *instantaneously*? Are we entitled to assume that they do? May not such thoughts be delayed for hours, days, months or years before onward transmission?

The following account appears in the *Memoir of Sir John Coape Sherbrooke, J.C.B.*, by A. Patchett Martin, published in 1893:

'No account of Sir John Sherbrooke could be complete with-out a reference to the famous story of the Wynyard apparition. It occurred in Sydney, Cape Breton, when Captain Sherbrooke, as he then was, was stationed for a while with the 33rd Regiment, before his memorable achievement in covering the retreat of the Duke of York in Flanders.

'One evening Captain Sherbrooke and Lieutenant (afterwards General) Wynyard were seated in the latter's room, which had two doors, the one opening into an outer passage, the other into the bedroom. These were the only means of ingress or egress, so that anyone passing into the bedroom must have remained there, unless he returned through the sitting-room.

'The story goes that Sherbrooke suddenly perceived, standing by the passage door, a tall youth of about twenty, pale and wan, to whom he called his companion's attention.

' "I have heard," said Sherbrooke, "of a man becoming as pale as death, but I never saw a living face assume the appearance of a corpse except Wynyard's at that moment."

'While they were gazing, the figure, which had turned upon Wynyard a glance of sorrowful affection glided into the bedroom. Wynyard, seizing his friend's arm, said, in a whisper, "Great heaven! My brother!" "Your brother?" replied Sherbrooke, "what do you mean? There must be some deception. Let us follow."

'They darted into the adjoining room, only to find it empty. Another young officer, Ralph Gore, coming in at this moment, proceeded to join in the search. It was he who suggested that a note should be made of the day and hour of the apparition.

'The mail brought no letters from England for Wynyard, but there was one for Sherbrooke, which he hastily opened, and then beckoned Wynyard away. When he returned, alone, to the messroom, he said in a low voice to the man next to him: "Wynyard's brother is dead!" The first line in the letter had run "Dear John, break to your friend, Wynyard, the death of his favourite brother." He had died at the very moment when the apparition appeared in his brother's room.'

Most people over thirty-five years of age will remember the appalling shock to the nation when it learned that at 1.30 a.m. on October 14, 1939, a German U-boat penetrated the defences of Scapa Flow and sank the British battleship *Royal Oak*. Mrs. Edna Mary Hunt, an infant school teacher, of Midanbury, Southampton, tells me:

'I have a vivid recollection of a personal experience on the evening of October 14, 1939. The tragic news of the sinking of H.M.S. *Royal Oak* at Scapa Flow had been broadcast on the one o'clock news. My fianceé, a Leading Signaller, Albert S. Baldwin, was serving in that ship at the time. During the night I had a distinct dream or vision of him standing close by with a dreadful expression of anguish on his face, and his lips were closed as if he were speechless. Then his whole figure seemed to become elongated and faded away.

'Early next morning I was asked to look at the newspaper to see if his name was amongst the list of survivors. I refused to do so as I was quite convinced of his death (a conviction proved to be correct). Later that day I had my last letter from him. It had been written and posted October 13th. Since then I have only cherished memories.'

Mr. Charles E. Marn of Little Meads, Romsey, Hants, has given me an example of a 'death visitant' which appeared from only a short distance away.

'It happened about sixty years ago ... but it is as clear today as when it happened. First I must tell you that when I was young I used to wear a sort of apron when playing in the garden. In the next house lived an old gentleman who had several nice apple trees, and when he was picking apples he would call me to the wall and tell me to hold out my apron to catch the apples he dropped in it.

'When I went to bed my mother used to leave the bedroom door open with a light on the landing. On the night in question I seemed to wake up to see the gentleman from next door standing at the foot of the bed, dropping apples over the footboard. The vision was so clear that I got out of bed and started to look for the apples. The heavy movement made my mother come and see what it was all about, so I told her that Mr. Walker had been in the room and had put apples on the bed. My mother said that I must have been dreaming, because Mr. Walker had not been in the house as he was unwell and had not been out for some time. In the morning we learned that Mr. Walker had died the previous night.'

A curious story comes to me from Mrs. Doris Pilkington of Manor Road, Horwich, Bolton, Lancs. A passage of sixty years has in no wise dimmed the detail of her recollection of the following:

'When I was seventeen years old my mother had to undergo an operation at Manchester and the specialist said that she had one chance in six of recovery. We were living in Moss Bank Cottage, Smithels, Bolton. I had the job of looking after the house and my father and small brother while she was away. The night before she left for hospital I lay in bed feeling awfully worried. Suddenly, I saw a woman—probably in her early forties—standing at the foot of my bed. She was on the small side, had bright blue eyes, colour on her cheek-bones and hair smoothly parted in the middle. She wore a slate-grey dress with the bodice buttoned with tiny black buttons in a point over the skirt. The yoke was outlined with a band of velvet about one and a half inches wide. When mother had been home again for a few weeks after a successful operation, one of her elder sisters came to see her. After tea, I asked them: "Do either of you know anyone like this?" and described the woman. Mother replied "I'm afraid I don't" but Auntie looked at me with astonishment and said "Why, child, you have described our mother just as she was when your mother was born. She was very fond of that dress."

'Granny was forty-five years old when mother was born and died aged seventy-three when I was three months old. The only photo we have of her was one taken shortly before she died, showing her to be very different from the lady who visited my bedroom.'

I asked Mrs. Pilkington whether the ghost of her grandmother appeared to be transparent or solid. 'When she appeared at the foot of my bed' she replied, 'she looked just like an ordinary living person.' No one else saw the phantasm, but when Miss Pilkington told her family about it, the news was received in a matter-of-fact sort of way. Apparently they had got used to that sort of thing since the day the whole family first moved into Moss Bank Cottage in 1907, where they soon became accustomed to a kind of 'residential' ghost.

The cottage, which had once been the gatehouse to Moss Bank Hall, was rather isolated. After a few days' residence they got the impression at times that somebody was coming to the back door, 'but they never arrived.' Visitors often got the same impression. It had, apparently, nothing to do with the time of the day or the weather. 'Once,' Mrs. Pilkington recalls, 'mother went downstairs during the night and saw an old woman with a red shawl sitting in front of the fire. She described the lady to an old man who often walked down the lane. He said it was very like his aunt who had lived in the house when it was first built. Some years later his family had to leave for business reasons and the aunt didn't like having to leave the house.'

The interesting aspect of the grandmother's appearance is that Mrs. Pilkington had never seen an early photograph of her. Incidentally, she felt certain, when she saw the ghost, that her mother would recover from her illness because 'granny's face was so placid and contented.'

A strange story of a death visitant or apparition at the moment of death, was related to me by Mr. W. H. Curtis, of Northam Avenue, Upper Shirley, Southampton.

In 1914 he was serving with his regiment in India, and ' ... in due course we were sent on service to Palestine where we drove Johnny Turk up into the hills of Judea and there, one morning, got surprised by a shower of Turks. During the resulting battle I was wounded, but managed to obtain first aid then, by stretcher and mule cart, I reached the first casualty clearing station, a small place situated in an orchard and looking very clean and pretty in the early morning sun. They carried me in and as we paused for a moment outside the Medical Officer's tent, I was surprised to see young Scott come up to me' ('young Scott' was a member of his regiment whom he did not know particularly well though they exchanged occasional pleasantries).

' "Hullo, Scott old man, you here?" were my first words, but he did not speak—only smiled. I noticed how pale he looked, and how the freckles on his face stood out in marked contrast; I also noticed what seemed to be a large patch of dried blood on part of his head and neck. I thought it rather odd for a man to be walking about without a wound-dressing of some sort, but at that moment I saw the M.O. coming towards me, so I said to Scott: "Come along and see us when I've got through with this lot." Then the M.O. came up and seemed to jostle with him somewhat; with that Scott walked away.

'Next I was in a tent looking through the flies, when I saw a pair of of legs come along. Someone bent down and I recognised a corporal of my company who came out with the all too familiar query: had I seen any of our fellows on the way? I said "No, only Scott, he's here somewhere." With that the corporal said "That's queer, I thought I was the only one until you came."

'Later on I started my journey to hospital. On the way I encountered some men, one of whom threatened to knock my block off when, in answer to his questions, I said I'd seen Scott; but neither of us was in any condition to fight, so we went our different ways. Feeling a bit mystified, I decided to say no more about it. Then, about two years afterwards when I was back in Blighty, I met the Quarters of my old company and we fell to talking about the different battles. I asked him if he remembered Scott. "Yes, indeed I do," he said, "Corporal Brown and I helped to bury him and his comrades just behind the ridge where they fell." Did he, I asked, happen to notice where Scott was hit? "Yes, at the back of the head and neck," he replied. I then found the corporal, who verified this.'

Some time later, in conversation with his mother, Mr. Curtis learned that his father had met young Scott's father.

'Then,' says Mr. Curtis, 'a great light seemed to dawn on me, for I remembered years before, as a young boy, travelling round one summer with my parents when they were looking for a suitable public house to take over. During the course of our travels we visited a certain village, where we stayed longer than usual and while my parents talked business I spent the afternoon playing with the innkeeper's son. We got on first-rate, what with his rabbits, and he had some boxing gloves, but I never met him again. So did not know what to think, and still do not; suffice it to say that it made a lasting impression on me all my life.'

It is indeed extraordinary that Scott should have appeared to him so plainly at the time of his death, since there was only this tenuous link between them. Had poor Scott's mind, in the instantaneous impact of death flashed back to that childhood encounter, thereby establishing some telepathic link with Curtis? Or had his brain continued to work for a few moments after death, sending out its thoughts in some mysterious manner? Whatever the reason, we can well understand what Mr. Curtis means when he says that the impression remained with him for the rest of his life.

From another informant I have a strange story which I give in her own plain but graphic words. Mrs. A. Spicknell, of Felwood Broadway, Knowle, Bristol, told me:

'One night I went to bed but could not sleep. Then, suddenly, I felt my body travelling in space; the funny part was, I wasn't a bit afraid. Presently I came to a door, and the door slowly opened. I was looking into the loveliest of rooms, being in pink and green marble; at one end was a magnificent stairway, and over everything was an ethereal light. As I watched, so my dear mother came gliding down the stairs, and in her arms was my nephew's baby. As she drew nearer, I noticed the baby was wearing a greeny-blue nightdress with pink rosebuds on the bodice.

'The baby was so strong that my mother had a job to hold it. When Mother came close I said "Mother, why have you got Billie's baby?" Mother replied "That is why you have visited me. I want you to tell Doris (the baby's mother) she is not to grieve, for her baby is in better health now than it has ever been in its short life on earth, and I am looking after it until such time as she can claim it. You won't forget to give her the message, will you?" I answered, "No, Mother, I won't forget." Mother then said, "Goodbye. I shall see you again one day." I came to, and I was in bed again.

'Next morning, as I was telling my dad, my sister came in (this was the baby's grandmother). She was crying and she said that Billie's baby had died in the night, after a sudden illness lasting only three hours. When I told her what had happened in the night, and I described the nightdress, she said that was what the baby was wearing when it died. I must mention that I had never seen the nightdress before, and when my sister brought the nightdress for me to see, it proved to be exactly the same as the one the baby was wearing when I saw it in my mother's arms.'

A dream? But why should Mrs. Spicknell have dreamed about the baby *of whose illness she had heard nothing*—and furthermore have seen in detail the pattern and colouring of the baby's nightdress?

A strange story indeed—but Mr. C. G. Barrie of London Road, Blackburn, Lancashire, tells me of an experience he had in Kirriemuir, Scotland, forty years ago:

'As I passed a house, what looked like a piece of diaphanous material appeared from the top of a *closed* window and disappeared rapidly upwards. I learned later that a newly-born child died in that room of the house at that time ...'

7

Noisy poltergeists

Of all ghostly manifestations guaranteed to make the hackles rise and the hair stand on end, the activities of the poltergeist come high on the list.

It is easy to understand why this should be so. Apparitions defying natural laws by appearing through walls and disappearing through closed doors; disembodied voices; sepulchral shadows or the unnerving menace of sounds without vision—all these things, except for those with the toughest nerves, are terrifying enough. But when stones appear from nowhere; when furniture is shifted by unseen hands; when objects levitate themselves—not to say when somebody has the physical sensation of being attacked (the terror of the unknown being added to the terror of the tangible), then the abyss of fear is being plumbed.

Whole families have been known to flee from their homes at dead of night or in severe winter to escape the depredations of these invisible influences, whatever they are. Clergymen in Britain and elsewhere are constantly being called in to exorcise these noisy 'spirits'. Psychologists and psychiatrists have tried in vain to define in scientific terms the basis of these extraordinary manifestations; but their vocabulary, as pitifully incomplete as their knowledge of the occult, fails them. They have had to content themselves with the observation that these disturbances are often acute in homes in which one or more members are going through the stages of puberty. This is an interesting, but unconvincing observation, because there are few homes in which at some time or another somebody does not go through the inevitable transition of puberty, and if poltergeist activites were an inevitable complement, poltergeists would be the rule rather than the exception.

Poltergeist is a German word for 'racketing spirit'. Accounts of poltergeist activities are not simply folk-lore—picturesque tales based on a tiny residue of fact or no facts at all. They are not the morbid inventions of the unhealthily credulous nor, generally, the impostures of impudent or mercenary fakes; nor are they atavistic memories of the trials and terrors of our ancestors as experienced thousands of years ago, so that these secret fears are in the very genes that gave us being. There are hundreds of well-authenticated cases of such hauntings, reliably corroborated by witnesses of unquestioned probity and reason. The neurotics and frauds may have added their noise to the ghostly clamour, but in proportion to the whole it has been little indeed.

Consider, for instance, how extraordinarily persistent are reports of unexplained showers of stones. In A.D. 530 according to Cyprian's *Life of St. Caesarius of Arles* one reads that Deacon Helpidius, physician to King Theoderic, was troubled in his house by noisy spirits and by showers of stones actually *inside* the house. Showers of stones afflicted the house of Bishop Hugh of Maus in 1138. In 1170, the hermitage of poor St. Godric was hit by showers of stones. The Cieza de Leon (1549) describes how, during his conversion to Christianity, the cacique of Pirza, in Popyan, was bombarded by a hail of stones appearing from out of the air, while Mr. Dennys in *Folk Lore of China*, published 1876, tells of a Chinese householder who fled from his home to a temple for refuge from poltergeists which threw crockery about and made life intolerable by their heavy footfalls.

In 1612 M. Perrault, a Huguenot minister, described at length and in considerable detail, poltergeist phenomena that continued, including stone-throwing, for two months. When a poltergeist ran amok in the monastery of Malbroun in 1659-60, stones were hurled, fire started and bedding torn from beds, and these phenomena continued despite the guard of a regiment of soldiers.

One of the best-documented visitations of a poltergeist is contained in the letters and diaries of the Wesley family (see Southey's *Life of John Wesley*) and these happenings between 1716 and 1717 are chronicled with such care as to leave no room for doubt. There are letters written to Samuel, the eldest son, by his parents and two sisters, and the personal accounts of the Reverend Samuel Wesley and Mr. Hoole, a local vicar. A manservant, Robert Brown, testified to the veracity of the accounts, and so did John Wesley. There is absolutely nothing in the lives of this worthy, God-fearing family to support even a suspicion that they could or would be capable of fraud.

At the time of the visitations the Reverend Samuel Wesley was living at Epworth Rectory where he spent most of his time

writing books and poetry. His life, even before the appearance
of the poltergeists, had been far from easy—once he was thrown
into prison for debt; twice his rectory went up in flames. His
wife, Susanna, was a strong character with decided ideas of her
own. She expressed disagreement, for example, with her husband's politics—an unusual thing in the eighteenth century.

In 1716, his household began to complain of strange happenings: ominous and inexplicable rumblings were sometimes
heard in the basement and attic. Loud knocks would shatter
the reverent silence of the rectory. Throughout the night the
heavy footfalls of a man could be heard walking up and down
the stairs.

One night Samuel Wesley heard nine loud bangs on the walls
of his study, the sounds appearing to come from the adjacent
room. Dashing into the room, he found nobody there. His
children, and the staff of servants, all heard these knocks at
some time or other. Wesley tried keeping a dog, but it was
as frightened as the rest of the household. Once, accompanied
by his wife, he went to investigate noises so uproarious that
sleep for both was impossible—and to the consternation of this
stout-hearted couple the noises followed them wherever they
went in the rectory, as though they were accompanied by invisible and malignant hosts. As Wesley put it: 'We still heard
it rattle and thunder in every room, locked as well as open,
above and behind us.' Once, chasing the invisible 'thing' with a
club, Wesley was astonished to discover that when his aim
'missed' and struck the house, a complementary knock was made
as if by an unseen presence.

Sometimes the door latch would lift itself, and when Emila,
one of Wesley's daughters, tried to hold it down, it would be
beyond her strength. The latch would go up and the door
burst open, sending the girl flying.

Angry and defiant, Wesley challenged what he called 'thou
deaf and dumb devil' to come into his study and stop terroris-
ing small children; the records say that the challenge was
accepted with alacrity—one might almost say—for Wesley
found himself pushed about in his study by an unseen presence. As for the Reverend Mr. Hoole, the near-by clergyman
to whom Wesley appealed for comfort and support, it took only
one night in the Wesley household to persuade him to take to
his heels.

A weird phenomenon was reported in *The Times* of April
21, 1821 and subsequently. In Truro, Cornwall, stones descended upon a house in Carlow Street. They came out of the sky,

hitting the roof and eaves with a resounding crash. There was absolutely no explanation as to their source or how these stones, heavy as they obviously were, came to be in the air in the first place. The Mayor, alarmed at what all took to be a super-natural visitation of some kind, visited the house—and left in a hurry. He called out the military guard and on his instructions soldiers kept stern watch for intruders, practical jokers and any human interference. The possibilities of slings, arrows and concealed strong-arm men were all considered. But the stones, anyway, didn't come on a trajectory from afar; they *fell* as hailstones fall, sometimes on a slight slant like driving rain. Five days later, according to *The Times* of May 1st, the weird inundation still continued.

I have mentioned these old cases because the distinguishing characteristic of poltergeist disturbances is their violence. Per-haps, too, their uselessness; their almost juvenile vandalism. Assuming there are what are loosely called 'spirits', that is, some discarnate intelligence capable of thought and physical action—and reaction, for there are examples of poltergeists responding to orders and queries by means of an agreed num-ber of knocks or raps—why should they bother with such ab-surdities as throwing stones, smashing crockery, and the stealing of such trivial objects as thimbles, shoes, and so on? One's rea-son boggles and protests at such an affront! Does a spirit, then, come through the boundless ether on missions of such triviality? But before attempting arbitrary criticisms, we should know more of the nature of the energy let loose on these strange occa-sions but as we do not, we come back to the realisation that perhaps all energy, even mental energy, is basically electrical, and we are reminded that although electricity is a power making possible many technical, man-organised marvels (I al-most said 'man-made' but checked myself in time) nobody really knows what it is. We know simply how to produce it and ex-ploit it, yet it is invisible except for its manifestations. On the other hand, we have no scientific grounds for assuming that only those manifestations which are basically electrical can be seen. Lightning we can see as a grandiose demonstration of heavenly pyrotechnics; but there can be electrical disturb-ances following laws not yet comprehended, which may be felt but not seen at all. I remember the late Professor Margaret Murray, that remarkable authority on witchcraft, magic and what I would call the darker labyrinths of human thought and anthropology, telling me what she thought about ghosts. We had been discussing witchcraft—a favourite subject of hers

—and she had agreed to appear on a television programme
about witches which I was then organising for a television net-
work.

She was ninety-six years old at the time, and so clear in her
thoughts and so self-reliant that she had attended every session
of the British Association in Edinburgh, even to the point of
making copious notes on the subjects that interested her. Our
conversation drifted to ghosts, a subject on which I had frequently written and broadcast. 'Has it ever struck you,' she
asked me, 'that ghosts are so frequently seen in places where the
air has been left comparatively undisturbed, such as rooms in
castles which have been unoccupied perhaps for centuries?' I
confessed that this aspect had escaped me, and pointed to the
evidence of apparitions having appeared in places where the
air was not only 'disturbed' but frequently in a tumult, such
as far out at sea, and on country roads exposed to the flail
and fury of the gales. 'True,' she agreed, 'but consider how
many haunted houses are old and have sections which, because
of the very size of the place, are not used ...' 'Agreed,' I said,
'but what inference emerges?' 'Perhaps the dust, in some strange
way, "photographs" what has happened,' she said, 'for you must
remember that dust is not a flat surface. These tiny particles
may settle, but the atmosphere still retains some of them in a
suspended state; and they form a three-dimensional surface.' A
sort of three-dimensional plate ... it set me thinking, but I
found that line of thought too inconclusive to be satisfactory.
What about *sound*? What about heavy footfalls—and positive
assertions of energy implied in the opening of doors and lifting
of latches? And what of poltergeists?

What indeed? What are we to make of the young Pliny's
account of a freedman he knew, by name Marcus, who, lying
in bed with his younger brother, saw a vision of somebody
sitting on the bed cutting the hair from the top of his head?
And his statement that on awakening he found his hair cut
and the loose strands scattered about the room? The same thing
happened to another boy. Must we conclude that Pliny was a
charlatan telling stories for effect? There is nothing in his
life and reputation to justify any such suspicion. What are
we to make of the stories, far too numerous to be quoted in a
single chaper in a general work of this kind, of showers of
stones reported in A.D. 534, 535, 540, 558, 559 and 562 in Italy?

And what, indeed, can we make of the well-documented
case of Gilles Blacre who, in the year 1580, rented a house in
the suburbs of Tours from a Peter Piquet and then found, to

use his own words, that it was already tenanted—'by all the fiends of hell?' Sleep became utterly impossible. There were loud knocks and bangings on the walls; the chimney echoed with unearthly noises; window-panes were smashed and pots and pans flew about his kitchen as though hurled by an invisible drunkard or lunatic. The disturbances attracted large crowds and it is even recorded that bricks 'detached themselves' from a wall and hurled themselves at selected individuals among the spectators—allegedly those who had not been devout in their prayers that morning!

The last detail, one suspects, was an invention of the priests, anxious to reap some sort of harvest from these disturbances.

Matters reached such a state that the unlucky tenant appealed to the Civil Court at Tours for his tenancy to be annulled as being unworkable. The Court agreed that the residence was not a desirable one, and ruled the lease invalid. Landlord Piquet, bothered more by the thought of lost rent than of spirits, went over the heads of the Court to Parliament itself and succeeded in having the Court's verdict squashed and his own rights restored. But Parliament did not dispute the validity and genuineness of the poltergeist disturbances—it upheld the landlord's lease on a legal technicality.

There is also the well-attested story of the haunting of the Palace of Woodstock in 1649. Cromwell's envoys were ordered to take it over, because it had been a royal seat. From early times Henry II had courted Rosamund Clifford ('fair Rosamund') there, and in the magnificent park there was a well, called Rosamund's well, near the bower where in the tender flush of youth she fell to the monarch's wooing. Charles the First had often stayed in the palace when he was on a hunting holiday in the royal forests.

The Commissioners arrived at Woodstock on October 13, 1649 and immediately demonstrated their anti-royalist sentiments in an orgy of vandalism. Apartments rich with dignity, tradition and the treasured momentos of generations were treated with ostentatious contempt: meats and roast game were eaten from priceless tables; tapestries and rich hangings served as bedspreads; lovely apartments were used as kitchens and sculleries; priceless china and glass were smashed, and old masters slashed. Just as soldiers at their best cannot be equalled in courage, so at their worst nobody can excel them in vandalism. The dining-room became a firewood store; the council-chamber became a brewery, heavy with the fumes of fermenting hops and the spillings of the drunken soldiery. Heraldic

devices and coats of arms, whether carved in wood or stone or
engraved in metal, were broken or destroyed, and a magnificent
oak tree of noble proportions was wantonly uprooted and
burned because it carried the name of the Royal Oak.

If anything survives of human personality, surely a whole
army of people who had lived and died at Woodstock would
have been appalled at this frenzied destruction and indignity.
Perhaps they were, for within a few days, weird things began
to happen at Woodstock—things which neither pikes nor
blunderbusses could dispel. The commissioners would be
troubled at night by a ghostly dog whose growls from underneath their beds were truly terrifying. Tables and chairs were
moved by unseen hands, and even danced a kind of jig in the
air. On the fifth day, ghostly footsteps, loud and distinct, were
heard in the bedchamber; then plates and dishes were slung
around the dining-room with demoniac frenzy. On the following day ghostly presences invaded the bedchamber, throwing
logs of wood around. The nuisances became more fantastic and
alarming as they continued. Chimney bricks dislodged themselves and danced about the floor, occasionally whizzing around
the heads of the usurping commissioners. Breeches disappeared; beds mysteriously became filled with pewter; glass shattered simultaneously throughout the house and after a fortnight there was a tremendous noise as of a shower of pebbles.

In November, after a slight lull, violent disturbances recommenced with unabated fury. In the 'withdrawing room', loud
and measured footsteps were heard; the following day a warm-
ing-pan crashed on to a table, followed by a shower of stones
and—of all things—the jawbone of a horse. Water cascaded
down chimneys, extinguishing fires; candles were blown out.
There is good reason, however, for suspecting the authenticity
of these phenomena. The Clerk to the Commissioners, Giles
Sherp, was trusted by them but was at heart a convinced
royalist; furthermore, he knew every nook and cranny of that
vast, rambling house which, to the occupants, was a sealed
mystery. He knew every cupboard, every chimney-stack, every
trapdoor, false wall and hiding place. Once, it is true, the servants themselves were drenched with scummy water from a
ditch, but the major discomforts were reserved for the commissioners themselves, with their apple-pie beds and bricks whizzing around their ears. But if Giles Sharp, whose real name was
Joseph Collins, *was* responsible, he must have been a man of
quick wit and resource. His head would swiftly have followed
King Charles's had he been detected.

Most famous and over-publicised poltergeist of all was the noisy 'ghost' of Cock Lane near West Smithfield in London, in the house of Mr. Parsons, the Parish Clerk of St. Sepulchre's. Parsons was perpetually hard up, and it is reasonable to suppose that the 'ghost' that set all Britain talking was his own idea.

The year was 1862. Parsons had let rooms to a stockbroker named Kent, who cohabited there with his sister-in-law Miss Fanny, who had originally come to town to keep house for him when Mr. Kent was left a widow. Parsons borrowed money from Kent and being sued for its return, conceived a great hatred for him. Kent and Miss Fanny had both made wills in each other's favour, and in the course of the litigation between Kent and Parsons, Miss Fanny suddenly became ill and died, being buried in a vault under Clerkenwell Church. But it is worth recording (since the real truth about the subsequent occurrences has never really been established) that before leaving the Cock Lane house to live in Clerkenwell she complained of violent knockings which kept her awake at night; knockings which occurred when the landlord's twelve-year-old daughter slept with Miss Fanny in her bed. One reason for Miss Fanny's departure for new lodgings in Clerkenwell was, undoubtedly, the curiosity of the neighbours whom Parsons invited to the house to hear the mysterious noises.

During the eighteen months between her departure and her death in Clerkenwell, all was quiet in the Cock Lane house. But after her death all bedlam broke loose. No matter in which bed Parson's young daughter was placed, violent noises and scratchings were heard underneath. Parsons questioned the alleged 'ghost' and elicited that the disturbances were caused by Miss Fanny, who declared she had been poisoned by her lover.

'A gentleman of quality' was invited to the house and, informed by the girl that she regularly saw the ghost of the deceased Miss Fanny, returned in due course with three clergymen and twenty other witnesses. The child was in bed with her sister, and the bed was carefully examined for any concealed object such as a board, on which loud raps could be produced. Mary Frazer, servant of Parsons, acted as a 'medium' through which the ghost was believed to address itself to its questioners. Answers were given by knocks of a particular number in response to questions. The 'ghost' was then asked: 'Do you make this disturbance on account of the ill-usage you received from Mr. Kent?' and replied: *Yes*.

'Were you brought to an untimely end by poison?'—*Yes*.

'How was the poison administered, in beer or in purl?'—*In purl*.

'How long was that before your death?'—*About three hours*.

'Can your former servant, Carrots, give any information about the poison?'—*Yes*.

'Are you Kent's wife's sister?'—*Yes*.

'Were you married to Kent after your sister's death?'—*No*.

'Was anybody else, besides Kent, concerned in your murder?' —*No*.

'Can you, if you like, appear visibly to anyone?'—*Yes*.

'Is it your intention to follow this child about everywhere?'— *Yes*.

'How long before your death did you tell your servant, Carrots, that you had been poisoned? An hour?'—*Yes*. (Carrots was present at this séance and declared that this statement was quite untrue, as her mistress had been speechless for over an hour before her death.)

'If Mr. Kent is arrested for the murder, will he confess?'— *Yes*.

'Would your soul be at rest if he were hanged for it?'—*Yes*.

A number of questions were then put regarding the composition of the gathering present, and description of such objects as watches, and so on. Once the ghost, asked at what time it would depart, said it would leave at four o'clock—which it did, entering the near-by Wheatsheaf public house and scaring its innocent habitués out of their wits.

But *was* there a ghost? Or was this a case of mass hysteria, sparked off by a usurious landlord with a bitter hatred of Kent? For the manifestations, one must remember, always centred around Parson's daughter, while his servant was the 'mouthpiece' of the supposed spirit. And the questions and answers were directed specifically to accusing Kent of murder and bringing him to trial.

A number of factors fed this suspicion: Cock Lane was thronged with curious sightseers with the result that Mr. Kent's reputation was maligned throughout the capital. Further, the 'ghost' promised to accompany the little girl to the vault of Clerkenwell Church, where Fanny was buried, and strike the coffin to convince the assembled clergymen and witnesses (who included Dr. Johnson, the lexicographer) of the genuineness of the manifestations. But the inquirers noticed that when they held the hands of the little girl, the strange noises ceased, and no amount of questioning through a medium or by any other means would induce the alleged ghost to manifest itself. Furthermore, when the whole retinue of investigators trouped off to the vault on their lugubrious mission, nothing whatever happened. No one knocked on any coffin, and the supposition of imposture gained its strength.

That supposition seemed confirmed when Mr. Kent, understandably tired of all this publicity, decided to reinstate his reputation. He indicted Parsons, his wife, his daughter, the servant Mary Frazer, the Rev. Mr. Moore and several tradesmen, who were tried before Lord Mansfield at the Guildhall, by a special jury, and convicted of conspiracy against the life and character of Mr. Kent. But seeing that Mr. Kent had suffered so much damage, sentence on the clergyman and tradesmen was postponed for from seven to eight months so that they could make good their misconduct by paying several hundred pounds to Kent. The father was condemned to the pillory (a punishment which was both comfortable and profitable, for the populace, convinced that an underdog was being victimised by a villainous aristocrat, refrained from pelting him with the customary rubbish and stones and instead, collected money for him) followed by a year in King's Bench Prison. Elizabeth, his wife, went to prison for a year; Mary Frazer went to Bridewell for six months' hard labour and the publisher of some letters relating to the affair was fined. Oliver Goldsmith wrote a pamphlet (featured in his collected works) for a mere three guineas, and eventually, it is said, the girl Parsons confessed.

Confessed? There is such a thing as brain-washing. Accuse somebody long enough, and if all voices are raised in accusation the victim may begin to doubt his own experience or judgement. Besides, are we so sure that Mr. Kent was innocent? Is it not possible, by the laws governing averages and coincidences, that a haunting might be faked in a place already genuinely haunted? I raise the point for this reason:

Long after the event, an artist, Mr. Wykeham Archer, was drawing in the crypt of St. John, in a narrow cloister on the north side. The attitude to interment and death was not always quite so reverent—behind the scenes—as the solemn church ritual implied. In this instance, coffins, fragments of shrouds and even human bones lay strewn around in some disorder. The sexton's boy pointed out to Mr. Archer a coffin which, he declared, contained the mortal remains of 'Scratching Fanny' as the girl in the Cock Lane Ghost affair was known. The lid of the coffin being loose, Mr. Archer lifted it and peered inside. No effluvia of ammonia was wafted up; the flesh had not contracted inwards against the bony structure, nor was there to be

seen the usual discolouration, mouldering and flaking associated
with bodily disintegration. There, in her shroud, lay Miss Fanny,
her handsome, oval features lifelike and unimpaired, the delicate aquiline nose still beautiful in death. In medical terms, her
corpse was *adipocere*.

The supposition that she had been poisoned seemed at that
moment stronger to Mr. Archer than it had been to the outraged Lord Mansfield—for arsenic, which the 'ghost' alleged had
been administered, has been known to cause the condition of
adipocere.

If the sexton's boy was right, and the coffin which he singled
out was truly that of the woman whose spirit was supposed to
have haunted Cock Lane, we are left with the alternative hypothesis that Mr. Parsons, bitterly antagonistic though he was,
may genuinely have believed, and have had good reason for
believing, that Mr. Kent murdered Miss Fanny in order to profit
from the will she had made in his benefit and that believing
Mr. Kent guilty of murder and determined to draw attention to
his guilt, he resorted to trickery. But at the point at which his
daughter and servant, in obedience to his promptings, began
to fake certain manifestations, a genuine ghost may have decided to take a hand. If so, it was an ironic situation. Perhaps in
that house of fakery—assuming that there was, in fact, fakery—
a bewildered ghost was providing disturbances and noises as
an overture to the symphony of manifestations conducted by
mere mortals!

8

More poltergeists

The history of poltergeists is a fascinating one. It also rules out any question of universal faking, or even of universal lying. For, considering the accounts which are available in all countries and in all centuries, one fails to see how there could be unanimity on certain points. To name one only: objects set in motion by invisible forces often move in mild curves, and on occasion they 'wobble'. No trickster, throwing objects from some concealed vantage point, could control the behaviour of objects as unwieldy as warming pans, vases and boots once they had left his hand.

The annals of poltergeists through the ages are too numerous to be assembled by one person. It would take several lifetimes to read the depositions alone. A further selection will be rewarding, however, because the point needs to be made that there *does* exist some invisible force (however projected, from whatever source, point or person emanating) equal in its power to that of human hands, and exceeding human potentiality in what it is able to encompass and achieve.

The *Western Gazette* of January 11, 1895, contains a long and detailed account of a remarkable haunting: 'The little village of Durweston, situate about three miles from Blandford, has been for some weeks past the scene of considerable excitement in consequence of the supposition that one of its cottages is haunted. The cottage in question is one of a double tenement, situate at Norton—a spot isolated from the rest of the village, some considerable distance from the highway, and on the outskirts of a wood. The cottages are owned by Viscount Portman; his keeper (named Newman) occupies one, and the other until recently has been in the occupation of a widow (named Mrs. Best), her daughter, and two little orphan girls who were boarded out to Mrs. Best by the Honourable Mrs. Pitt of Steepleton. It is in the latter house that these occurrences, which have caused such a scare in the village, took place.

'More than a month since, Mrs. Best—who, it may be here

stated, is a most respectable woman, of a quiet, inoffensive disposition, and on good terms with her neighbours and the village generally—became puzzled by faint knocking and scratching in various parts of the house, and could account for the same in no possible way. As days passed there was a repetition of these strange noises, which gradually increased in loudness until they could be heard by the keeper Newman in his own house.

'About a fortnight since, these sounds—which the village blacksmith described as then being as heavy as sledge-hammer blows—were succeeded by more startling events, for, according to Mrs. Best's version, stones came violently through the bedroom windows, smashing the panes and then returned through the windows. The neighbours instituted a thorough search of the surroundings to see if there was anyone hiding who was playing a joke upon the woman, but there was not the slightest trace of a human being, nor of footprints.

'In the latter part of January, Mr. Westlake proceeded to Durweston and took down the statements of some of the principal witnesses—about twenty in all.

'The disturbances, it appears, began on December 13, 1894. On December 18th Mr. Newman witnessed some of the phenomena.

'The following is an extract from Mr. Westlake's notes of an account given to him by Mr. Newman (whose cottage was adjacent to the haunted cottage) on January 23, 1895:

'"On Tuesday (December 18th) between 10 and 11 a.m., Mrs. Best sent for me, and told me that Annie (the elder girl, about thirteen years of age) had seen a boot come out of the garden plot and strike the back door, leaving a muddy mark. I went into Mrs. Best's, and I saw a bead strike the window; and then soon after, a big blue bead struck the window and broke it, and fell back. Then a little toy whistle struck the window, but did not break it. Then I sat down in the chair, and said: 'You're a coward, you're a coward; why don't you throw money?' I was looking at the door opening into the garden; it was wide open, leaving a space of fifteen inches between it and the inner wall, when I saw coming from behind the door a quantity of little shells. They came round the door from a height of about five feet. They came one at a time, at intervals varying from half a minute to a minute. They came very slowly, and when they hit me I could hardly feel them. With the shells came two thimbles. They came so slowly that in the ordinary way they would have dropped long before they reached me. They came from a point some, I think, a trifle higher, and some no higher, than my head. Both the thimbles struck my hat. Some missed my head and went just past, and fell down slantingwise (not as if suddenly dropped). Those that struck me fell straight down. The two children were all the time in the room with me. Then straight from behind me a slate pencil came as if from the copper. The pencil was about two and a half inches long and went slowly on a slant to a bowl on the floor in the pantry; and another piece went in the same direction, just over the bowl, and fell into a pot of dirty water.

'"Then a hasp, like a hasp of a glove, was dropped into my lap from a point above the level of my head. I never saw any of the things begin to move. I saw some of them just after they had started. The time was between 10 and 11 a.m.—a nice, clear day. I don't remember whether there was sunlight.

'"A boot then came in from outside the door. It came in moving along a foot above the ground, and pitched down. The boot had been lying right in front of the door, where it had previously fallen. This boot came towards me and fell down just at my side. Mrs. Best took it and threw it out—it was an old, dirty boot from off the garden plot (it was a woman's boot). I think the boot moved about as slowly as the other things, but cannot quite remember. It finally fell softly.

'"After the boot was thrown out into the garden, I went out and put my foot on it and said 'I defy anything to move this boot'. Just as I stepped off, it rose up behind me and knocked my hat off; there was no one behind me. The boot and the hat fell down together.

'A few days later the two children, with their foster-mother, Mrs. Best—a woman, it should be said, of about sixty years— went to stay in Mr. Newman's cottage for some days. Whilst they were there the Rector of Durweston, the Rev. W. M. Anderson, came to witness the phenomena. On his first visit (Friday, January 4, 1895) nothing took place. On Thursday, January 10th, he went again, accompanied by Mr. Shepherd, the schoolmaster. Mrs. Best took the two children upstairs and put them to bed, herself lying down on the bed with them.

'Loud rappings were heard, apparently on the walls in different parts of the room. Mr. Shepherd went outside to see that no one was playing tricks from outside, whilst the Rector remained within, the noises still continuing."'

The Rev. Anderson declared: 'I put my ear and hand to the wall but could not detect any vibration; but when resting my hand on the rail at the bottom of the bed, I could distinctly feel a vibration varying according to the loudness of the knocking. It is, perhaps, needless to say that I searched the room and the house, also Mrs. Best's house, from top to bottom. Occasionally there was a noise on the walls, as if someone were scratching with their nails. This scratching also appeared to be produced on the mattress of the bed, although I am sure it was not produced by any of the occupants of the bed, as I could see their hands, and watched them very closely all the time.

'There was a lighted lamp, a small hand-lamp giving a good light, on the washstand the whole time. When the rapping first began, I noticed that it frequently ceased when I came into the room, but after a short time it made no difference, and was loud and continuous when every inmate of the house was in the room. About 2.15 a.m. it was suggested that the "agency" should be asked whether it would write any communication on a slate and the number of raps requested for an affirmative were given. There was no slate in the Newmans' house, but Mrs. Best told us where we should find one in her house. Newman, Mr Shepherd and myself went into her house, found the slate and a piece of pencil, and returned. In reply to several questions as to where the slate was to be placed, the number of knocks given indicated the window-sill (inside, of course), the sill being nine or ten inches wide. I may mention that every conceivable place was mentioned one after the other, but the right number of raps was not given, only a short, sharp knock, which seemed always to be given for a negative. We almost gave up at this point, until, as an after-thought, I suggested the window-sill, which was at once accepted. The next question was as to who was to remain in the room, and according to the knocks everyone was to leave, except the two children and Mrs. Best; the light was also to be removed. The sign to be given when the writing was finished was four raps.'

They retired from the room, leaving Mrs. Best on the bed with the two children. Fifteen minutes elapsed, and then the scratch of the pencil on the slate was heard (Anderson and Shepherd, with Newman, were on the stairs). Four raps were given, the slate pencil dropped and simultaneously Mrs. Best shouted 'Come!'

The marks on the slate were meaningless, but another similar test was made, producing a flowing, script-like line but having in itself no apparent meaning. The curves, said the Rev. Anderson, 'were beautifully drawn, with firm, bold lines, such as no child could produce ...' Having seen the lines, I would not accept that as axiomatic. On the third occasion the letters M and MONY were written; on the fourth the word GARDEN with an 'o' above and below the centre of the word, and on the right-hand side of it the French word JARDIN, the o's being similarly placed.

If they were looking for any message that made sense, they must have been disappointed. Mr. Anderson declared himself absolutely convinced "that no one had moved in the bed, much less left it ... I am absolutely certain that the writing could not have been done by anyone in the room without my knowing it." Mrs. Best was prepared to swear that no one had moved out of bed.

The sequel to these happenings is interesting. The children were taken to another house in the village, where raps and noises were again heard, and were finally separated; the elder child, Annie, being removed to the house of a single woman in another village: Iwerne Minster. There the disturbance still continued: noises were heard, generally on the outer walls of the house; a big stone was flung on the roof of the porch, and snowdrops were dug up out of the garden and flung about. On March 7th, Miss W. H. Mason, Local Government Board Inspector for Boarded-out Children, came down and took the child Annie to stay in her flat in London for a week. No disturbance worth recording took place during her stay in London.

Annie was examined by a doctor and was found to have a tendency to consumption and to be of somewhat hysterical disposition. One witness maintained that in the early stages of the 'poltergeist' noises, Annie had seen 'a queer animal with green head and green eyes and a big bushy tail, sitting up and pulling her doll to pieces with its paws. Gertie, the young girl, had seen the same apparition when Annie called her.

A strange story. Suspicion fastens upon Annie; but did the occurrences cause her hysteria or her hysteria cause the disturbances? When minds are unhappy or disturbed the mental energy, it seems, has been known to create the most curious disturbances.

Perhaps a more dramatic example of a poltergeist at work is described by Podmore in the *Proceedings of the Society for Physical Research*. Volume XII, pages 45-58. On February 20 or 21, 1883, a Mrs. White was washing up the tea-things at the table in her cottage at Worksop, while two children were in the room, when the table tilted of its own accord at a most extraordinary angle.

On February 26th, when Mr. White was away from home, Mrs. White invited Eliza Rose, supposed but not proved to be a rather backward girl, to stay with her. On March 1st a number of objects which had been in the kitchen a few minutes ago 'came tumbling down the kitchen stairs', at a time when Mrs. White and the girl were in the kitchen together. Lumps of hot coal arrived, inexplicably. Once, when Mr. and Mrs. White and Eliza were together in the kitchen all manner of bits and pieces and objects came in as though carried or propelled by invisible hands (and, as in the case of the objects which came towards Mr. Newman, in conditions which really defied the laws of gravity). Mr. White dashed upstairs, where his brother Tom was, but found nothing unusual, and returned to the kitchen in time to see a little china figurine leave the mantelpiece and fly into a corner. Picking it up and replacing it on the mantelpiece, he and the others were astounded to see it fly away again, this time smashing into pieces. A doctor, and a policeman (P.C. Higgs) were called. What *are* you to do in face of such a situation? It is as well the Whites did call them in or they might have been tempted to question their own sanity for before the astounded eyes of the policeman and doctor, a basin and cream jug arose of their own volition, fell on the floor, and smashed. The following morning, a clock which had not worked for eighteen months, struck the hours as though nothing had ever happened; it was found to have leapt over a bed and crashed to the ground. For days things kept flying and leaping about—but with the departure of Eliza Rose, nothing further happened. Was Eliza up to some mischief? Hardly. For she was often seen picking up objects flung into a room when other objects came hurtling after them. The village policeman, Higgs, actually saw White shut some cupboard doors, only to see them burst open and a large glass jar fly out of the cupboard into the yard, to be smashed. Podmore, of the SPR, who spent thirteen years investigating poltergeist disturbances, was inclined to the belief that Eliza was to blame. But it is difficult to see how a dull-witted girl, even if endowed with a kind of low cunning, could cause such disturbances undetected under the very eyes of Mr. and Mrs. White, a doctor and a policeman. Why should the village policeman have attested to the glass jar apparently breaking itself? Why should White, who can scarcely have welcomed the expensive damage and constant breaking of glass and crockery, have testified that Eliza had been picking up some objects while fresh objects were arriving? And once again the depositions show the wholly inexplicable behaviour of objects on occasions of this sort, e.g.: speaking of the glass jar incident, he says 'The jar could not go in a straight line from the cupboard out of the door; but it certainly did go.'

And what on earth can explain the depositions of Mr. Newman in the earlier case I have quoted?

So long as ghosts and poltergeists are talked of, so the name of Borley Rectory is bound to be mentioned. I will not retell the story at length, for the late Harry Price, the ghost-hunter whose University of London Council for Psychical Research attracted much publicity in its day, wrote two books on the subject, *The Most Haunted House in England* and *The End of Borley Rectory*. I met Price quite often in those days, and never doubted his integrity as a researcher any more than one could question his business acumen. In the first place he tackled psychic research with an enthusiasm and energy not always apparent in those who interest themselves in it, and in the second place, his writings were a sound commercial proposition for him and for those who published them. I see nothing against that. Since his death detractors have come forward to say that he had been known to exaggerate. He once pleased the spiritualists (many of whom he had exposed as frauds) as much as he astounded sceptics by his declaration that, at a spiritualist séance in a London suburban house he had, after taking the most inordinate precautions against fraud, actually felt a spirit of a dead six-year-old girl called Rosalie. The materialisation, he reported, was a flesh-and-blood affair. Her flesh was warm and living: he could feel her cheek, hear her breathing. He placed his hand on her chest and even put his ear to it, while with his luminous plaque he saw by its reflected glow 'the normal feet of a normal child.' The soft flesh, the bright, intelligent eyes, were very unlike what most people imagine when they think of a 'spirit'. Price had to stand a good deal of criticism over this particular affair and declared afterwards that because war broke out and he had therefore lost touch with the mother in France, he must regard the case as incomplete. Yet he told the Ghost Club in London in November, 1939 that it would have been impossible to smuggle a child into and out of the room without his knowledge. The seals he had placed, and the starch powder he had scattered to preclude the possibility of windows and doors being opened would appear to have excluded any possibility of fraud, conscious or unconscious. But one doctor, criticising the whole affair, said that the whole thing was a 'definite and rather brazen fraud'.

The war having intervened, and the case having never been satisfactorily resolved by investigations other than Price's, the matter must be left there.

No such limitation applies to Borley Rectory. It is one of the best-documented ghost stories in the world. Even so, no ghost book would be complete without at least a reference to it, but I will be content to summarise the facts, leaving the reader who is sufficiently interested to read about it more fully, if he pleases, in the existing works.

Borley is a village between Sudbury and Long Melford in Suffolk, with long and fascinating historic associations. In 1362, Edward III granted the Manor of Borley to an order of Benedictine Monks. Subsequently, the Manor was for three centuries in the hands of the Waldegrave family and between 1862 and 1892 the Rev. H. D. E. Bull, a relative of the family, was the Rector of Borley, building himself a fine new rectory—on the site of the old Benedictine monastery. His son, the Rev. H. F. Bull, succeeded him and lived there until 1927. From then until October, 1928, when the Rev. G. Eric Smith took over, the Rectory was deserted.

For many years, from 1886 onwards, people saw there—amongst other things—a ghostly nun. A nursemaid left precipitately in that year because of weird and inexplicable footsteps. In 1900, the two sisters of the Rev. H. F. Bull both saw the ghost of the nun in full daylight on the lawn of the rectory, and shortly afterwards the phantasm was seen yet again by one of the sisters and a servant. In that same year the occupants of a cottage within the rectory grounds, Mr. and Mrs. Edward Cooper, saw the ghostly nun on numerous occasions, and were terrified by a looming black shadow in their bedroom. They even saw a ghostly coach and horses career through the rectory garden. It is not surprising that in March, 1920 they sought more peaceable accommodation.

Associated with the place was a legend which might well have been founded upon fact, since it concerned times when vengeance was swift and salutary, and punishments grim and deliberately cruel. The story has it that in the thirteenth century a nun fell in love with a lay brother in a near-by monastery. They eloped in a coach drawn by two bay horses, were chased, captured and—in their respective ways—harshly and ignominiously punished. The monk was hanged. The nun was walled up alive in the confines of her convent.

However, although the legend is interesting the facts are even more so. Over two centuries, something like two hundred people have seen the ghostly nun at one time or another. The scientific assessment of all these strange happenings, however, began in June, 1929 when the Reverend G. E. Smith, telephoned the *Daily Mirror* and told of strange happenings there. The news editor telephoned Mr. Harry Price, who by then had gained national reputation as a scientific ghost 'hunter'. Soon Harry Price, accompanied by Mr. V. C. Wall, a well-known reporter, was on his way to Borley.

A strange story unfolded—and took little time in doing so, for on the evening of their first day at Borley, after laboriously sealing the doors and windows upstairs, panes of glass in the front hall crashed down in front of them. The seals were undisturbed, yet a glass candlestick from a deserted room upstairs (a room firmly locked and sealed) came flying at them through the air, crashing into pieces as it struck the hall stove. Moth balls, a piece of slate and pebbles followed in due course, in the best poltergeist tradition. Bells rang—as they had rung so often without human agency, despite the fact that the rector was so sick of these manifestations that he had cut the wires.

A séance was then held in what was known as the Blue Room in which the late Rev. Henry Bull, his wife and son Harry had all died. Harry Price, addressing the 'empty' air, asked whatever was present to give three taps for 'yes' and one for 'no' and then proceeded to ply the 'presence' with questions. The ghost, it seemed was that of Henry Bull. The session lasted for four hours, and at one stage a piece of soap jumped from its dish and struck the edge of the water jug with such force that it became dented in the process.

In July, 1929, the Rev. G. E. Smith left the Rectory, and was succeeded by the Rev. Lionel A. Foyster who moved in with his wife and two children. The poltergeists renewed their efforts: Mrs. Foyster found herself locked in her bedroom, so her husband recited the Lord's Prayer and touched the door with a religious relic—and the bolt shot back. Once Mrs. Foyster found herself flung out of bed, and was struck by a ghost in a passage, blackening her eye. Other phenomena observed included the appearance of mysterious writing on the walls addressed to 'Marianne', and showers of pebbles.

Subsequently, Mr. Foyster asked a friend, Dom Richard, to stay in the house with his wife while he went out. During this time Dom Richard and Mrs. Foyster had dinner in the kitchen, attended by the maid. Suddenly a wine-bottle, from nowhere, burst into fragments under Mrs. Foyster's chair. Another smashed under Dom Richard's chair. As the three were standing with their backs to the fire an astonishing thing happened; a bottle materialised from nowhere before their eyes, changed its shape from that of a mushroom to that of an ordinary bottle, and then crashed to pieces before them. So goes Price's testimony. It strains credulity ... and yet, when Price rented the house in 1937 and appealed for intelligent and educated people to help him keep a day and night watch, numberless people reported phenomena of the strangest kind.

Mr. Andrew J. B. Robertson, M.A., of St. John's College, Cambridge, then formed a commission composed of university students and teachers to investigate the alleged hauntings. The co-ordination of the many reports from this team showed that there were no less than twelve spectres of one kind and another, ranging from the now familiar nun to the ghost of Harry Bull; from headless men to the ghost of a girl in blue. Apart from these tangible visual phenomena, no less than twenty-six types of audible phenomena were reported, from the sound of galloping horses to whisperings; from ghostly footsteps to the sound of rushing water. There was also a large category of physical happenings unaccompanied by any spectre, but alarming enough, nevertheless, such as the unexplained writing on the wall; keys falling from locks; doors locking themselves; objects rolling about, floating through the air, or appearing to be thrown; luminosity, and attacks on individuals by unseen hands. There was also a rag-bag of eerie odds and ends, such as fragrant scents and horrible odours concentrating in particular spots at certain times for no obvious reason, and unexplained footprints in the snow. With such a catalogue of evidence, even the most sceptical could hardly deny that Borley Rectory was haunted. However, with admirable scientific zeal, Mr. Robertson and his team spent five years on observation, using relays of men of high intelligence and acute observation—people with no preconceived ideas but used to noting and recording facts objectively and without elaboration. This team compiled as impressive and fantastic a record of strange happenings as did Harry Price.

Out of the mass of phenomena reported, however, there is one deserving of particular emphasis.

On March 27, 1938, Miss Helen Glanville was using a planchette which produced writing alleged to be that of the nun who was killed at the convent. After a while another 'entity' announced itself by rappings and, asked for its identity, gave its name (in writing, by means of the planchette) as 'Sunex Amures'. Sunex, in untidy scrawl, warned that he proposed to set fire to the rectory at nine o'clock that night. Asked in which room the fire would start, the reply was 'over the hall'. It was said that this would be the end of the haunting, and that the bones of somebody murdered there would be revealed. The nun, on her alleged visitations to the séance room, revealed her name as 'Mairie Lairre'.

Dr. Phythian-Adams, Canon of Carlisle and then Chaplain to the King, investigated the phenomena closely and did extensive research into the historical possibilities. He decided that the ghost was that of a girl who had lived in the seventeenth century and was French. A member of the Waldegrave family had met her while visiting Papists in France. Perhaps the Roman Catholic girl was brought to England and taken to the old manor of Borley, seat of the Waldegrave family and perhaps her presence, like their marriage, was a secret. 'Perhaps', he said, 'the husband departed, leaving his French bride a foreigner among strange faces, waiting only for his return. But when he does return, when at last that long-expected coach swings round the bend, he comes back not as a loving husband, but as a pitiless enemy resolved to remove the barrier which he finds between him and a more 'suitable' and profitable marriage. Deep in this fantastic record there is a poignant agony neither lightly caused nor lightly solaced; an agony not of remorse but of young innocence, foully betrayed and murdered.'

The reader who is interested will find fuller accounts in Harry Price's own books and in Paul Tabori's excellent biography of Harry Price. I can do no more than refer to the bare facts as widely publicised throughout the world at that time. But two sinister footnotes have to be added to a story which has to be accepted as a genuine poltergeist 'infestation' since it is inconceivable that so many people, including men of the calibre of Harry Price and the late Professor C. E. M. Joad, could have been imagining it all.

The nun, Marie Lairre, as she called herself at a séance, declared that she was murdered in 1667. The presence giving the odd name of Sunex Amures had declared that the rectory would be set on fire, the fire starting in the room above the hall.

Both predictions came to pass.

Eleven months to the day after Amures' threat, Captain Gregson, who had purchased the house, was arranging books on a shelf in the hall when, for no accountable reason the books fell straight on to an oil lamp which was overturned and caught fire, the flames licking up the wall to the room above the hall. Within minutes the old rectory was a blazing furnace. The death of Borley Rectory occurred on February 27, 1939; the prediction of the fire was made on March 27, 1938. But ghosts, walking wanly past the open windows of the ruins, have been seen since.

Some human remains, believed to be the bones of a nun, were found. They were interred with proper reverence in Liston churchyard in May, 1945.

The supposition that Borley Rectory, or at least the site on which it stood, was the scene of some great human tragedy which had left its indelible imprint is, in face of the facts, overwhelming. And there is real poignancy in the underlying assumption that evil cannot be erased even by time, and that fear, panic, indignity, pain and grief may have some permanence of their own, if only in being able to affect the senses of living people. There is little enough comfort in contemplating the extent and enormity of human cruelty; but there had been a limited if melancholy solace in the thought that death brought release.

On the subject of poltergeists whose activities, as I have shown, imply the actual projection of some form of energy, and to some extent of conscious will, no account would be complete without a reference to the sinister and inexplicable story of the Barbados Coffins.

Barbados, the lovely 166-square-mile island set in the golden Caribbean, with its green and pleasant countryside reminiscent of England, seems hardly the place for such a story. It has English place names—a reminder that it was occupied by the English in 1627—and Anglican churches. The story of the haunted vault starts in one of these churches, and perhaps finishes there.

In the Parish church of Christchurch is a large vault. For thirteen years there occurred in that vault, without human agency of any kind and without any scientific or natural explanation, weird happenings of violence: A hundred years ago the Rector, the Rev. Thomas Harrison Orderson, D.D., who was an eyewitness of many of the occurrences, set down for his friend Mr. R. Reece the following weird chronology:

'July 31, 1807—Mrs. Thomasin Goddard was buried in the vault which, when opened to receive her, was quite empty.

'February 22, 1808—Mary Anna Maria Chase, daughter of the Honourable Thomas Chase, was buried in the same vault in a leaden coffin. When the vault was opened for the infant, the coffin of Mrs. Goddard was in its proper place.

'July 6, 1812—Dorcas Chase was buried in the same vault, and the first two coffins were in their proper places.

'August 9, 1812—The Honourable Thomas Chase was buried in the same vault. Upon its being opened, the two leaden coffins were dislodged from their situation, particularly that of the infant, which appeared to have been thrown from the corner where it was first placed, to the opposite angle.

'September 25, 1816—Samuel Brewster Ames, an infant, was buried, and when the vault was opened the leaden coffins were found to have been thrown from their positions and were in much disorder.

'November 17, 1816—The body of Samuel Brewster was removed from the parish of St. Philip and was buried in the vault, and great confusion was discovered among the leaden coffins.

'July 7, 1819—Thomas Clarke was buried, and there was much disorder among the coffins. N.B. Each time the vault was opened the coffins were placed in their proper order and position, and the mouth of the vault was regularly closed by masons. The vault is twelve feet long and six and a half feet wide, and is partially hewn through a flinty rock. The entrance to it was secured by a massive stone, which it required six or seven men to remove.

'April 18, 1820—The vault was opened in the presence and at the request of His Excellency, the Governor, Lord Combermere. The Hon. N. Lucas, R. B. Clarke (now Sir R. Bowcher Clarke, Chief Justice of the Barbados) and R. Cotton Esquire, were attending.

'The condition of the coffins on this occasion can best be appreciated by a reference to the engraving below, which exhibits on one side the position in which the coffins were left on July 7, 1819, and on the other the disorder that was presented on April 18, 1820, the day on which Lord Combermere inspected the vault.

'These are the simple facts of the case. Nor can the writer venture to make any suggestion that might give a clue to the cause of these amazing occurrences. The approaches of the vault render it virtually impossible for any ingenious or mischievous person to tamper with its contents. Further than this, had it been practicable for anyone to have entered the rock, the achievement of dislodging the coffins single-handed would have been superhuman, and it is not easy to be credited that a piece of mischief of such a character would have been entrusted to many hands to carry out.'

What other theories justified consideration? Volcanic disturbance? That could be discounted, because only the coffins were disturbed; a force strong enough to dislodge and throw heavy leaden coffins about would have damaged or disturbed the precision-fitting masonry of the vault itself.

An influx of water? Did water somehow penetrate and shift the coffins? But how would water rise to a heigh of 100 feet through the flint rock? In any case the vault was a considerable distance from the sea.

Obviously, the story of the haunted vault and its restless dead sent a shiver of apprehension through the island, and no Negro would go near the churchyard at nightfall, except an occasional bravado who, even then, would whistle loudly to scare away the 'duppies' as ghosts are called there. In their minds, at least, the supposition that supernatural causes were behind the disturbance of the coffins was unanswerable. They pointed to the fact that Colonel Chase was a man of cruel disposition and ungovernable temper, and that his daughter, because of his cruelty to her, had starved herself to death and the assumption was—since the disturbances dated from the interment there of the Honourable Thomas Chase—that the dead newcomer was unwelcome and that there had been a violent though ineffectual effort to expel him. So great was the alarm felt that, for the peace of mind of the inhabitants of the island, the coffins were buried in earth and the vault closed.

An interesting note on the occurrences is contained on page 385 of *Memoirs of Viscount Combermere* by his widow:

'In the spring of this year (1820) an event occurred which was so inexplicable—we may almost say supernatural—as to merit a place in these pages. For some years previous to Lord Combermere's arrival in Barbados, the inhabitants had been startled by reports of mysterious occurrences in a family vault of Christchurch, where, it is said, some supernatural agency always upset or displaced the coffins deposited there. No Negro would approach the burying-ground after nightfall. Women whispered wonderful stories of apparitions and children were threatened with its horrors to ensure their good behaviour. Lord Combermere, hearing of the terror occasioned by these rumours, and ascertaining that the coffins had actually been several times displaced, resolved on investigating the matter personally. The family to whom the vault belonged were anxious to have it examined, and as an interment was immediately to take place, he determined to be present at the ceremony. Barbados is formed of calcareous rock, over which

lies a very inconsiderable depth of earth, but that portion of
the island immediately connected with our story, viz.
Christchurch and the adjacent burying-ground, stands upon a
shelf of coral which rises to an eminence of one hundred feet
above the level of the sea. The church, dedicated to our
Saviour, is one of eleven founded two centuries since, when
various members of the district erected family vaults in the
burying-grounds appointed to each church. From the nature
of the foundation these tombs were formed partially above,
partially below, the surface, a circumstance which may have
served to protect them from the fury of the hurricanes that
from time to time have devastated the island.'

The vault, it seems, was solidly constructed of local sand-
stone which had hardened to stone, while the door was a huge,
heavy slab of stone firmly fastened round with cement. The
unexplained happenings aroused not simply fear but excited
curiosity, and thousands began to flock to the scene of the
happenings. The 'haunting', if haunting it was, threatened to
become a public nuisance and macabre obsession. Accordingly,
the methodical, phlegmatic, no-nonsense Lord Combermere got
to work;

'In his presence,' his widow wrote, 'every part of the floor
was sounded to ascertain that no subterranean passage or entrance was concealed. It was found to be perfectly firm and
solid; no crack was even apparent. The walls, when examined,
proved to be thoroughly secure. No fracture was visible, and
the three sides, together with the roof and flooring, presented
a structure as solid as if formed of entire slabs of stone. The
displaced coffins were rearranged, the new tenant of that dreary
abode was deposited, and when the mourners retired, with the
funeral procession, the floor was carefully sanded with fine
white sand in the presence of Lord Combermere and the assembled crowd. The door was slid into its wonted position
and, with the utmost care, the new cement was laid on so as
to secure it. When the masons had completed their task the
Governor made several impressions in the cement with his
own seal, and many of those attending added various private
marks.'

Nine months afterwards the commotion in the island over
the alleged haunting of the vault reached such a crescendo
that Lord Combermere, to quieten apprehension, agreed to the
vault being opened and inspected. For Barbados, it was the
sensation of the year. Whole towns were deserted as on a
public holiday, and thousands made their way to the church-

yard. 'Europeans and Negroes all crowded together in their varied attires, and scarcely less varied complexions, upon the brow of a hill, with the massive stone tombs rising here and there above them, and the old church standing forth in sombre relief, as if a connecting link between the living and the dead, made the scene altogether one which beggared description, while perhaps its peculiar interest was in the death-like silence that reigned over it—the silence of mute anxiety and superstitious awe.

'Lord Combermere now arrived, and if his own interest in the mystery could have failed in inducing him to seek the reopening of the vault, the assembled masses gave ample testimony of the universal gratification caused by his intervention.

'He at once proceeded to examine the structure. All was secure, and the vault appeared exactly as when he had left it after being closed. The cement was unbroken, and the large impressions of the Governor's seal were as sharp and as perfect as when made, but now hardened into stone. Each person present who had before made private marks, satisfied himself that they were untouched and unaltered, and, the command being given, the masons proceeded to break the cement and slide off the door. The cement yielded as usual to their implements, but when they endeavoured to remove the stone, it resisted with unwonted weight. Increased force was applied, but still it remained immovable. For a moment all hands were paralysed, and a look of wondering dismay passed from each to each, but it was only for a moment. The next, excitement lent a powerful energy to their efforts, and the stone yielded half an inch—enough to afford a glimpse inside.

'Increased force was tried to remove the stone, and inch by inch it yielded till it was slid sufficiently aside to admit of a person's entering, when it was discovered that a huge leaden coffin was standing upon its head, *with the end resting against the middle of the stone door.*' (My italics.) 'Though this coffin, which it required seven or eight men to move, was thrown from its central place and left in this remarkable position, yet the sand on the floor bore no trace of footprints, or of being in any way disturbed. The coffin of the infant had been hurled with such force against the opposite wall, near which it was lying, that a deep indentation had been made in the stonework by the corner which struck it.

'The Chase family immediately ordered the coffins to be removed and buried in separate graves, after which the vault was abandoned and has never since been used.'

It should not be thought that the only contemporary accounts are those of the Governor and his wife. There are the notes of the Rector, while the Hon. Forster M. Alleyne prepared an account of the vault, based largely on an account he received at first hand from Sir Robert Boucher Clarke, who was present when the vault was opened, and partly from the church's archives. Another witness, the Hon. Nathan Lucas, left detailed accounts in his carefully written manuscript volumes. There is also a description of events by the Rector of Christchurch and the Hon. Major Finch, Lord Combermere's A.D.C. It is commonly asserted that Lord Combermere sent home a detailed and official account of the affair to the Public Records Office but it has never been traced. It is possible that officials in charge of the Office at the time thought the subject too frivolous to deserve posterity.

Nobody has yet adduced a satisfactory explanation of the mystery of the Barbados vault. Some explanations have been more preposterous than the phenomena they attempt to deal with. As for vandalism, voodooism and suchlike thoughts— who, or what lifted that incredibly heaven leaden coffin and leaned it against the *inside* surface of the tomb's stone door?

9

Ghostly lights

Of all categories of paranormal phenomena (so far as one can attempt an acceptable classification) I suppose that ghostly lights are, scientifically, the most interesting. The prevalence of reports of the appearance of ghostly lights in all countries and all periods makes it difficult to accept the premise that all are hallucinations, or capable of some 'natural' explanation. Here, again, I should say that we are accustomed to use the word 'natural' loosely, the inference being that anything beyond our understanding is '*un*natural'. It could be said that all facts and all laws are part of nature in the broadest sense, and therefore being of nature are 'natural', whether within the range of our comprehension or not.

Sometimes, of course, there *is* an explanation. I remember being out in a dinghy, at dead of night, off the coast of Maine. The night was inky-black. There was no moon—something I hadn't noticed. There was something soothing about the utter silence, of being away from crowds and tumult and noise; only the phut-phut of the outboard motor and the occasional grunt of a porpoise broke the silence.

I was contemplating how attractive the spume of the churned-up water seemed in what I supposed to be the pale moonlight, and idly dragging the ends of my fingers in the water, noticing how every tiny bubble and microscopic touch of spray was illuminated. Then, looking up at the sky, I found nothing to relieve the inky darkness, nothing piercing the Stygian gloom. It seemed quite eerie that the spume should be illuminated, until I realised that the motion churned up phosphorescent animalculae in the water.

Similarly, the flames seen over graveyards or marshy ground may well be gases released from the graves themselves, or from the marsh. Such lights were known in England and Ireland as will-o'-the-wisps, but in various regions they had their distinctive names—Joan-in-the-Wad in the West Country, Sylham Lamp in Sussex and, why I am not clear, in Newcastle they went by the name of Weize. Such lights were commonly supposed to be heralds of death or even the actual spirit of a relative come to guide the spirit of someone about to die. Indeed, in Wales it was believed even as late as last century that a light emerging from the house of a dying man, would make its way to the cemetery, along the path which the funeral would one day follow.

In support of the theory that phantom lights presage a death, there is a legend in Llangatten, Carmarthenshire, that five ghostly lights were once seen by a housekeeper in a mansion there. Some months later, the walls having been replastered, a roaring coal fire was lighted to dry the damp plaster off. Five servants were found the next morning suffocated by the fumes.

Ghostly lights were frequently seen at the now world-famous Borley Rectory. A patch of light would flicker and move along the ceiling of the Blue Room, scene of so many hauntings and other phenomena.

In Homer's *Odyssey*, when Odysseus and Telemachus were removing the weapons from the hall, the latter exclaimed: 'Father, surely a great marvel in this I behold! Meseemeth that the walls of the hall, and the fair spaces between the pillars, the beams of pine, and the columns that run aloft, are bright as it were with flaming fire ...'

A spectre known as the 'Lady and the Lantern' was said to haunt the beach at St. Ives, Cornwall. She was supposed to be the ghost of a mother who, with her child, was being rescued from a wrecked vessel when the child slipped from her grasp and got carried out to sea. A light, once said to hover about 'Madge Figgs' chair', was supposedly the ghost of a heartless woman, Madge Figgs, who robbed of her jewels a woman washed up on the shore. Mr. Baring-Gould, in *Yorkshire Oddities*, tells of a farmer who, riding one night to Thirsk, was passed by 'a radiant boy' on a white horse. The phantom made no noise whatever, yet cast a shadow before it on the road. The child was about eleven years of age, with 'a fresh, bright face'.

Early in the nineteenth century the village of Black Heddon, near Stamfordham, Northumberland, was much troubled by a gleaming, brightly-lit ghost called 'Silky' which would appear on lonely roads and terrify travellers. Once a wagon bringing coals to a farm was held up for hours because the horses would not budge in its presence. A traditional Welsh ghost called 'Cyhyraeth', (mentioned in *British Goblins* by Wirt Sykes) used to trouble the beaches of Wales with its shrieks and groans, and appeared as a floating light. The appearance of a flame as high as a man, which moved about as though by conscious movement, was often reported between the German villages of Alversdorf and Rost during the last century. There had been a dispute between the two villages over their respective boundaries, and parochial bitterness had gone so deep that the arbiter of the dispute, supposedly a fraudulent measurer, was assumed to be so oppressed by conscience that he hovered for ever in the area of his misdeeds. The people, seeing the light, would exclaim: 'Dat is de Scheelvagt!' —'that is the land-divider'. Whatever the merits of the explanations, the reports were numerous enough to establish one thing: there *were* ghostly lights.

In Sussex there have been numerous reports of 'ghostly lights' being seen over the heads of sick persons. In *Evolution of Light from the Living Subject*, by Marsh, we can read how 'a pale moonlight-coloured glimmer' was seen playing around the head of a dying girl shortly before she died. The light seemed to emanate from her head, and to flicker. There is a story in Carmarthenshire that a coach, running between Llandilo and Carmarthen, was passing by Golden Grove, part of the Earl of Cawdor's estate, when three ghostly lights were seen gliding down the surface of the stream near the road. A few days later three men were drowned there. Shakespeare refers to the idea, common even centuries ago, that these lights were the lights of spirits:

> The lights burn blue. It is now dead midnight,
> Cold fearful drops stand on my trembling flesh . . .
> Methought the souls of all that I had murdered
> Came to my tent. (*Richard III*, Act v. sc. 3.)

Notes and Queries mentions a haunted house at Taunton which had a room with an inherent illumination of its own. One witness declared that long after the house had been deserted by its occupants, when all the other windows in the house were dark, this particular window emitted an eerie, greenish-blue light.

We must not suppose, however, that ghostly lights are the monopoly of folk-lore. They are seen frequently all over the world, and the reports of such instances within a single year would fill a whole book. Take, for instance, the case of the phantom bus.

Phantom *bus*? A modern vehicle, with body and wheels, tyres and engine, and *lights*?

In 1934 a young metallurgical engineer, Ian James Steven

THE PINK STAIRCASE, CULLEN HOUSE   *Photo: British Travel Association*

Reputedly haunted. The house, over 700 years old, is linked by underground passage, built and used by monks, to the parish church. It is the home of the Countess of Seaford.

GLAMIS CASTLE   *Photo: British Travel Association*

This castle, the ancestral home of the Earl of Strathmore and Kinghorne and the birth-place of Princess Margaret is said to be haunted by two ghosts—of a woman burned as a witch in the 16th century, and of Earl Baerdie, said to have staked his soul in a card game with the devil and, having lost, was condemned to haunt the castle in perpetuity (see page 39).

Photos: University of London (Harry Price Library)

BORLEY RECTORY

Top left (before the fire): Built in 1863, Borley Rectory was the scene of many strange happenings and the subject of investigations by Harry Price, which began in 1929 and continued until 1938. *Bottom left (after the fire)*: A year after the Rectory was bought by Captain Gregson it was destroyed by a myster-

THE HAUNTED FIREPLACE AT LITTLECOTE   *Photo: Studio Wreford*

Legend says that after the murder of a newly-born baby—which was thrown into the fire—
this part of the ancient manor became haunted (see page 58).

THE HAUNTED GALLERY AT HAMPTON COURT PALACE   *Photo: British Travel Association*

Leading off it is the chapel where King Henry VIII was brought supposed proof of the
infidelity of his wife, Catherine Howard. He ordered her arrest and execution. Her ghost
still repeats her panic-stricken flight along the gallery to the chapel, where she hammered
at the chapel door, begging for mercy (see page 157).

A HAUNTED HOUSE IN BEDFORD
Photo: The Bedfordshire Times

This handsome building, erected in 1760 was until recently used as the offices of the Clerk to the Justices, and for occasional court sessions. One of the Deputy Clerks thought the house 'quite definitely haunted' and said that a ghost would knock sharply on the office door (see page 148).

A HAUNTED COTTAGE *Photo: Mrs Grace MacRae*

Walnut Cottage, home of Mr and Mrs MacRae, has been the scene of many strange happenings. The most extraordinary was 'a great glow spreading over the roof and chimney stack, as though the cottage was on fire' (see page 123).

THE ARTIST WHO PAINTED GHOSTS

Austin Osman Spare, a distinguished artist who lived as a near-recluse in South London, also studied the occult and once painted a ghost. He also drew 'magical stelles' which one possessor believed to be haunted (see page 233).

MYSTERIOUS FIGURE ON THE STAIRCASE AT RAYNHAM HALL
Photo: Shira

otographer and his assistant who took this photograph at the Norfolk home of the Marquis of
ishend found, on developing it, a luminous figure whose brilliance seemed to be throwing
ights on to the surrounding woodwork (see page 151).

JAMES TURNER

Pictured left, he was one of 300 seamen drowned when the
Eurydice foundered in a gale, and sank off the Isle of Wight on 24th

CRADLE TOWER, TOWER OF LONDON   *Photo: British Travel Association*

The turbulent history of the Tower of London is known all over
the world, but what is less known is the fact that its ghosts have

PHOTOGRAPH
NEVER BEFORE
PUBLISHED

It was taken by the Marquis of Ely in a house in Bryanston Square, London, in 1936. Neither he, or his assistant, or the sitter noticed anything unusual, but when developed, the dark shadowy figure on the right appeared. Note the period dress, the mantilla and the necklace (see page 197).

Photo: Marquis of Ely

THE HAUNTED CLOCK
On three occasions, separated by many years, this old clock has stopped at the precise moment that a member of the family owning it has died. Its present owner (shown on the left) is Miss Helen Verba, a writer on the staff of the *Denver Post*, Colorado, U.S.A. The clock was subsequently

Photo: Denver Post

Beaton, of Hamilton Road, Dollis Hill, London, N.W., was killed
when his car crashed in the middle of the night at the junction
of St. Mark's Road and Cambridge Gardens, North Kensington.
He had collided with another car driven by a chauffeur,
George Pink.

At the inquest held at Paddington Coroner's Court on June
15, 1934 a witness, Mr. Frank Robinson, was describing the wet,
slippery roads and poor lighting when he was questioned by a
solicitor about a 'phantom bus'. Mr. Robinson replied that at
the point of the accident a ghostly bus was said to tear along
at night, all its lights blazing, empty, and with no driver at
the wheel.

Apart from the physical impossibility of the idea, there never
was a bus service along the route alleged. And yet ... there
were plenty of others who came forward at the time to tell
newspapers that the report was not so outlandish as it
sounded. A Mr. Durwan, who lived in Cambridge Gardens,
declared that he saw the phantom bus racing past, saw its
lights lighting up his ceiling, then heard a great crash. Jerking
up the sash window, he looked out into the cold night air. On
the pavement against the wall was a shattered motor-car. The
driver, pale as a ghost, was slumped over the steering wheel.

Durwan dashed downstairs to help. The driver, as he re-
gained momentary consciousness, looked at Durwan with eyes
dilated with horror. 'You might not believe this,' he said, 'but
when I came round that corner I was suddenly confronted
with the most hellish-looking bus that you could imagine. Its
lights were full on, it was going at full speed, and it didn't
seem to have a driver.'

A Mr. and Mrs. George Sutton said that they had come across
a bus, strangely empty and unattended with all its lights blazing, near the top of St. Mark's Road. It was February, and a cold
night. A friend had given them a lift that far, and thinking it
might be an all-night service they considered boarding it, but,
understandably enough, the fact of it being empty, stationary,
and without driver or conductor made them hesitate. However,
a few yards in front of the bus stood two busmen in peaked
caps. In the ill-lit, misty rain Mr. Sutton moved forward, intending to speak to them. At that moment, to their utter amazement, the bus, without driver or conductor, moved off down
the road, turned at the junction with Cambridge Gardens and
disappeared. But, as I have said, there was no bus service there.
The supposition at the time was that the dead driver of the
crashed car may have swerved to avoid the 'phantom bus' and

in so doing crashed into a real vehicle. The individuals who gave their testimony at the time have long since dispersed, but the Coroner's Court proceedings may be read by anyone who cares to peruse the local newspapers filed in the British Museum Library at Colindale.

Let me now adduce some stories of ghostly lights reported to me, while mentioning that I have, in every case, questioned the people concerned and am satisfied absolutely as to their integrity and intelligence.

Mrs. Molly Balderson and her husband, Alfred, of Glaxheugh Road, Hylton, near Sunderland, brought to my notice the following experience of theirs, which I set down here in Mrs. Balderson's own words:

'About twenty years ago (but still as vivid in my mind as though it had happened only yesterday) I was lying in bed one night looking towards the window. This window was of the type found in a tee-fall room, with slanted side panes above roof level. I must add that these side windows did not open. It was fairly late, as dark as a still summer's evening can be, when I saw something appear at the side pane and float right through it into the room. I can only describe it as being about the shape and size of a swansdown powder-puff, the kind one buys in a box of bath talc, but this phenomena was a beautiful blue, glowing and pulsing as it moved; an electric blue is the only word I can use to describe it. It moved slowly across the room and hovered about eighteen inches above my head. Then my husband, whom I thought asleep, said in almost the same breath as myself, "What's that?" I think that afterwards I could have easily been persuaded I'd dreamt the whole thing if we had not both watched it float across the room, hover again over our two small girls asleep in their cots, and disappear through the bedroom wall. My husband and I were too awestruck to move or do anything, but I've felt since that I wasn't really afraid—it was too beautiful and I somehow felt it was good. Nothing ever happened afterwards, and we've been neither lucky nor unlucky, so it could not have been a warning of anything to come.'

I asked Mrs. Balderson to supplement her account. I asked for the address of the house where it occurred, whether the house was an old one, whether any noise was heard when the ghostly light was seen, and so on. Since a phenomenon of this type is always more interesting when more than one person has seen it, I asked Mr. Balderson to be good enough to tell me in his words, too, exactly what he saw.

The house, described as 'quite old' was in New Street, Hylton. 'I remember my father saying it was there when most of the village was just a ploughed field,' says Mrs. Balderson. 'My sister bought the house when I married, but I believe it is now due for demolition.'

When the light appeared through the window there was what she describes as 'a most intense silence' and she felt herself unable to get out of bed, as though paralysed: 'Anything other than that would have roused me in a second to go to the children's side. They were then about six years and one year old respectively . . .'

And here is Mr. Alfred Balderson's account of the incident: 'I had been sleeping when I suddenly became wide awake in an instant and saw a luminous, blue, pulsating ball of light float through the window. This was accompanied by a dead silence: the absence of any extraneous noise was strange as even at night-time there is a certain amount of noise in this area. I thought my wife was asleep but she gripped my arm and whispered *"Can you see that?"* This glowing, blue object slowly floated through the air and came to rest about three feet above our heads and I had an uneasy feeling that it was inspecting us. After about, say, thirty seconds, it slowly moved to the other side of the room and then stopped above the heads of our two children. It hovered over them for a while and then just floated through the wall. There was no sequel to this—no sudden deaths of relatives or anything like that.'

Mr. Balderson adds, 'I am an engineer and always believe there is a scientific explanation for these occurrences but this I have not been able to solve. The house was lit by gas at the time so no electrical short circuit was responsible, nor were there any electrical storms about at the time.'

What was the ghostly light, and how could it seem to move of its own volition, *through* a closed window, and *through* a wall? A final note on this incident: A man once hanged himself in an outhouse attached to this house, in which he then lived.

On the old Roman road to Southampton, in Old Chilworth Village, stands the charming old Walnut Cottage. Here live Mr. and Mrs. MacRae. It has been in Mrs. MacRae's family for generations and is between 300 and 400 years old. Her grandfather once told her that before they came the house had been empty for a long time because of 'ghostly happenings'. She told me:

'When my husband and I were walking home one dark

night about twenty years ago, we were about 100 yards from the cottage when we saw a great glow spreading over the roof around the chimney stack. We both dashed into the cottage expecting to find it on fire, but everything was in order. When we went outside again the glow had disappeared. A good many years before that, my aunt found an eiderdown which appeared to be on fire. She turned to beat out the flames with her hands and then realised there was no heat or light emanating from it. My grandfather and grandmother heard someone come up the stairs one night and wash their hands in the wash-basin but on lighting a candle they could see no one and there was no water in the basin. My husband heard the same thing about twenty-five years ago. My husband and I once heard a very loud rat-tat-tat on the front door but there was no sign of anyone. Twelve years ago my mother and I heard a lot of horses trot up to the back door—when we looked out there was not a sign of a horse anywhere. People have been heard going up and downstairs many times. My mother sat up one night and put out her hand, thinking it was my husband bringing her an early morning cup of tea. It was midnight when she looked at her watch. All my family have heard loud crashes in the night and the sound of smashing china. I myself have heard something or someone fall down the stairs, bumping on each stair. Before we were married my husband slept alone here for a month or two. One night he had a sort of picture or vision of a lot of old men talking in low voices, wearing cloth caps with a tassle on the side. A friend of mine brought a medium here a few weeks later, and although we had not told her of Donald's vision, she described it just as he had seen it. We bought the cottage from the Fleming Estate twelve years ago and since we have done a few alterations we have heard no more ghostly happenings.'

The ghostly glow, the shifting light on the roof is an extremely interesting example of a phantom light. It was witnessed by these two people in November, 1939. The aunt, Miss Hilda Smith, who thought the eiderdown was on fire because of its glowing 'fire', saw this in 1924. I would have asked her for her account too, but she is no longer alive.

Another 'ghostly light' report is from Mr. Eric Cully of Westfield Road, Chandler's Ford, Eastleigh, Hants:

'One night during the last war I was in bed when the air-raid warning sirens hailed the approach of enemy planes. My mother and father went down to the shelter and pleaded with me to go with them but I had always said that the shelter was of no value and would collapse as easily as the house in the event of a near miss or direct hit. I stayed in bed in absolute darkness looking at the ceiling when I became conscious of a luminous ball of grey light in the corner of the bedroom towards my right. The light began to travel very slowly along the ceiling and went in a straight line in the direction of the foot of the bed. It continued very slowly around the room, but always close to the ceiling. I thought it was the reflection of a searchlight or a warden's torch and I sat up in bed and looked through the window on my left but could not see any sign of a light. I then looked to the right and behind me through the partly open bedroom door to see if there was a light shining through the landing window but again there was no light. I was completely puzzled and when the light started to approach in my direction along the ceiling and wall my hair began to bristle and my heart began to beat fast. I dived under the bed-clothes and went to sleep. I cannot help but feel that this was my guardian angel standing by to protect me.'

Strange patches of light used also to be seen by Mrs. E. M. Stephenson who, for twenty-five years, lived at the beautiful old Manor House in the village of Humberston, near Grimsby. Her friend, Mr. W. Barry Herbert, of Humberston Avenue, Grimsby, recalls that 'a mysterious patch of light would appear on the ceiling of one of the bedrooms ...' This, of course, was awe-inspiring enough. A shadow cast by no discernible light, a light which casts no shadow, or a light which has no explanation, are all calculated to chill the spine and set the heart pounding. This, however, was not the only phenomenon at the Manor House. Doors opened and shut of their own accord; loud knocks on doors were heard, furniture could be heard being moved violently downstairs and, when investigation was made at once, everything would be in order. Some years ago, when a new fireplace was being installed, a skeleton was discovered under the hearth. A monastery and a convent stood on this spot, and the remains might have been of a nun punished, in the cruel manner of the times, for some misdemeanour.

A rather terrifying experience—that of seeing something *black* yet visible, in a pitch dark room—was described to me by Mrs. Burtenshaw of Toronto Terrace, Brighton, Sussex. One night, glancing towards the door of her bedroom at 3 a.m. she saw what she describes as 'a small, jet black skull. The skull floated towards me and finally stopped at half an arm's length from my face. I dived under the bedclothes. When I came up from under the sheet I found I was looking straight at the skull ... the room was pitch dark but the black skull stood out very clear ...'

From Miss Rose Campbell of Heavitree, Exeter, comes this strange story:

'I was taking a walk with my fiancé one evening in late October, 1919, through some allotment gardens at St. Layes where there is a derelict monastery church below. On entering, a man with whom I worked in my office came towards us and said, "I should not go down by those ruins as it is getting dark." When I asked him why, he replied, "You might see the red lamp and if you do, it denotes danger for you, I've seen it, also the man working with me." We thanked him and just laughed it off, treating it as a joke. We arrived at a stile below the ruins and started talking about our forthcoming marriage when suddenly I saw a bright red light in the top of the ruins. My fiancé said: "It's those two men playing tricks on us—I will go and investigate." He went into the ruins, but returned saying, "I can't see a thing in there, so it can't be them." Anyway the light got more prominent than ever. It looked like a very large monstrance with a red light inside. I was terrified so we decided to go home.

'The next morning, on entering my office, the man who had warned us came and asked if I had seen the light. I told him, "Yes, we thought you were playing us tricks." He replied, "It's an ill omen for you."

'Two weeks later I saw in the E. & E. that the other man who was with Mr. F. had been killed by his son-in-law at the allotment. Then November came and we avoided the St. Layes walk, and did not refer to it again. Alas, on November 19, 1919, I had a telephone call to say that my fiancé had met with an accident by car, here in Pinhoe Road. He was taken to the R.A. & E. Hospital but was dead on arrival. I heard afterwards that the red lamp appeared as a warning of bad news to follow. When we had our blitz it was seen several times, and quite a number of people who had reported seeing it were later killed.'

Of the many stories which have reached me from various parts of the world, and of which there is space for but a few examples, the common factor that emerges is the capacity of such lights—as with many species of ghosts—to go through solid objects such as walls, doors and windows.

Generally, such lights appear to be pale blue or purple (a fair number of accounts of ghosts mention the phantasm as being enveloped in a kind of haze, mist, halo or aura of bluish or purple light), but Miss Campbell's account of the ghostly lights near St. Layes mentions a red glow, while Mr. and Mrs. MacRae saw a glow like fire flickering about the roof of Walnut cottage, so distinct even from a distance that they imagined for a moment that the roof was on fire.

A red glare, resembling that of a fire or furnace was, late in the last century, reported as being seen through the crevices and loopholes of an old barn near Birchen Tower, Hollinwood. On many occasions the glare was so pronounced that neighbours thought the barn was on fire and raised the alarm. But on rushing to the barn to put the fire out they found nothing wrong. Lest it should be supposed that some tramp or intruder was making use of the barn, it should be said that the reported lights were not of the kind to be accounted for in that way: the fire was almost like molten lava, seeping through cracks and openings. The fitful illumination shed by an oil lamp or candle would not produce such an effect—nor would an intruder (none was ever discovered) advertise his trespass so absurdly.

In Normandy, folklore has it that unquiet spirits flit around the countryside. One such light was reputed to be that of a priest who violated his vows of perpetual chastity and now endures an endless purgatory around the scene of his misdemeanours.

A curious legend concerning phantom lights is linked with the Chapel of Roslin, which was founded in 1446 by the Prince of Orkney. Apparently, whenever one of his descendants was about to die, the chapel appeared to be on fire—a phenomenon which sounds very similar to that observed by Miss Rose Campbell. In *The Lay of the Last Minstrel*, the long poem by Sir Walter Scott, published in 1805, we find a graphic description of these ghostly lights in Harold's Song:

> O'er Roslin all that dreary night,
>   A wondrous blaze was seen to gleam;
> 'Twas broader than the watch-fire light,
>   And redder than the bright moonbeam.
> It glared on Roslin's castled rock,
>   It ruddied all the copse-wood glen;
> 'Twas seen from Dryden's groves of oak,
>   And seen from cavern'd Hawthornden.
>
> Seem'd all on fire that chapel proud
>   Where Roslin's chiefs uncoffin'd lie;
> Each Baron, for a sable shroud,
>   Sheathed in his iron panoply . . .

10

Ghostly sounds

As long as history has been written, and ghosts mentioned, there have been accounts of ghostly sounds. The sighing of the wind ceases at times to be natural, assumes an entity of its own, and chills the heart of the solitary tenant or lonely traveller. The heavy, measured tread of invisible feet; the clanking of chains; the rustling of silk and linen; the creaking of doors upon their rusty hinges; sharp, minatory knocks having all the rhythm and definiteness of noises produced by some conscious agency; music from nowhere; sighs, cries, screams, shrieks; the dragging of heavy objects; inexplicable and nerve-racking crashes and bumps make up a cacophony of ghostly sounds to be reckoned with.

> From ghoulies and ghosties and long-leggity beasties
> And things that go bump in the night
> Good Lord, deliver us

went the ancient country prayer. It was often uttered, I dare say, with fervency. A stout heart can deal with the tangible; the intangible can terrify the bravest.

Sounds, of course, often accompany the actual appearance of a phantasm, and they are an almost inevitable feature of poltergeist hauntings, many of which I have already mentioned. But ghostly sounds are often heard unaccompanied by any other phenomena; which is not to say that they are any the less alarming. Shakespeare drew often enough upon his own knowledge of life and local beliefs to illustrate his points, and although his description of the gloomy night in which Duncan is murdered sounds like dramatic licence, it is no more spine-chilling than the actual experience of many people living today:

> Our chimneys were blown down: and, as they say
> Lamentings heard i' the air; strange screams of death:
> And prophesying, with accents terrible,

Of dire combustion, and confused events,
Now hatch's to the woeful time.

Strange screams of death ... do they ever happen?

The following story has been related to me by young Mr. Jeremy Pender of Portslade, Sussex.

'It was about one o'clock in the morning of January 5, 1964 that I returned to a flat which I was then sharing with a friend in Barnes. The night was quiet and still, and I was in good spirits and not over-tired, for I had had a pleasant evening with friends.

'I looked at my watch, and decided it was time for bed. Then, shattering the night silence, came the most appalling scream from the field opposite. I have never heard or even imagined such a cry before and hope never to hear such again: it was a mixture of terror, agony and grief, and at first seemed like the cry of some animal. It changed and became half animal, half human, and took on a note almost of pleading, and in a strange way directed at me. I rushed out to the field, but there was absolutely nothing to be seen. The sound went on and on, coming at me, and persisted for almost fifteen minutes. I was terribly shaken and completely mystified and went to bed tense and worried in my mind. I have heard the phrase "the voice of doom"—well, I heard it myself.

'In the morning, a telegram came to tell me that my father had died at about 8 p.m. the previous night—about five hours before I heard that strange, protracted cry. Now I know that the "wailing banshee" of legend does exist as a reality for I heard it myself.' Mr. Pender's father, a retired manager of the British American Tobacco Company in India, had died at Brighton, about fifty miles away.

A rather similar account was vouchsafed to me by Mr. Brendan Fathaigh, of Achill Island, County Mayo, Ireland. He describes his experience in these words:

'While I was a student at University College, Dublin, I had accommodation at a hostel situated on rising ground in a Dublin suburb. The hostel, a large one, looks right across the city.

'Three of us students who were engaged in the same work arranged to do some study together in Tom's bed-sitter one night. At midnight approximately I decided to retire as I was feeling rather tired and had to be in the University College, Dublin, by 9 a.m. next day. As I was about to leave the room Tom moved quickly to the window, opened it up from the bottom and leaned out. The night was absolutely still (in mid May).

' "Listen," said Tom, "Do you hear anything?"

'I went to the window and looked out over the city. All was quiet except for the distant drone of traffic. Tom spoke again.

' "Do you not hear that long wail? It's the Bean-sidhe cry—some member of my family has died!" Dick laughed in uncertain fashion. As for myself, I merely remarked in a light-hearted manner that it was time for all of us to retire. As I left the room Tom was still straining out of the window and listening attentively.

'Next day I attended my morning lectures in U.C.D. At 11 a.m. there was a knock on the door of the hall where Professor D. J. Hayes was lecturing to over 150 students. The professor himself went to the door, returned in a moment and asked if there was a Mr. Tom O'Boyle present. Tom duly presented himself and was told he was urgently required on the phone. An hour later when I met my friend Dick during a break for coffee he told me that Tom's mother died suddenly at midnight—at the time Tom himself had said he heard the wailing . . .'

This is a version of the 'wailing banshee' of Irish folk-lore and legend—the Bean Sidhe, called in Gaelic Ban Sith, whose awful cries and shrieks or 'keening' were said to presage the death of a member of the family visited. Many Irish legends mention the banshee as appearing periodically, immediately before, or at the time of, or immediately after, a death or tragedy. Folk-lore in Brittany contains many references to the banshee, which corresponds to the Welsh Gwrach y Rhybin (witch of Rhybin). The Highlands of Scotland also had a similar legend, mentioned by Sir Walter Scott in his *Demonology and Witchcraft*, page 351. The Welsh also had the *cyhyraeth* or 'groaning spirit'.

The hearing of some supernatural or terrible sound in connection with tragedy is many times recorded. Walter Gregor in *Folk-lore of North East of Scotland*, page 205, relates of a murder committed at Cottertown, of Auchenasie, near Keith:

'On the day on which the deed was done, two men, strangers to the district, called at a farmhouse about three miles from the house in which lived the old folk that were murdered. Shortly before the tragic act was committed, a sound was heard passing along the road the two men were seen to take, in the direction of the place at which the murder was perpetrated. So loud and extraordinary was the noise that the people left their houses to see what it was that was passing. To the amazement of everyone, nothing was to be seen, though it was moonlight so bright that it aroused attention. All believed something dreadful was to happen, and some proposed to follow the sound. About the time discussion was going on, a blaze of fire arose on the hill of Auchanasie. The foul deed had been accomplished and the cottage set on fire. By the next day we all knew of what the mysterious sound had been the forerunner.'

It is interesting to compare that impressive account with the following recollections given to me by Mrs. M. Moonyeen Judge of Athnowen Glebe, Ovens, County Cork:

'In 1925, at the age of eleven years, I was sent to boarding school and spent most of my school holidays at Heathburn Hall, Riverstick, Co. Cork with my late grandparents who were farmers. A week before returning to school in September, 1927, my aunt asked me to go to Ahern's farm and collect a sitting of duck eggs she had ordered. Usually, I did messages on my pony, Kit (Ahern's farm was about one and a half miles from the Gate Lodge, along a lonely valley road), but that evening she was already stabled and I was told to walk. It was about 6 p.m. I called Shep, the collie, and we set off down the avenue at the front of Gate Lodge. Mr. Good, who resided there, was cleaning his car and when I told him where I was going he offered to drive me, but I refused as my aunt said the walk would do me good.

'One is rarely afraid in Ireland, but just before reaching a small bridge I was startled when Shep, normally a sweet-tempered creature, stopped and started to growl. Then I heard what sounded like an old woman sobbing and crying, loudly and clearly. I called out: "What is the matter? Can I help you?" Receiving no answer, I ran to the other side of the bridge and called again. Then the ghastly wailing started up again and I became really frightened and started to run. The wailing persisted, and followed me, but about a quarter of a mile from the farmhouse, it left me and went up a road leading up to other farms, getting louder all the time. When I reached Ahern's farm at the roadside, I ran to the kitchen door crying. The family and neighbours were playing cards and when I tearfully related what had happened the old lady was very distressed and gave me hot milk and biscuits.

'When they asked me where the wailing had gone, I told them it had gone up to Crowley's farm where two bachelors resided (Mr. Ahern had talked with one of them only that morning). Two of the men present then escorted me home and when we arrived they informed my aunt that I had had a "bad fright". She was most annoyed with me and called me a baby for causing so much trouble, but I recall a favourite uncle who was present at the time, saying: "You've heard the Banshee, my girl".

'I was sent upstairs to join my grandparents in the study, and found granddad to be very sympathetic to my story. A deeply religious man who believed in ghosts (we are Irish Protestants) he never tired of telling us that "Our Lord returned as a Ghost—the Holy Ghost", and I remember him telling me once that a pane of glass crashed when a member of their family died. That night, as he went down to see the Ahern boys who were still in the kitchen, I was told to go to bed and forget my experience.

'We were having lunch the next day when Mrs. Keefe, the old cook, came in and said that two policemen were in the kitchen and wanted to see my grandfather. After about a quarter of an hour, grandfather returned and said I was not to be frightened but just answer truthfully any questions they asked me. I told them I had seen no one on the road to the farmhouse with the exception of Mr. Good to whom I had spoken at the Gate Lodge.

'Later I learned that Paddy Crowley was found hanging by a rope in one of the outhouses of the farm where the wailing had gone. He had hanged himself about the time I was on my way to the farmhouse. Later still, I was told that, taking part in the War of Independence against his mother's wishes, he had blown up that same small bridge where I first heard the wailing, killing some men in the process. This preyed on his mind and he became very quiet and retiring. I never wish to hear another "banshee" again as long as I live.'

Whatever the reasons for these strange sounds, the nature of the 'banshee' wail has, clearly, not changed. One wonders, once again, whether the brain, whose workings are in part a form of electrical energy, sends out signals in times of intense and exceptional emotion; whether the extremes of pain, fear and terror are somehow transmitted and by a freak impress themselves, somehow, on the atmosphere. It is common knowledge that sounds travel better in some climatic conditions than in others, but in these accounts it is not just a question of sound travelling. The stories do not concern a noise made in a particular place and heard over a wider area than one would normally expect. It is almost as though emotion by some process we cannot even begin to guess at, became translated into sound.

Sometimes the sound is not just a wail, but actual words, as though of recognition. On August 9, 1876, Mr. George Smith, the famous scholar and authority on Assyria, died at about six o'clock in the afternoon. At exactly that time Dr. Delitzsch, a close colleague and friend of long standing, was passing near to the house in which he used to live when in London when he heard his name called out, loud and distinct 'in a most piercing cry' which 'thrilled him to the marrow'. The startled and puzzled doctor looked at his watch, made a note of the time of this strange occurrence and recorded the fact in his notebook. He discovered that his friend had died at the moment he had heard that agonising appeal.

Generally, ghostly sounds are unpredictable. But on one occasion at least they were recorded. A tenant who found herself in a haunted house went to the lengths of hiring an expert from a firm of recording engineers so that there would be some positive evidence to offer the local authorities, who owned the premises.

Mr. and Mrs. J. Britton were living with their three children in a three-room flat in St. James's Parade, Horsefair, Bristol. Only Mrs. Britton actually saw the ghost—a phantasm of a little old woman in brown who always made a habit of going towards her daughter's cot.

One night a vigil was kept in the house, with sound recording apparatus and an independent investigator in readiness. At two o'clock in the morning the sounds of ghostly footsteps and padding began. Suddenly, Mrs. Britton became rigid with fear, shrieked 'my baby!' and fainted. She had seen the ghost of the old woman again, making her way as usual to the infant's cot.

The recording captured the footsteps, and also produced a strange kind of metallic vibration sound throughout the recording, for which there was no technical explanation.

I am indebted to Mr. Leslie North, features editor of the *Reading Mercury* who, like myself, has been interested in ghosts and the supernatural for many years, for a tale of ghostly footsteps heard in Farnborough, in the heart of the Berkshire Downs. There, a schoolmistress lived alone in her timbered cottage and often heard footsteps treading slowly up the stairs, going along the landing past her bed-head and ending in a metallic thump. At first (not unnaturally!) she was scared, but she became accustomed to the noises, which did nobody any harm. She has not seen this spectre herself, but not long ago an

infant girl visiting with her parents cried out one evening in
the sitting-room: "Naughty lady! Go away, naughty lady!",
following with her eyes someone (who was invisible to the
others) round the room. A dog also confirmed the 'presence'
by growling and lifting its hackles.

From the headmaster of The Stroud School, Highwood
House, Romsey, Hampshire, I have the following remarkable
story of ghostly sounds:

'In the spring of 1946, while on leave from the army, I was
staying at a house at Banwell, Somerset, with the family of a
school-friend of mine (also in the army). He was not present
himself but there were in the house his mother, his aunt and
his sister, all of whom I knew well. The house was situated
next door to the Old Abbey.

'At about two in the morning I was awakened by the dog
barking. It was, if I remember rightly, some sort of terrier, and
it slept in the bedroom of one of the ladies. I was in a semi-
conscious state of sleep, when I became aware of steps outside
my bedroom door descending the stairs (I was on the first floor
landing) and the sound of a woman sobbing. She was slowly
feeling the way down, step by step, as she would in the dark,
and I could hear the rustle of a robe as she descended. The
sobs were subdued, but regular. When she reached the
bottom of the stairs, I had become more awake, and as it
could have been one of the ladies, I thought I had better investigate to see what was the matter.

'As I came out on the landing, my friend's sister, whom I
thought had possibly descended the stairs, called out from her
bedroom and asked what was the matter. She was joined by
her mother, and I told them someone had gone downstairs, so
we searched the house for burglars, and the dog got very
excited. When our search proved fruitless, they asked me
exactly what I had heard, and on hearing my story they both
said, "You've heard the ghost". I had previously no knowledge
at all that the house had a ghost. They told me that although
they had never heard it, it had been heard by my school-friend,
when he was sleeping in the same room as his cousin ... both
heard it together, and when I related the story to my friend
when I next saw him, we found that we had had exactly the
same experience. At the time he and his cousin had been very
frightened, but it did not affect me in the same way, probably
because I had not thought there was anything abnormal about
it until I had discovered that all the ladies had been in their
beds.'

'Haunting by sound' can be very unnerving, and it is probably just as well that Mr. Sanger-Davies did not know in advance that the house was haunted in this way. The house stood within its own grounds, next door to the ruined Banwell Abbey which itself was always said to be haunted. 'My feeling,' Mr. Sanger-Davies told me in response to further questions, 'is that someone did actually walk down those stairs sobbing, exactly as I heard it—but many years before. Obviously she was in an acute state of emotional stress—cannot this somehow be "recorded" in a place and in a way that we cannot understand at present, rather like a gramophone record?' He did not *see* anything. He was in bed until she had got to the bottom of the stairs, though he has often wondered if he would have seen anything had he come out sooner, when she was outside his room. The fact that several people have heard exactly the same thing rules out hallucination.

I agree with him that somehow emotional stress does get 'recorded' in some strange way; why or how, nobody can be sure. A silk dress cannot rustle interminably without wearing out. In hauntings, time seems to stand still: again and again the ghost mounts the stairs (or descends), or glides through the field, or disappears through walls and doors. It would be a sad, indeed, an intolerable thought that man-made agonies and the torment of the soul are repeated endlessly; that the grief-stricken woman must sob through eternity, the grief being never-ending, the awful emotional upheaval continuing unmitigated by any happiness through the centuries. That would be something near to hell, itself the creation of man in his vindictive and morbid moods. As the history of wars, massacres and tyranny shows, man can and does make a hell on earth when he wishes. 'This is hell' said the commandant of a concentration camp to a batch of terrified newcomers during the Second World War, 'a man-made hell'. He did not exaggerate; he was glorying in the orgy of evil which he and his henchmen maintained. In considering the misery and unhappiness inflicted upon humanity by themselves and by fate, one of the great consolations is that all bad things, as well as all good, must come to an end—with death. One hopes, therefore, that the distress and terror, panic and unreason inherent in most ghostly sounds will be explained one day in terms of the 'photographic' theory—that emotions and happenings register on inanimate things, or on the atmosphere, being picked up by living people long afterwards, long after the sad events have been shrouded by the silence and peace of time.

From another informant come details of a haunted house in High Street, Worthing. The house dates back to the 1830's and was used by smugglers at one time—a tunnel passes under the house from the old police station to a public house. The informant writes:

'Whilst we lived there, we all experienced the distinct sounds of heavy feet walking over the kitchen. These sounds were heard mainly in the evenings, but at no particular times—perhaps twice within an hour. The ceiling of the kitchen was quite low, and obviously there was no one upstairs at the time of the occurrences. We all heard five or six steps which were quite distinctly and definitely the tread of a man. One particular evening I fitted a curtain rail, with runners, on to a wooden slat on the ceiling for the purpose of providing a heavy curtain to partition the dining part from the sink and the cooking part of the room. Whilst screwing up the rail, I had my head close to the ceiling and, suddenly, I heard mice and perhaps rats scurrying above and I put my head against the ceiling. Then I felt the vibration of the feet walk over me. Quite uncanny.

'The room above the kitchen was also the kitchen of a flat, but the occupier—a lady—was certainly never in that room when the noises were heard. A long passage led from there to the front of the house where the living-room was situated, and where the lady spent her evenings.'

Mrs. H. Malby lived in the house from 1931 to 1963. During that period the ghostly sounds often recurred and an apparition—a greyish figure—was seen by her. She remarked to her husband (now deceased) 'I didn't know that Mrs. Mare (the lady who lived upstairs) was in'. When she looked again, the figure had disappeared. A lady next door had also seen it but never mentioned it to Mrs. Malby for fear of frightening her.

The disturbing thing about this haunting is that the son-in-law who put his head to the ceiling felt the normal vibrations which would accompany the physical act of walking with heavy tread. Even if one accepted without further reservation the theory that sounds leave some imprint discernible by specially sensitive people, how can a ghostly footprint cause a floor to 'give'? And how account for a latch being *lifted* as well as footsteps being heard? Mr. D. A. Clover of Pinner Road, Sheffield, tells this story:

' "Fordington Lodge" is a farm standing about half a mile back from the main York to Northallerton road. About fifteen years ago, my wife's sister and her husband lived in this Lodge and farmed its land. It was a pleasant house with a large kitchen, two front downstairs rooms, a beautiful staircase with large window overlooking the yard, and two large and one small bedrooms upstairs. There was no electricity—lighting was by oil lamps—but there was piped cold water.

'At that time we had no children and used to motor up to Fordington regularly at week-ends, arriving Friday night and stopping over until Sunday. On this particular week-end we set off as usual from Sheffield, our route taking us through Doncaster, Ferry Bridge, Tadcaster and York. As we approached York, storm clouds were gathering and thunder rolled over the city. From York onwards, the lightning was intense, sometimes flashing right on to the tarmac road and we were very pleased when we turned into the lane approaching the Lodge and went over the bridge into the farmyard.

'We ate a wonderful supper and sat talking in the light of the oil lamps until tired, then retired to bed. In the night, my wife and I awoke suddenly and simultaneously to the sound of footsteps coming up the stairs and along the landing towards our door. Then we heard the click of the latch as the door opened and the footsteps crossed the room, stopping at the fireplace. Yet we could see nothing.

'The next day, when I examined the latch on our door, I found it was a heavy, wooden, Norfolk type which fitted perfectly in its neck, and could be moved only by lifting. Feeling rather silly, I mentioned our experience to my brother-in-law but his immediate reply was: "Oh, it's only the ghost." It appears that he had got quite used to it and went on to relate an experience he had one night when he went downstairs to prepare the baby's bottle: He was standing at the stove when he heard the sofa move behind him and spun round to see someone sitting there (though he saw no actual figure). Then the sofa moved back to the wall.

'Another night, he was alone in the house when he saw a figure appear at the kitchen window pointing a shotgun to the sky. He arose and went out to investigate, but whoever it was had gone.

'Subsequently, my sister-in-law went to York Museum to find that Fordington Lodge was mentioned a long time ago and that the present house was probably built on the site of the old one. She also found that a prince or nobleman had stopped there once on his journey north and that just north of the Lodge there is a tree where a highwayman was hanged.'

Mr. E. Hutchins of Essex Road, Hoddesden, Hertfordshire,

had a curious story to tell of noises heard during a year's stay at Sunderlandwick Hall, near Driffield, a market town in the East Riding of Yorkshire. Both he and his wife heard footsteps passing along a stone-flagged passage, always in the same direction and sounding as though they were made by feet that were wet and in a hurry.

In response to inquiries, he gave me the following details:

'The front of Sunderlandwick Hall had been destroyed by fire leaving the servants' wing occupied by farm foreman Mr. Cayley, and the nursery wing in which I lived with my wife and family. I do not know the name of the last resident at the Hall, but I was told that a son of the family was in trouble in Africa for shooting and killing a Negro servant.

'There was gas for cooking and lighting, and water came from a tank in the attic above the servants' quarters. The wing in which I lived had a stone-flagged passage running from the entrance door to a door (which was kept locked) leading to the other wing. There were four rooms and a staircase at the side of the passage and the layout upstairs was similar but with wooden floors. There were no pipes in the passage where the footsteps occurred, and there is no pond at the Hall nor, as far as I know (I am a water-diviner), any underground stream.

'We were never told that the house was haunted and in any case did not believe in ghosts, until we heard the footsteps. When we heard these footsteps, there was no lowering of temperature, nor did we see anything unusual.

'I lived at the Hall because of my work as a beck watcher on the Driffield Beck, which was over five hundred yards away.

'One night—I do not remember the date—we had all gone to bed except my wife, who was darning socks, but she came up after a few minutes, looking pale and nervous. She did not mention the footsteps at the time, though I heard them some time later—bare feet, at a fast walk, going through the locked room and fading away. When I told my wife about it she told me about the night she stayed up saying that she was so frightened that the hair at the back of her head stood straight out. As soon as she had recovered her composure, she decided not to tell anyone about it. My wife heard the footsteps again, but this time she was able to master her fear. Then I heard them once more.'

Between Uxbridge and Slough is an old house which had remained unoccupied for two years before Mrs. M. Hills, who now lives in Moulscombe, Brighton, went to live there as a young widow with a son of four years. 'Daily,' she says, 'there was a noise like a lot of army boots stamping about louder and louder.' Another curious noise was that of a car screeching to a halt, usually at about 1.10 p.m. Under her maiden name of Chamley, Mrs. Hills was running kennels there, and would often go out after hearing the car expecting to find a visitor; but there was nothing there. Making inquiries, she discovered that before the house was vacant as many as twenty-two children had been raised there. Also, a previous tenant reported that her brother had died when his lung was penetrated, and that vain last-minute attempts were made to get him into hospital before he died. Later, when two brothers of Mrs. Hills tried at different times to rent the house, people living in near-by caravans told them about hearing the noisy footsteps from the empty house.

Sounds of doors being opened and shut, and of 'something being dragged along the passage' were frequently heard by Mrs. Constance Thomas, of Hillcrest Park, Exeter, when she was living at another house in that area. 'I was in my mid-twenties and had never been scared or encountered anything of the supernatural,' she told me, 'but sometimes I would wake up at night and see a figure looking at me (my husband's work kept him away from home a good deal at that time, and during the week I would sleep there alone with my young son). I'd rub my eyes and then it (the ghost) would vanish. I told my husband, who laughed it off . . . until I left him alone there once. He told me on my return that all sorts of strange things had occurred. He had seen someone standing over him, heard a door being opened, and something being dragged along the passage . . .'

But the 'things that go bump in the night' often go with a very loud bump indeed. Mrs. C. Maclean Davidson of Merchison Place, Edinburgh, has uneasy recollections of a house in which she once stayed a few years ago. 'In the early part of the first evening I was awakened by strange noises which I put down to imagination, having awakened from a deep sleep. But these noises continued at nerve-racking intervals. The following evening my sister called and when I mentioned the noises she looked incredulous; however, not long after this an explosive sound was heard, so hearing was believing. Although I was left alone I was not afraid even when the loudest noise of all came after midnight, and which sounded as though a piece of furniture had lifted and fallen. On going through the house I found nothing amiss.'

A curious feature of this haunting was that at the time the

hall was being decorated. The stripping of the wall revealed, drawn on the plaster beneath, the pencilled head of a bearded man 'the only likeness to whom I could ascribe it was Kruger.'

Banging and knocking are features of innumerable hauntings, sometimes as an accompaniment to visual phenomena but more often not. Some people seem quite impervious to these uncanny noises; others are frightened. From Mr. Buhot of Ingouville Place, St. Helens, Jersey, Channel Islands, comes the story of a haunted house in Great Union Street where he stayed as a small boy. It was a nine-roomed house but 'there were two rooms that never felt right, and they were the lounge and the dining-room, because the dining-room was used as a place to rest coffins from the church opposite, when anybody died.' No one, however, was unduly bothered by this sombre civility: it was a small service, to allow a coffin to rest there, within easy proximity of the church opposite, until the last sad rituals had been enacted.

However, in 1957, when the landlady of the house died, there was an outbreak of completely inexplicable noises, including loud bangings and knockings in the middle of the night. Once, when his mother went to have a rest during the day, she felt somebody get on the bed at the same time, but could see nobody there. On another occasion her clothes, which she put at the foot of the bed, rose about two feet and went down again. On one occasion, when the young lad came home from school for lunch, he heard voices coming from the empty lounge, which stopped the moment he entered. A dog would not go into the dining-room without barking furiously, while the cat refused to go in at all—it stood at the doorway, back arched, hair on end.

The old superstition, or tradition, that 'three sharp knocks' often precede, accompany or follow death in a family is a recurrent theme in many accounts vouchsafed to me by people of rational judgement, having no record of or predisposition to, nervous instability or impaired observation. From Mrs. Gilchrist of Leith comes the following story:

'For eight months I lived in a haunted house, and I shall never forget it as long as I live. Every night, at twelve o'clock sharp, rappings came, *three times, three hard knocks*, in turn. When I went into the bedroom one night to get something out of the chest of drawers I found that I couldn't move, for there, floating through the room, I saw a figure in white ...'

It will be remembered that the mysterious patch of light which appeared in the Manor House at Humberston, men-

tioned in my chapter on Ghostly Lights, was preceded by
knocking sounds. And from a correspondent in County Durham,
Mrs. Maisie Gent, comes this account which she received from an
old lady, now dead, whom she knew well and who by temperament was a cheerful, vigorous realist with no fears and
phobias and who still insisted that she did not believe in
'ghosts and things like that':

'When she was sixteen, which was in the year 1890 approximately, she worked as a cook in Bradford. Her name was Kate
Collins and her home village was about fifteen miles away. One
day, Kate received a letter from her sister telling her about
mysterious and tragic happenings at home. The Collins house
was back-to-back with another house where an elderly couple
lived. One night, the family was awakened by three loud knocks
on the door, which not only aroused everyone in their house
but also those in the neighbouring houses. The father put his
head out of the window and seeing someone at the window
of the house on the opposite side of the street, said "It's at
your door, Mr. Collins". There was no one there and the gate
was closed.

'That week, three people in the house died, and they were
the only ones in the house who had not heard the knocks.
The first was the old lady at the back of the house who, admittedly, was a bit deaf. She was out milking the cow the next
day when she dropped dead. The second person was her husband (but I have forgotten the circumstances of his death), the
third was Mrs. Collins, who had a stroke while out in the horse
and trap and was brought home dead.

'Incidentally, on the night of the knocks, the policeman on
his beat went home feeling poorly as a result of shock because
he saw "a white thing which rushed past him like the wind"
as he was going up the hill.'

The following story concerns ghostly happenings, including
ghostly sounds, at a well-known inn, but since it has blossomed
to considerable prosperity since these events, and because not
every guest likes to feel that his night's rest may be interrupted by some terrifying experience, I will withold the name.

'In 1934, I was working as a domestic help at an inn near
Rugby. I slept in a large attic room, access to which was
through a smaller, unfurnished room. The electric light switch
was just by the door and as my bed was quite a distance away
from it, I used a candle to find my way to the bed when I put
the light off. On the night in question I needed a handkerchief,
so I lit the candle, crossed the room to the chest of drawers and

got one. Then I went back to bed and put the candle out. Almost at once I heard a noise like a fluttering, which came nearer and nearer to the bed. In the end, I clapped the clothes over my head in terror and stayed under them for I don't know how long. When the fluttering seemed to have stopped, I lit the candle, got out of bed and searched all round the room. I looked in the wardrobe which was a home-made affair and behind the chest of drawers, but found nothing.

'When I told my employer about it next morning, all she said was: "It must have been a bird in the tank room next to the attic", but when I looked in there it was obvious that no bird could have got in.

'I used to work for the people who occupied the inn before my employers at the time in question, and when I told my former employer, Mrs. Rangely, what had happened, she said: "You don't mean to say they put you in those attics? Why, they are haunted." To which I replied: "Well, thank goodness I did not know that—or wild horses would never have got me to sleep there again." '

In the case of a haunted house in Camberley, Mrs. N. Burnett, of Freemantle, Southampton, was not only awakened at midnight by someone knocking on her bedroom door but, when she said 'come in', the door opened. She could see nobody, but 'it' moved to the washstand, moved the wash basin, jug and soap dish, put them down again and, when Mrs. Burnett said 'who's that?' the invisible visitor went out and shut the door. Two weeks later, when she went into her room (the window was closed, and there was no draught) the heavy curtains on the door 'blew out into the middle of the room' as though the force of a hurricane was behind them.

Madingley Hall, Madingley, near Cambridge stands on a hill in gardens planned by the famous landscape gardener, 'Capability' Brown and was first built in Tudor times by Justice Hinde, being altered by his Elizabethan descendant. From a lady in Cambridge who visited the Hall comes the strange story of a very real-looking ghost, whose appearance was preceded by the distinct sound of ghostly voices:

'I have found it difficult to describe what I experienced last September (1963) at Madingley Hall.

'Briefly, these are the circumstances. Almost every day, over the last six years, I have taken my poodle for a walk round the gardens at the Hall to play ball and give him exercise. This is allowed during most of the year but during September the place is shut and the staff, gardeners included, are all away.

I forgot this last September, and as the gates were open, I drove up the drive and left my car outside the front of the Hall, as I usually did.

'I walked through the little iron gates to the lawns and gardens and was stooping to undo my dog's lead and throw his ball, when I heard a very loud sound of voices and laughter. I at once thought: Oh dear, there is a garden party on; I should not be here, but when I looked there was no one in sight. As I stood spellbound, the voices continued, especially a deep laughing woman's voice. My dog put his tail between his legs and showed all the signs of being frightened. It was late afternoon. The sun was brilliant but the wind was blowing so I thought I was just imagining things and started to walk on. It was just then that I felt somebody looking at me from behind and I just had to turn around. There was a young man hanging in the most awkward position over the stone balustrade in the garden above. His hair was dark and cut jagged over his forehead. He had a white ruff round his neck and his arms were hanging over the low wall in a most peculiar way. But his face was horrible. More like a skeleton's—greenish-white— and he looked at me with such hate that I found myself shivering. I walked on, not knowing what else to do. As the path is circular I had to come back to the same gate, but when I did pluck up courage to return, there was nothing unusual going on at all.

'I told my husband about it but he just laughed and said I had imagined it and after a day or so I thought that perhaps he was right. Then I started going for my usual Madingley walk and completely forgot about the 'garden party' until one day I walked through the little iron gate and exactly the same thing happened. I definitely wasn't thinking about voices. I was in the act of throwing the ball for the dog and there certainly wasn't a wind that day.

'Some time after this happened I met one of the under-gardeners and he remarked: "We were speaking about you the other day, saying we hadn't seen you lately." When I told him why, he replied, "I don't disbelieve you. Some rare old funny things go on up there, more than one can tell you. I saw and heard a couple of them myself once."

'Of course, Madingley is old. The earliest part was built in Henry VIII's reign with stone from the church of Histon. Rupert Brooke says in his poem, *Grantchester*—"And things go on, you'd ne'er believe, at Madingley, on Christmas Eve".'

An Outward Bound training course in the mountains isn't

the sort of occasion one associates with ghostly voices; nor are the down-to-earth, tough participants, trained to face and cope with realities pleasant or unpleasant, the type to be given to illusions and dreaming.

Mr. M. J. Watler of Southampton related to me how a voice, shrill and distinct, sounded from nowhere in the most unlikely circumstances:

'One December, about seven years ago, I was attending an Outward Bound course at Eskdale in Cumberland. This was for a period of one month, and in the early part of the course we were sent on a Reliability and Initiative Test. Basically, we were sent individually to certain map reference points to see whatever was there and then to another camp for the night. We found we were all camping in one wood two or three miles above Wast Water, in the direction of Santon Bridge (very near to Mort Galesyke) the object being to test our actual camping ability for picking team leaders later. I bivouacked by a dry stone wall in the wood by the edge of the road, cooked my supper, climbed into my sleeping bag and went to sleep.

'I have a happy memory of dreaming of open coffins; which I would have forgotten but for the fact that I was awakened by a devil of a noise—something like being in a crowded room. At first, I couldn't fully realise what was going on; but the noise was coming down the road from the direction of Santon Bridge. The nearest I can get to a description of it is that it sounded like a mixture of dogs barking, a gabbling noise like geese and, above all, high-pitched laughter (hysterical). My first thought was: it's a group of drunken cyclists driving a flock of farmer's stock down the road for a laugh. But on getting up and looking up the bright moonlit road (then fading away up the valley), I saw it was completely empty. Then, to my complete astonishment, a voice shrilled out, "It's twelve, boys, time to get up."

'I should have said this sound was passing over the woods at the time. It went on down the valley and away. The wood was full of some twenty blokes like myself, and we all heard it but could not offer any explanation. I don't know at what time it happened as it got dark at about four—it could have been any time during the night. The area was far too remote for anyone to be playing tricks with sound equipment. I know the voice sounds ridiculous, but it did say that.'

Indeed, a curious story. I put various supplementary questions to Mr. Watler: Was the voice which was heard that of a man or a woman? Mightn't somebody have concealed themselves and played a practical joke? Mightn't somebody have hidden themselves with a loudhailer—the electronic voice magnifier used by police, yachtsmen, etc., and quite commonly encountered nowadays—though even if they had, it could hardly account for the other strange sounds, such as the 'gabbling of geese'.

As for the wording of the shouted command: 'It's twelve, boys, and time to get up', this seems an odd command whether from human or any other agency, because most people don't rise either at noon or midnight!

Mr. Watler was quite direct and firm in all his answers. The voice was 'definitely that of a woman, very high-pitched, and elderly'. He was not frightened at the time, but 'just couldn't believe my senses'. He is perfectly satisfied that nobody was using a loudhailer.

My friend Bernard Kelly, a feature writer on the *Denver Post*, Colorado, received a strange letter from a reader who describes how an occurrence which can broadly be described as a typical poltergeist phenomenon, was accompanied by a good deal of noise.

'We were entertaining relatives and were sitting quietly conversing' said the writer, Mrs. Marguerite Miller of Loveland, Colorado, 'when a report sounded with almost deafening loudness and an object fall to the floor behind the chair of a guest. No one had been moving about and all windows and doors were closed due to the coolness of the night air. For a time, we just sat there, looking all about us with astonished, ludicrous expressions. Upon investigation, I found a large but common button lying on the floor. None of my guests had seen it and neither had I, although I know every inch of that room from much house-cleaning activity.

'The question is: Where did it come from and why did it hurtle in among a quiet group, like a projectile flung with tremendous force? It had struck the gas heater, which accounted for the reverberating sound. I am only stating facts. We are all of us reasonable, common-sense people. The men offered the explanation that someone was playing a trick, but that was recognisable as mere whistling in the dark. We live in a cabin high on a hillside overlooking a lake and no one was about the place except ourselves ...'

Mrs. Muriel Hinrichs, of 420 Clayton Street, Denver, reported that one day, when she was a child, there was a constant knocking throughout the house where she lived. The next day her aunt died. Later, there was a continual disturbance of the cook-

ing utensils, and strange noises, followed the next day by
the death of her mother.

But for a true American ghost story it would be hard to
beat that of Mr. J. Earl Stone of Malaga Road, Santa Fe, New
Mexico. His memory is as sharp as a diamond cutter and his
narrative style very expressive:

'I had gone up to Kiowa, in Elbert County, on a vacation at
my uncle's horse ranch out there. At this time (1894) I was
around seventeen years of age. A neighbour rancher-stockman
living not far from my uncle's place, named Dick Grubb, induced me to come to his place to help him out as his hired
hand had quit him pronto, giving as his excuse that Grubb's
house was haunted. Grubb asked me if I was afraid of ghosts,
and I replied that I was not. It seems that a few years prior a
man by name of Nelson had been murdered while sleeping in
his bunk, where I would have to sleep.

'So, for the munificent sum of eight dollars per month I
went to work on this ranch, doing the chores, ploughing the
corn, cooking breakfast at 3 a.m. and getting supper in the
evening. Grubb intimated that his wife was visiting in Denver.
The house consisted of two large rooms and an attic, which
was used as a store room, covered by a pitched roof—a typical
bunk house of those days. A stairway led to the attic along
one wall of my room. Grubb, on showing me to my bunk,
pointed to the blood-stains on the wall where Nelson had been
shot. Each morning, after breakfast, I had to draw water for
some forty hogs, feed and curry the work team, and start to
the cornfield to be ploughed, which was some two miles from
the bunk house, and be at work at sun up. I was instructed
never to trot the horses, but to walk them to and from work.
On Sundays I rode some fifteen miles of drift fence.

'Grubb was a taciturn man who kept an immense dog and a
loaded shotgun in the room in which he slept, with the door
between his room and mine kept locked at night. I always
left a side door of my room open at night for fresh air, as it
was summer time. Whenever a pig or strange animal mosied
into my room, Grubb would yell, "What's all that racket?"
and I would respond, "Oh, just some of your damned pigs!"

'I was left alone nearly every night and did not know where
Grubb was, nor did I ask. He at one time volunteered that he
had been driving cattle to Denver. One night, as I was sitting
at a table in the centre of the room reading, I heard footsteps
going up the stairway leading to the attic. I stiffened in surprise, as no one could have reached the foot of those stairs

without first passing me. I could hear them distinctly as they crossed the attic floor. There was a basket of empty bottles in that corner to which the footsteps led and I could hear those bottles being removed one by one and set upon the floor. I counted, and fourteen bottles were set down. I'll have to admit that by this time my hair was kind of standing on end. I was puzzled, but refrained from mentioning it to Grubb that next morning. However, to satisfy my curiosity I went up into the attic and counted those bottles; there were fourteen of them in that basket. Checking the windows, which were of four panes each, I found them built solid in the wall, with no broken glass in any of them.

'Not many nights thereafter, while again seated at the table reading, and alone, I noted the ceiling vibrating to the rhythm of dancing feet, and could distinctly hear what seemed to be a square dance in progress, overhead. There was no music, but the rafters were swaying and quivering. Again I refrained from mentioning this to Grubb. After all, I wasn't supposed to be afraid of ghosts; but I was mystified.

'One Sunday morning while Grubb was, I presumed, in Denver, a woman came to me at the corral, stating that she was Grubb's wife, and telling me to ride the drift fence. I assumed that she had returned from Denver. While following her instruction I came upon some thirty feet of wires that were dropped down as though the staples had come loose, and one post was down. Climbing down from my horse I repaired this.

'Upon returning to the house Grubb met me at the corral, demanding as to why I had been riding drift frence and upon whose authority. He was furious. I replied that his missus had told me to. He looked at me, both surprised and suspiciously, and roared, "I'm giving the orders around here, and you are only to take orders from me, understand?" Incensed, I demanded my pay and quit. Confidentially, I was glad to have an excuse to get away.

'Returning to my uncle's ranch I related to him why I had quit. "Grubb's wife gave you those instructions? Why, Grubb's wife died a year ago! We all attended her funeral," my uncle exclaimed.

'I've been scratching my head and wondering who DID give me those orders.'

There seems to be no limit to the nature and variety of sounds heard, either singly or together. Shrieks, cries, groans, whispers, strident voices, clanking sounds, dragging sounds, knocks, crashes, banging, tapping, scraping. Are these sounds made by some supernatural agency, or are they the product of the subconscious mind of the hearer, just as the eye can 'perceive' hallucinations? But even if one accepts such a thesis, it leaves an added mystery to which an answer seems impossible. For the bunkhouse described by Mr. J. Earl Stone had already the reputation of being haunted. Others had heard strange things. Why should one place, the scene of tragedy or emotional upheaval, have a something about it which registers and impresses itself upon a succession of people, while other places soaked in human tragedy do not appear to be haunted? The torture chambers of the Inquisition, the Roman amphitheatres in which every imaginable—and unimaginable—cruelty was perpetrated for the diversion of bloodthirsty decadents, the gas chambers where, in more recent times, millions were done to death—these places appear to be no more haunted than the odd garage or factory or suburban house. Hauntings seem commonly linked to tragedy, but only a tiny percentage of tragedies culminate in haunting.

Geoffrey Wilson, chief reporter of the *Bedfordshire Times*, has drawn my attention to a very interesting haunting—of what until 1964 were the offices of the Clerks to the Justices in Bedford, at 38 Mill Street, a fine old building which was built in 1760 and is scheduled for preservation as an ancient monument, from which the Clerk and his staff have recently moved to other premises in St. Paul's Square. In the opinion of Mr. Derek Payne, one of the deputy Clerks to the Justices, the premises are 'quite definitely haunted'. He has described how 'the ghost used to knock sharply on an office door, but when the door was opened there was no one there. On one occasion I was working alone in my office at a time when there was no one else in the building. There was a sharp double knock on my office door. I opened it—and no one was there'.

Mr. T. B. Porter, of West End, Pavenham, who was brought up at 38 Mill Street, Bedford, confirmed that there was something decidedly strange about the place. In a letter to the *Bedford Record* he says:

'The sound of unexplained footsteps at 38 Mill Street is no unusual event. My father, a man of strong will, refused to have the matter mentioned, saying the subject was quite unfit for discusssion by educated people. As the orders approximated closely to those of the Medes and Persians, this was quite sufficient. In later years my mother did occasionally mention the matter.

'As small boys we used to come in to dinner at one o'clock, passing the kitchen door and going upstairs to tidy up. Mother then served the dinner and took it into the dining-room. On one occasion we seemed to be a long time, and she called us to come down, but got no answer. Then we actually came in. "Have you been in before?" she asked. We had not, and wondered why she had asked. She went back into the kitchen and told the old servant what had happened.

' "There must be somebody upstairs," my mother said, "I am going up to see."

' "You're not going up alone," said the servant, snatching up a carving knife, "I'm coming too."

'They searched the house from top to bottom, but found nobody. Both my mother and the servant were convinced that they had heard us come in, and could not understand it. They carried out my father's orders and told us nothing about it at the time.

'Another experience my mother told me about happened one winter's night. She was sitting in the dining-room when she heard two heavy knocks on an old oak back door which had a heavy iron knocker. Screwing up her courage, she opened it—but no one was there. She called, but got no answer.

'When my father came back at nine o'clock (he had been to the Town and County Club to play billiards), she told him what had happened. He said it could be simply explained by the fact that the big gates facing Mill Street could not have been bolted.

'Upon investigation, however, he found that they had been bolted, so he then said that there must be somebody in the garden—this was about a quarter of an acre and well planted. He asked for the hurricane lamp, took a heavy stick, and searched the garden, but he found no one there, and said that my mother must have been dreaming.'

Mr. Porter also remembers a two-storeyed, half-timbered cottage at the back of 38 Mill Street which had a coach-house, stabling and a loft. On one occasion the gardener had to search the loft because of mysterious noises, for which no explanation was ever found.

Singing by ghostly choirs is, on the whole, not so rare—there are very many records of singing heard on sites where monasteries and abbeys once stood, or still stand either ruined or intact.

Miss Anita R. Wills, of Dunster, Twiggs Lane, Marchwood, recalls a visit to Palace House, Beaulieu, Hampshire, the ances-

tral home of Lord Montagu of Beaulieu. When she was seven or
eight years old, she took a French boy to look over the Abbey
ruins, and distinctly heard the chanting of monks there. Palace
House was originally the gatehouse to a Cistercian Abbey
founded in 1204, the house being converted into a private residence in 1538.

Workers engaged in building Wylfa nuclear power station at
Anglesey have both heard and seen a singing ghost. Surface
workers and others engaged in excavating a tunnel saw, in
1964, the shade of a woman in white, humming. The tunnel
passes through land on which a house called Galan Dhu
(Black Bank) once stood. This house was the home of a famous
opera singer from New Zealand, the late Rosina Buckman, and
it was during the excavations that a casket containing her cre-
mated remains was discovered, and reinterred in a local churchyard.

The first time the ghost was seen in the moonlight, the men
thought it was a girl out for a swim; but she would go to
the edge of the cliff and disappear, and often could be heard
singing. The atmosphere was so eerie that several men quit the
job, saying that they could not stand the unnatural strain.

Haunted houses

For over all there hung a cloud of fear,
A sense of mystery the spirit daunted,
And said, as plain as whisper in the ear,
The place is haunted.—*Thomas Hood.*

Ghosts appear sporadically and unpredictably in thousands of different places all the time. Nevertheless, particular houses, castles, buildings and localities are described as 'haunted' because phenomena appear to manifest themselves to different people at various times.

In the course of nearly two centuries, for example, 'The Brown Lady of Raynham' has been frequently seen. It is many years since I spent the day there, but on that occasion the late Marchioness of Townshend told me that she herself had seen the Brown Lady several times. The present Marquess does not share his parents' enthusiasm for the ghost and tells me he has never seen it.

One detailed account of the appearance of the ghost was written by Lucia C. Stone in 1835. Her facts, which were obtained from an eye-witness may be briefly summarised as follows:

Christmas celebrations were in full swing and a large house party was in residence. The hosts were Lord and Lady Charles Townshend, whose guests included Colonel Loftus, Mrs. Loftus and her cousin, Miss Page. Colonel Loftus was a relative of both host and hostess—brother of Lady Charles and cousin to Lord Charles.

Colonel Loftus and a man called Hawkins, settled down one night to a game of chess. As both were experienced players, the tussle was a protracted one, but the match at long last resolved, and midnight long since passed, the two tired players went upstairs to bed. They were saying 'good night' to each other when Hawkins drew the Colonel's attention to a lady standing by his sister's door. 'How strangely she is dressed!' he remarked. The Colonel, being short-sighted, did not im-

mediately see her but by the time he adjusted his monocle he
saw the figure of a woman in period dress who walked along
until she gradually faded from view. He saw her again before
his departure and this time with brisk strategic intent the
Colonel out-manoeuvred her, going up the staircase in such a
way that they came face to face. It was as well that he was a
soldier to whom a display of nerves would be shameful for
there, facing him, was the detailed figure of a spectre of an
aristocratic-looking lady dressed in brocade, her hair done in
a coif, her features clearly delineated in a kind of unearthly
light and—a very unpleasant feature, common to many ghostly
appearances—she had no eyes. Her face was normal except for
the stygian, empty caverns of her eye-sockets.

The Colonel afterwards drew a sketch of the ghost, but
nobody laughed at him because, although her appearances
were infrequent and followed no recognisable pattern of behaviour, she had been seen many times before 1835. Furthermore, when Miss Page asked Lord Charles if he believed in the
ghost he replied, 'I cannot but believe, for she ushered me
into my room last night'.

The Brown Lady of Raynham seems to take special pleasure
in scaring men in uniform. Captain Frederick Marryat, the
famous author of sea stories, saw the apparition when he was
once a guest at Raynham, being one of a large party assembled
to celebrate the redecoration and refurnishing of the mansion.

Anybody who has read Captain Marryat's salty, racy stories
will know that he was the last man to believe in ghosts, so
when he heard of guests scurrying off because of a supposed
haunting he was indignant both with them and with the people
who he really believed responsible—the poachers and smugglers
whose hidey-holes were near by, and whose comings and
goings, normally furtive and unnoticed, were now noisy and
publicised because of the dogs. 'Let me sleep in this so-called
haunted room,' he told Lord Townshend, 'we'll soon show 'em
what nonsense it is.'

And so he slept in the 'haunted' chamber, in which hung
the portrait of the Brown Lady of Raynham, in her brown
satin dress and elegant ruff. Even so, as he retired, he glanced
with appraisal—he would not admit to apprehension—at the
portrait as it flickered in the candlelight. There was *something*
odd about it. The eyes? Could any mortal eyes be as deep-set,
luminous and even evil-looking? Was it imagination, or did
the expression on the face change, from impassivity to dynamic
malevolence?

He undressed, and had reached his undergarments when two young men came to his room. There was to be a shooting party the following day and they wanted some technical tips about their gun. Discussion about firearms could not, of course, be postponed whatever the hour of day or night; the rest of the guests being long abed, Captain Marryat went just as he was to their room, inspected the gun and then returned with the two men to his room. As they proceeded along the semi-dark, gaunt corridor all three saw the figure of a woman approaching. Worried about his undress, he and his companions hid behind the door of a vacant room. But as he observed the figure coming closer, Captain Marryat experienced what it was like to feel his flesh creep. He had seen the portrait in his room—the picture which had given him such uneasy feelings and here was the 'living', or at any rate moving, embodiment of it. On, on it came, holding a lamp which reflected against its brown dress. It made no noise on the oak flooring. And as it passed the door where they were partially concealed it looked at them 'in such a diabolical manner', to quote Marryat's own words, that it struck terror in their hearts. It is not normal to shoot at guests, so we can be sure that at this stage Captain Marryat knew that it could not be human, whatever else it was, because he fired point-blank at the figure. His bullets went through the phantasm, embedding themselves in the door of a room opposite.

In 1926, a sensation was caused by the reappearance of the ghost: Lady Townshend stated that her son and a friend had encountered the Brown Lady on the famous staircase. Both identified the figure they had seen with the portrait of the Brown Lady, although neither had been told that the place was supposed to be haunted.

The most sensational sequel to this long story of haunting happened ten years later. On the afternoon of September 19th, two photographers, Captain Provand and Mr. Indra Shira were taking a series of photographs of the interior of Raynham Hall. Captain Provand had taken a flashlight picture of the ancient oak staircase and was preparing to take another when Mr. Shira noticed, to his amazement, a shadowy form on the stairs. The figure was gliding down the staircase towards the photographers, so Shira, standing behind his colleague, urged him to take an exposure whilst there was yet time. As soon as Provand indicated that he was ready, Shira fired the flash gun. Provand ridiculed the idea that there could have been a ghost, and added that even if there had been it wouldn't register on the plate, but when the negative was developed, the shadowy form of a hooded figure of a woman was discernible. The picture now reposes in the *Country Life* photographic library. Experts who examined the plate at the time were satisfied that there had been no element of faking. It is certainly a curious one. The outline is *suggestive* of a figure, as can be seen from the illustration in this book. More one cannot say.

The Brown Lady of Raynham Hall is an example of a 'residential' ghost, and a rather unpleasant one at that (nobody knows, incidentally, who the Brown Lady of the portrait is). But some permanent ghosts are often quite acceptable to the mortal tenants of the premises haunted.

A few years ago I visited a haunted rectory where two apparitions were seen fairly frequently. The family became so used to them that they regarded them as friends and a natural feature of the home's amenities. Indeed, they called one of them: 'Mrs. It' and appear to have given no offence to the subject of their facetiousness. My first intimation of what, next to Borley, must be one of the most haunted rectories in England, came to me in a letter from the wife of the Rector, the Rev. A. B. Farmer:

'We have definitely seen ghosts in this home—many times— the last being a week ago. Five people living here have all seen the same thing. Not frightening, but a charming elderly lady, *circa* 1735, and also another lady of the same date. We can identify them with people who lived there then, and lately they have become very active . . .

'Our little lady is seen so often that it is quite impossible to give exact dates; it is such a usual occurrence. I saw her go up our attic stairs one morning. Ten minutes later she went past the kitchen door. Generally, she is like and of the same consistency as smoke—grey black. At other times only her skirt materializes, or part of it, and is then much more dense. In fact I have been able to see that the skirt is made of thick, black, watered silk. It has a full round bottom, is very voluminous and the top part of her is covered by a dark shawl, probably wool, under which she carries a basket or handle— her head is covered by a hat (with cap underneath) which is tied on with ribbon under her chin.

'She is always in a hurry and takes great interest in all we do. She *loves* a party. During the preparation for my daughter's wedding she was seen inspecting the wedding presents and the arrangements in the kitchen, and was also seen in places where she has never been before or since. One day in particular I must tell you about: I had made a good many of the cakes for the wedding myself, then I was held up for want of eggs. My usual source of supply having failed, I happened to be in the garden when I looked up and saw "Mrs. It", as we call her. I went over to where she stood and as she hurried away up the garden, I followed her. In the middle of a flower bed, she vanished, and on looking down at the spot where she had disappeared I found thirteen eggs! All excellent. At other times, when we have been away, delicious smells of cooking have issued from the kitchen, on the day before our return, even though all the fires have been out. The other tenants in the house have told us about this (they have seen her, too). She has been seen and heard by all five members of the family, and the dogs. The dogs generally give a little growl. She rustles as she goes, and sometimes we feel a cold draught of air.'

The Rectory, with its simple yet elegant façade and ivy-covered brickwork, has absolutely nothing sinister about it; its mellow appearance exudes a welcome. The building fits snugly and comfortably into its country surroundings without looking as if it had been added. In a book of 1608 it is described as standing 'on the east end of the churchyard, having a kitchen standinge on the north side thereof. Item: a garden adjoininge thereto.' The north front of the Rectory was built in 1740 and the south front seven years later. In 1906, fairly considerable alterations were made, the dining-room being incorporated in the entrance hall, and the kitchen, with its piece of old passage, being made into a dining-room. A new kitchen was added and new bedrooms were built. There is a coach-house and stable, rebuilt in 1804 and splendid gardens with yew and privet hedges.

The alterations are of some interest, because the bustling lady with the basket frequently followed the track of a staircase long since removed—a common feature of hauntings of this type.

During my visit to Yattendon Rectory I took evidence from four people who had seen the ghosts—from Mrs. A. B. Farmer, who had written to me in the first place; from the Rector, who was then the Rev. A. B. Farmer; from his young daughter and from a guest who had come to stay for a period. Mrs. Farmer told me: 'I was standing in the basement the other day—it was very hot outside and I'd left the door open to let a little cool air through the house—when I decided to go along the passage and look into the cellar. There I saw a lovely lady walking away from me a little above the floor. She'd got a

most beautiful dress on and a lovely tall headdress, and as
I've always been very interested in clothes, and in period cos-
tumes, I thought that I'd go and look up the date of that
dress, which I did, with the result that I think she is the un-
married sister of the old Rector who lived here in 1725. She
kept house for him during that time.'

The Rector referred to was the Rev. William Puller, who
was inducted on September 27, 1724, and died in 1735.

The Rev. Farmer himself told me that he had seen 'Mrs. It'
twice. He emphasised that he was 'not at all psychic' and never
saw 'things' as a rule. The first occasion on which he had seen
the ghost was outside the kitchen door about 1948. 'I felt her
presence rather than saw her ... I got an impression of a
rustling mass of black silk just slipping through the door, and
on another occasion I saw her in the garden, but strangely
enough, this time she was wearing white, not black. I couldn't
see *through* her ... she glided more than walked, but she
moved very quickly as if she was in a very great hurry ... I
can only surmise that she was going to do the village shopping,
as she used to do in the days when she walked on earth ...
that's all I can think of.' There was absolutely no sensation of
fear. 'It's just like a very friendly presence, and we've grown
attached to her; we all love her as a friend of the family.'

Mrs. Barton of Goring-on-Thames, who stayed at the Rectory
for six months in 1949 told me that although she had never
believed in ghosts, she went through the kitchen door one
day and saw the figure of a woman walking across the top of
the cellar stairs. 'She looked rather pretty, really, with a sort
of silvery grey frock, and a light seemed to be shining around
her. And the funny part was that she was not walking on the
floor. Her feet were sort of *off* the floor—about a foot off—
and she disappeared through the wall.'

Miss Farmer, a younger daughter, told me how she had been
to a dance and, coming back, brought some friends in with her
for a cup of tea because it had been raining and they were
all feeling very cold. They went into the kitchen, shut the
door, and sat down. 'Then,' she said, 'we heard some footsteps.
Three of the people, I may say, had never heard anything
about our ghost before, and they heard the footsteps too.
We saw a figure pass as we looked through the frosted panes
of the door.' Her immediate thought was that she and her
friends must be making too much noise, so she went out to
explain; but there was no one there. 'I'm sorry,' she told them,
'but you've seen a ghost.'

When Mr. and Mrs. John Grange and their three children went to live in this Rectory a few years ago, they did not share the enthusiasm of the outgoing tenants for the residential ghosts, especially as the children were very young. They therefore asked the outgoing Rector if he would be kind enough to conduct a service of exorcism, which he did. There were no manifestations after that, Mrs. Grange informs me. Sir David Llewellyn, the present tenant, also tells me that no ghosts have been in evidence since he moved in.

Britain has so many haunted houses that a mere catalogue of them would fill a book. Of those 'permanently' haunted, Burton Agnes Hall, near Bridlington, Yorkshire, would come high on the list. It is a fine Tudor mansion, and in its Great Hall is preserved—in accordance with her dying request—the skull of a girl who died there three hundred years ago. Once when her skull was removed from its customary niche behind the panelling, such noisy disturbances ensued—doors banging, weird noises and inexplicable knocks and crashes—that with no more argument the skull was restored to its rightful place.

Levens Hall, near Kendal, Westmorland, parts of which date back to the twelfth century, houses a veritable colony of ghosts, and reports of them over the centuries are too numerous to permit the assumption of mere suggestion or superstition. And very peculiar ghosts they are. They have appeared in daylight, and instead of a phantasmagoric, wraithlike swirling presence they appear surprisingly solid—until—POUF!—they vanish. There is the Grey Lady, who has several times been the cause of near-accidents by stepping in front of horses, coaches and (more recently) motor-cars as they made their way up the drive to the house. Many a driver has pulled up, sick with fear at the thought of having run over an elderly lady, to find ... nothing. Not so long ago a member of the Bagot family, which owns the house, *bicycled* through her! There is also a homely little lady in cap and print dress, who appears only when children are present. The strangest ghost at Levens Hall is a small black dog which, when it appears, is seen by some but not by others.

Hampton Court Palace, now no longer a royal residence but used as 'grace and favour' apartments for those who have given long and loyal service to the State, has very many ghosts, each of which has been reported as having been seen—usually in terms very similar to others long since dead and buried—by very many people. There is a deceptive amiability about the palace's physical aspect. Its red brick is cheery, unlike the mellowed stones of ancient castles and mansions; its lovely river-side site, its forty-five acres of gardens (the palace itself covers eight acres), the Great Vine planted in 1768, the deer park and its wonderful old chestnut trees provide a pleasing blend of idyllic pastoral life and elegant comfort.

King Henry VIII, with his revels and rages, who usurped the building after the disgrace of Cardinal Wolsey, brought many of his wives there. The ill-fated Anne Boleyn joined in the royal carousels; Jane Seymour was there and died there in childbirth; Catherine Howard, who was arbitrarily and prob-ably unjustly accused by her husband of infidelity and executed for it, still re-enacts her panic-stricken flight along the Haunted Gallery to the Chapel, where the wine-bibbing womaniser was too absorbed in his prayers to heed the pitiful screams and appeals for mercy from the woman who hammered at the locked doors of the chapel.

Anne Boleyn, whose head also rolled beneath the axe of Henry's busy executioner, is said to appear—headless and in a phantom coach drawn by headless horses—at midnight along the roads to Bickling Hall in Norfolk, on the anniversary of her death. It was at Bickling Hall that Anne Boleyn spent her childhood. Another of Henry VIII's wives, Catherine of Aragon, is said to haunt the gallery of Kimbolton Castle in Huntingdon-shire.

Royalty, on the whole, is well represented in the ghost world. The apparition of Queen Elizabeth I has been seen in the lib-rary at Windsor Castle and, as I mentioned before, Sawston Hall, the fine old mansion in Cambridgeshire, enjoys an occa-sional visit from the ghost of Queen Mary I. On the night before she left, she sat at the virginal, playing music—and the ghostly strains can still be heard, occasionally. This is a rare example of a smiling ghost. It is a happy smile, for she was content and (so far as possible anywhere in those days) secure at Sawston Hall. She bears herself proudly, holding her prayer book in such a way that the etheric beauty of her sensitive hands can clearly be seen.

Scores of castles have the well-documented reputation of being haunted. Corby Castle, Cumberland, had a ghost known as 'the radiant boy'—a description merited by the effulgence of light that emanated from him; Peel Castle was noted for its ghostly dog; Cortachy Castle is said to be haunted by a ghostly drummer who was once flung from the battlements because of a suspected intrigue with the Earl's wife. Hinton Ampner Manor House in Hampshire, demolished in 1797, was persistently haunted, and a detailed account of its happenings, well worth reading, can be seen in *Lord Halifax's Ghost Book,* one of the most readable ghost books ever written. A detailed statement by Mary Ricketts of Hinton Parsonage gives chapter and verse of innumerable appearances and strange happenings at this manor house: the rustling of silk; noisy footsteps; a ghost of a man in a drab-coloured coat; a tall woman in silk; 'dismal groans' which terrified a servant; 'three knocks'; sometimes 'a shrill female voice' and two other voices 'deeper and more manlike'; heavy doors slamming so violently that the building was shaken; a rushing noise; a shrill and dreadful shriek becoming fainter as it was repeated.

During the work of demolition of Hinton Ampner (for such was the evil reputation of the place that nobody would live in it at any price) workmen found, concealed underneath the floorboards, 'a small skull said to be that of a monkey'.

Lord Halifax simply repeats the fact for what it is worth but the remains were never proved to be those of a monkey, nor can one think of any reason for interring the remains of a 'monkey' beneath the floorboards. No real and methodical inquiry was made into the matter, nor was any real expert consulted when it came to identifying the bones. It would seem more probable that they were the relics of a concealed birth, or a murdered baby. Since hauntings so often attend upon tragedy, the last explanation seems the most likely.

Penkaet Castle (originally Fountainhall House, a 400-year-old mansion near Pencaitland in East Lothian) is constantly resounding to the sound of something being dragged and heavy footsteps. Its 'resident' ghost, whom nobody really fears, is said to be the phantom of a former owner, John Cockburn, who is believed to have murdered a man called Seton. John is a 'rackety' ghost, occasionally given to banging and knocking. Once, when members of a local antiquarian society were on a conducted tour of the house, a glass case split with a resounding crack—and it was never discovered why it should have done so.

Penkaet Castle has amongst its furnishings a peculiar four-poster bed bearing a death mask of King Charles I, who was hanged in 1649. It was meant as a patriotic gesture, I suppose; but whether the bed is haunted or simply the room, the fact remains that on several occasions it has given the impression of having been slept in when no one has been near it. Fortunately, the Holbourn family, who bought the property in 1923, happen to like ghosts.

Holland House in Kensington was reputed to be haunted by the Earl of Holland (Lincolnshire), who became the owner in 1614 and was executed by the Roundheads during the Civil War. It was much damaged in the last war by air raids, and the only remaining part now forms an annex to a hostel. But reports of the haunting were persistent for many centuries. They are too numerous to list here, but Holland House could truly be called 'a haunted house' in contrast to a place where only one phenomenon has been seen by one or two persons.

Number 50, Berkeley Square was long reputed to be haunted. There is a long correspondence on the subject in *Notes and Queries* in which some people declared that the sounds had a natural explanation, namely: 'its neglected condition when empty, and the habits of the melancholy and solitary hypochondriac when occupied by him.' But Lord Lyttleton said that the house had been long unoccupied because it was haunted, and claimed that there were 'many strange stories' about it. One of these is told in the magazine *Mayfair* of May 10, 1879:

'The house in Berkeley Square contains at least one room in which the atmosphere is supernaturally fatal to mind and body. A girl saw, heard and felt such horror in it that she went mad, and never recovered sanity enough to tell how or why. A gentleman, a disbeliever in ghosts, dared to sleep in it, and was found a corpse in the middle of the floor, after practically ringing for help in vain. Rumour suggests other cases of the same kind, all ending in death, madness, or both as the result of sleeping, or trying to sleep, in that room. The very party walls of the house, when touched, are found saturated with electric horror. It is uninhabited, save by an elderly man and woman who act as caretakers; but even these have no access to the room. That is kept locked, the key being in the hands of a mysterious and seemingly nameless person, who comes to the house every six months, locks up the elderly couple in the basement, and then unlocks the room and occupies himself in it for hours.'

A 'strange story' indeed, and the mysterious owner seems to have had the most compliant housekeepers. A firm of antiquarian booksellers have occupied the site for years. Its proprietor once told me that the original premises were once supposed to be haunted, but that he himself had never seen anything.

Berry Pomeroy Castle, in Devonshire, was once said to be haunted by the daughter of a wicked baron who, as a consequence of an enforced incestuous relationship with her father, bore him a child, which he strangled. Bagley House, near Bridport, was haunted by the ghost of a squire who committed suicide. Bisham Abbey was haunted by the ghost of Lady Hoby, who, having married again, conceived an unnatural and bitter hatred against the son of her first marriage. In that loveless and fear-ridden home he found it impossible to study well enough to please her, and she beat and mistreated him so appallingly that he died as a result. Samlesbury Hall, near Blackburn, was, according to Ingram's *Haunted Houses*, haunted by a lady in white attended by a handsome knight.

Hermitage Castle, once an important border fortress, is said to be haunted by the ghost of Lord Soulis. According to legend, William de Soulis made a pact with Satan who appeared to him wearing a cap stained red with the blood of his victims. In exchange for his soul he was rewarded with the right to summon the Devil by rapping three times on an iron chest. As a result of his demoniac compact, so the story goes, Lord Soulis was impervious to injury from rope or steel. Bonds would not hold him nor steel kill him. A loathsomely cruel tyrant, his enormities caused his own vassals to rise up against him. He was dragged to Ninestane Rigg, a hill nearly 950 feet high, four miles long and one mile broad, and on two of the huge stones which once comprised a Druidicial circle, they gave him an end fitting, they thought, for one sold to devilry. Eschewing rope, which would not hold, and steel, which would not kill, they rolled him up in a sheet of lead and boiled him alive in a copper cauldron. But still, says the legend, the ghost of Lord Soulis keeps his tryst with Satan:

> And still when seven years are o'er
> Is heard the jarring sound
> When hollow opes the charmed door
> Of chamber underground.

Ghosts of Prime Ministers are rare. Queens, knights, squires and an unlimited assortment of distinguished and undistinguished people are reputed to appear as ghosts, but, so far as I know, only one British Prime Minister. That was Disraeli, Queen Victoria's Prime Minister who, only a few years ago, was seen standing at the foot of the cellar stairs of his Buckinghamshire home, Hughenden Manor. He has also been spotted on the upper floors of the house.

Some of the most sinister ghosts are associated with castles. Throughout the ages these fortresses also served as prisons, and the absolute power which feudal chiefs and nobles enjoyed perpetuated some pretty grim legends. Hurstmonceaux, a fine old Tudor castle built by Sir Roger de Fienne in 1440 is haunted by a giant nine feet in height, beating a ghostly tattoo upon a drum. A lovely young heiress, Grace Naylor, was starved to death in the Lady's Bower by a jealous and sadistic governess. A former owner was executed for murder at Tyburn (near Marble Arch in London), while at least three tenants died raving mad.

At Crathes Castle there is a quaint room with a gaily-painted ceiling, a fine old spinning wheel and a handsomely-carved timber fireplace. A second glance at the fireplace however, reveals something unusual. There is something not quite pleasant about the carved figures on either side which, caryatid-fashion, support the mantelpiece. This room is haunted. A woman known as the Green Lady was seen frequently to cross the room, reach the fireplace, and lift a ghostly baby from the hearth. An unpleasant sequel to this haunting is that a few years ago workmen discovered, beneath the fireplace, the bones of a woman and child.

A weird tale is attached to Scotney Castle in Sussex—named after its original owner, Walter de Scotney, executed at Winchester for poisoning Richard of Gloucester. His niece, Florence, inherited the castle, and married John Darrell. John's descendant, Arthur Darrell, died abroad, and people were told that his body would be brought back to his castle for interment. The funeral took place on December 12, 1720, and amongst the crowd watching the coffin being lowered was a tall cloaked figure. Several people round him heard him whisper: 'That is not me'—and as they turned curiously to observe him, he vanished before their eyes. The story sounds, no doubt, like the hastily-conceived plot of a second-feature film, but it has a macabre sequel.

In 1924, when one of the owners died, his coffin was placed next to that of Mr. Darrell. When the old sexton examined Darrell's coffin it was found to contain no bones at all—only a number of heavy stones to give it weight.

As I have mentioned in connection with Yattendon Rectory, many residents are content to live with ghosts, and while some estate agents guiltily conceal information from prospective clients which they fear might scare them away, some estate agents are more happy handling property which is haunted.

There have, however, been cases where people have made representations over property which they have found or believed to be haunted. A few years ago, Pembrokeshire County

Council found themselves sued for damages in respect of personal injuries sustained by a man and his son who were laying floors in a partly constructed school. The two men slept in an old adjacent mansion, Bush House. On the first night Mr. George Hesketh, the father, and his son saw the vision of a woman in a crinoline in the grounds of the house, and there were 'queer noises'. On the second night a paraffin lamp was turned down four times and their mackintoshes pulled off their shoulders. On the third night the eerie atmosphere so unnerved them that they left and returned to the school at 1 a.m., when the older man fell down some unlit concrete steps and fractured his skull.

Mr. Justice Salmon, who heard the case at Glamorgan Assizes, conceded that the experiences of the two men were 'ghostly and ghastly' but gave judgement in favour of the Council, who had denied negligence and breach of building regulations.

In May, 1948, however, there was a case in which the rating assessment on a house in Weathercock Lane, Apsley Guise was reduced from £62 gross value to £52 after the owner had called witnesses to prove his point that the value of the house had depreciated because of ghosts. Later on, a second attempt to get the assessment still further reduced in which the owner described how people had seen a horseman ride down Weathercock Lane and disappear into a hedge, and how they saw a phantom lady on a lawn found the Chairman of Bedfordshire Quarter Sessions appeals committee less sympathetic, however.

Complaints to local authorities that premises are haunted are not as rare as might be supposed, nor are such statements treated with the levity or bureaucratic inflexibility one might expect. A scared family is an unhappy family and in the long run, if nothing is done to remedy matters, an unhealthy family. Despite the virtual impossibility of assessing accurately the weight of the statements made about 'ghosts', Councils have heard enough about them to realise that to some people at least they are very real.

There was a case some years ago when Mrs. Evelyn Sayers, who was living in Coventry Hall, a block of flats owned by Wandsworth Borough Council, awoke with a vague sense of unease. She went to see if the children were all right; they were asleep, but were tossing and turning as though having bad dreams.

Wandering, depressed and moody, round the flat, she found herself drawn involuntarily towards the front door. It was locked and bolted, but she felt she must open it. She did so—and standing there in the cold night air she saw the spectre of a nun. She wanted to scream, but the sound froze in her throat. As though in solace, the nun raised her arm and it seemed she was speaking. 'Do not be afraid,' she whispered, 'just say God ... be ... with ... you.' Mrs. Sayers screamed, and was found distraught and trembling at the open doorway.

Her letter of complaint was not pooh-poohed by Mr. L. Dean, the housing manager. He suggested to her that she might like to contact the Society for Psychical Research.

The block of flats is built on the site of a nunnery. During the war, in 1944, two Irishmen, Tom Connelly and James Duggan, who had been working on bomb damage repairs, passed the spot one night on their way to their hostel. The Catholic Training College, as it had been when war broke out, was empty, for the students had been evacuated. Both men distinctly saw what seemed like a group of shadows, wearing cowls with their habits trailing on the ground. They could hear the rustle of garments and heard whispers. Other people declared that they saw flickering candles at the windows and heard chanting. When the time came to construct the flats, workmen constantly complained that tools and materials left in one place appeared mysteriously the next day in quite another part of the building; and it didn't seem to be vandalism or mischief, because the objects were so neatly stacked and piled where they were taken. The children of a tenant of the newly-constructed flats told their mother that they had seen a 'nurse' in the flat; but when she went to the spot they indicated, there was no one there. For the last few years, however, all has been well at Coventry Hall.

Comparing this particular haunting with what happened at Borley Rectory during and after its destruction, one wonders whether ghosts (or whatever they are) are 'stirred up' by the disturbances of conversion, repairs or demolition of old premises. But the manner in which, in just a few of the instances I have quoted, apparitions seem to frequent the spots where there have been secret burials is very curious.

It raises a query in my mind. Do the thoughts of the dying have any permanence? Can they 'register' on the atmosphere or on inanimate objects and materials and be picked up in certain conditions by living people? Or—a somewhat melancholy thought—is there a brief transition where the human brain still has thoughts and can project images *after* death?

It is not often one is in a position to consult a man who has died, but I have been able to do so. A friend of mine, a well-known journalist on the *Boston Traveler* in Boston, Massachusetts, U.S.A., died a few years ago under an operation, and was miraculously brought to life by the skill of the surgeons, after being dead for several minutes. Up to the moment that he awoke (lived again, for his heart had stopped) he dreamed, he told me, continuously. Theoretically, he should have had no thoughts during his death.

12

More haunted houses

The following story of a haunted house was related to me by Miss Radawich, of Regent Park Road, Baltimore, Maryland, U.S.A. It is an interesting and well-authenticated example of a persistent haunting, by a 'ghost' which did not content itself with the usual poltergeist manifestations (bangings, lifting, knocking and so on) but by actually attacking human beings:

'Shortly after the Civil War, in fact sometime after 1865, my great-grandfather, a professional soldier (Frank A. Boidie) was transferred to Fort McHenry in the area of Baltimore. Having a large family, he rented a house off the base, in a block between Fort Avenue and Clement Street at the spot which was then called Locust Point.

'He got the house very cheaply with no explanation, but neighbours warned great-grandmother Caroline that the house was haunted. An Englishwoman who had lived in the house had starved to death there. Before her death, she had been seen sitting in a rocker in a window of the second floor, rocking her two children. No one realised she was destitute, although the people in this area, being of a kindly disposition, would have been glad to help her out, had they known. She came from a good family but, it was said, had married beneath her —now there was no man in the house and no money. Apparently, she was too proud to ask for help, and eventually she was found, dead, with her two children lying dead in her lap, in the rocker at the window.

Subsequently, neighbours noticed noises coming from the house, and occasionally saw the shade of a woman in a rocking chair at the window. This went on for a long time, and was accompanied by the rapid departure of all those renting the house after just a few days in occupation. Then grandmother moved in. She was not to be scared off by ghost stories. After all, she had travelled by covered wagon and had had a child stolen by Indians in Florida shortly after the Civil War (the child was recovered), and one little biddy ghost wouldn't do what Indians had failed to do, so she thought.

'The family immediately became aware of the hostile atmosphere of the house. There was a cold spot over the third step leading up to the second flor. There was also a sense of not being able to pass that spot. Any lamp carried up the stairs went out there, no matter how carefully held nor how carefully shielded. The family heard crying in the night—a woman weeping softly but very sadly. But my great-grandfather, who was a Major of Music, was a very rational man, and his book had no pages on ghosts, so the family stayed.

'Shortly after they moved in, Harry, Caroline's child and grandmother's brother, took sick with typhoid fever. Typhoid used to be a real problem in Baltimore because the area was so low and wells were so easily contaminated. But that's another story. Anyway, Harry was very, very sick and was segregated in a room on the ground floor. Then one night, as the family sat at the table eating dinner, they heard him scream and the sound of a blow. They rushed in to him, to hear him say that he had been slapped by a lady, although he didn't know why she was mad at him. On his cheek he bore the red mark of a hand which faded in a normal fashion. At other times the ghost slapped John and Charles, two other brothers, and Caroline herself. The family could not move because the child was quarantined, so they got the full treatment.

'At night they would hear a noise that my grandfather describes as sounding "like a billy-goat running over the loose planks on a bridge" and the creaking of a rocking chair could be heard in the front upstairs room, also at night (there was no rocking chair in the room at this time.) Grandmother, who is still alive, and whose recollection is perfectly clear on these details, remembers particularly the "cold spot" on the stairs—she says it was a feeling as if a cold, strong wind was blowing against her, although there was no draught on this spot, which was appreciably colder than the rest of the house.'

As soon as Harry was better and out of quarantine, the family moved out post-haste. The house still stands, although its lovely old brick has been covered with stucco, tinted and shaped to simulate stone.

In Catonsville, in the same area, a pirate lived in one of the large houses there, and is supposed to have buried his loot in the garden, and still guards it. Many declare that on the first full moon in September he walks the yard until he reaches the house, then turns into a ball of fire and spins to where the treasure is buried. Then—POOF! he disappears. But the actual

occupants of the house take a more jaundiced view of this
ghost story as well as the exasperating procession of curious,
morbid or crackpot sightseers who try to invade their privacy
in search of the ghost. It is said the two spinster ladies are
so sick of sightseers that they almost felt like keeping a shotgun
in the house!

I am indebted to Lee Emerson Smith of Denver, Colorado, for
the following details:

There was a house in Denver, standing at 2334 Lawrence
Street, which was the scene of a quadruple murder in 1875
and which was haunted for many years afterwards.

It was on October 21, 1875 that a policeman called there,
because the inhabitants, a band of Italian musicians, had not
been seen for days. He found all the doors locked and the
window shutters drawn and every room blood-stained as by
recent carnage. Continuing his search, he opened the trapdoor of a small cellar to be confronted with the appalling
spectacle of the corpses of Guiseppe Peccora, an amiable old
scissors grinder known locally as 'old Joe'; his two 'sons' Gio-
vanni and Guiseppe, and his 'nephew'.

With the corpses there were blood-soaked mattresses, three
harps, two violins, a scissors-grinding machine and blood-soaked
weapons of various sorts including daggers, a hatchet and a
hammer. The throats of the four victims had been cut from
ear to ear and each body bore evidence of vicious mutilation.

The police did not take long to solve the mystery, although
tracking the miscreants took longer. It turned out that Peccora
had abducted the three children, who were in no way related
to him. Ragged, illiterate and often hungry, they played their
instruments in the streets to supply his income, and because
they could barely express themselves, the authorities never realised how they were being exploited on American soil.

Among the frequent visitors to the house were three Italians,
Filomeno Gallotti, Michiele Ballotti and John Anatta. All had
disappeared. Gallotti was found to have been leader of a gang
of bandits in Italy, and it was he who had organised the mas-
sacre, together with other accomplices, including a Mexican.
They had fled with the loot, intending to get to Mexico and then
raid and rob travellers and homes as they had done in Italy.

One of the murder gang made a detailed confession, which
I give in part as it is relevant to the subsequent reports that
the house became haunted:

'The band consisted of Gallotti, Anatta, Ballotti, Campagne
and a miner. I was forced to join them against my will, but was

powerless to resist Gallotti. The killing commenced on Friday, October 15th, at half past one o'clock. I was playing a harp in the front room. The old man, called Joe in English, the biggest boy and one or two brothers were playing cards in the front room. The cards lay on a box and the players were seated around in a circle. Ballotti, Campagne and the miner were playing, too. Gallotti, the boss tinker, was standing up and watching the game. Suddenly Gallotti reached under his coat, drew a knife, seized the old man by his hair, drew his head back and with one powerful stroke cut his throat from ear to ear. The blood flowed upon the cards and into the faces of the other players. Not yet content, Gallotti stabbed the old man in several places and, releasing his hold, he let the lifeless body fall to the floor. At the same time the others seized the big boy who was sitting at my side playing the harp, but he made a desperate resistance and tried to fight them off.

'Seeing that the others were not very successful, Gallotti left old Joe's body and, grabbing the boy, cut his throat, crying to me, "play louder!" In the struggle they all used knives, and Anatta cut his fingers so badly that when they ceased to bleed he could not close them. I kept on playing the harp for I dared not stop, and I was so frightened that I trembled violently. Once I stopped playing, but Gallotti shook me and, drawing his knife across my throat, told me he would cut my d . . . d head off if I did not play on. So I started up again.'

Later the two young boys returned, not together but one after the other. Each was brutally slain. 'Filomeno stood behind the door and, as the little one entered, carrying his harp, he said, holding up a fancy article he had purchased, "Look here, I have bought you something nice today," and just then he seized the poor boy, pulled him down on the floor and putting his knee on his head said in Italian, "Ah, my boy, I've got you now." With that he cut his throat.' The arrival of the other lad was even more tragic in its drawn-out horror. Seeing the blood and chaos, he attempted to flee, still grasping his harp from force of habit, although he was streaming with blood from stab wounds. Finally he collapsed, still holding the harp. With that the gang, after taking the old man's money-belt containing about £800, and throwing the bodies into the cellar, departed.

It was not surprising that no one wanted to live in that house of death. As for its reputation of being haunted, imagination might have accounted in part for the ghost stories associated with it; but not entirely. A Mrs. Althea Braithwaite, who lived four doors away, ran screaming to a neighbour when she heard the wild playing of a harp, accompanied by screams, coming from the empty house. Neighbours frequently heard screams, cries and groans. One family fled from the neighbourhood after seeing shadowy forms swaying in the moonlight at No. 2334. The house became derelict—windows were broken and doors gaped open revealing blood-stains to public gaze. At last, neighbours whose identity was never established, resolved to remove the house for good. One night, the haunted house was seen to be blazing furiously. By the time the fire department arrived the place was a raging furnace beyond all hope of saving it—and from it came the unmistakable smell of cans of kerosene. It was with relief, therefore, that the people of the neighbourhood saw, the next day, that the place had been reduced to a cinder. Too many people had already left their homes because they were frightened to live near it.

Mr. William Black, of Kensington Street, Donegall Road, Belfast 12, tells me of a decidedly alarming experience he had in the scullery of the house.

'When we came to this house twenty-six years ago the window in the scullery was twenty-four by eighteen inches, consisting of four small panes of glass, with rotting woodwork. So I made a one-pane window which could open out into the yard. The scullery is five feet square, with sink, cooker and a small two-door cabinet, and opens on to the yard which is three feet six inches wide but widens to five feet to the boiler and bin recess.

'One Saturday morning, near lunch-time some years ago, I was washing my face and hands and was just about to reach for a towel when I glanced through the small window in front of me and saw a baldy head with a round face looking at me. The face had a "still" look about it. I didn't get time to see a body, as I got such a shock and a pain in my heart that two jumps took me into the kitchen. The wife looked at me as I came flying through the door and said "What is the matter?" When I told her she said I was imagining things, so I walked into the yard, but there was no one there.

'The time I spent in jumping and then walking would have been enough to give an active man time to get over the six feet wall of the yard, but there wasn't a sound of a footstep or the scuffle of anyone climbing over the wall. If he had used the bin as a step we would have heard the sound of the bin rattle. I have never forgotten the face at the window ...'

An account which is subjective and uncorroborated is evidentially less impressive than one in which several accounts tally; but it does not mean to say that the account is not a correct one. In this instance, it is difficult to decide whether, in what he admits was a state of excitement and shock, he would necessarily have heard the noise made by an intruder in escaping over the wall. Prowlers *do* appear unexpectedly as a prelude to burglary or assault or even through being drunk or losing their way.

A feature of the appearance of apparitions is that the first indication of their presence is often revealed by an animal, usually a cat or a dog. Consider the experience of Mr. R. B. Brinkworth of New Villas, Lyncombe Vale, Bath:

'In reply to your letter in the press on the subject of ghosts, I had an unusual experience. This occurred in early September, 1953, at Grosvenor Place, Bath, in the second floor flat.

'As we were having the lounge decorated all the furniture had been crowded into the large bedroom, in which we were making do. At about eight o'clock in the evening, my wife and I were sitting before the electric fire reading the evening paper. I had my cat on my knees—she was a delicate little thing and had never been outside the flat in her life—when I became aware that she was digging her claws into my leg. On looking down I saw that her ears were pricked up and her coat ruffled.

'I moved my paper aside, followed her gaze, and saw a woman in an old-fashioned dress and bonnet pass across the room and vanish. She was hazy and moved through the conglomeration of furniture, but she was quite distinct to me and obviously to Rusty who, for the only time in her life, gave a low growl. When I told my wife, she laughed and said I was imagining things. The cat settled down again after a few moments.

'We lived there, sleeping in that room for several years after, but I never saw her again. I would like to point out that there was no chill, no "atmosphere" or any strange feeling at all. If it hadn't been for the cat I'd have seen nothing.

'Some years later I mentioned this incident to a spiritualist friend of my wife. He said that possibly the upheaval of the decorators had disturbed the lady.'

In reply to further questions, Mr. Brinkworth described the apparition to me more specifically. She was a middle-aged woman, in age about forty-five to fifty. The phantasm was not in colour, but monotone. Her appearance was not accompanied by noise or other manifestation of any kind. She appeared 'within' the furniture, which was altogether on that

side of the room. She appeared to glide along. Her features
were quite composed and in no sense sinister or malevolent,
and she was wearing an old high-necked dress with a sort of
Salvation Army bonnet.

I am indebted to Bernard Kelly of the *Denver Post*, Colorado, for bringing to my notice another unusual ghost story
which concerns the country home of Dr. and Mrs. Robert A.
Bradley in Cherry Hills, south of Denver.

The house, Bradmar, is spacious and beautiful. A mixture of
Tudor and Gothic in its setting and its aspect it looks very
English, and this had clearly been the intention when it was
built in 1920. The previous owner was Mrs. Ethel Work, the
widow of Dr. Hubert Work, former Secretary of the Interior and
Postmaster General during the presidency of Herbert Hoover.

It is said she asked that her body should lie 'in state' in the
drawing-room in front of the fireplace. She also told her servants that she would cause a huge beam in the ceiling to split
the night she came home in her coffin. The beam did split,
and a tremendous beam it is, nearly a foot square. The prophecy and its apparent fulfilment disturbed many people—but
it did not bother Mr. and Mrs. Bradley when they took possession. But in the course of preparing the house for occupancy
some very odd things happened.

On one occasion an electric light in the ceiling of one of
the bedrooms—it was a bare yellow bulb—went on of its own
accord, although no one had touched the fixture or the switch.
The electrician was completely nonplussed. On another occasion, at a time when water had not been turned on in the
house, a member of the family was hit in the face by a blob
of water. Yet the closest inspection of the ceiling could reveal
nothing to account for it.

The unhappy electrician had further complications ahead.
One day, when the lights went out in one wing of the house
he came to repair the fault. After installing three lines of
wire strung in a braid in a brand new conduit, he found the
three wires unbraided. On another occasion, a member of the
family cleaning a floor with a hand sander yelled and grasped
his face, dropping the sander in the process. Mrs. Bradley rushed
to see what could have happened. Something—though nothing
could be found and nothing was seen—had struck him in the
face.

When I asked Dr. and Mrs. Bradley if they had recently been
troubled by the ghost, if ghost it is, they reported: 'We have
heard but not seen. We have heard footsteps in the house,

doors slamming, a pet dog barking after its death, and this Christmas (1964) additional decorations appeared in stored containers which all members of the family denied having previously seen.'

In 'Ghostly Sounds' I have described the wide variety of completely unexplained noises which are heard in haunted places. We all know that to the apprehensive mind, noises of innocent origin can become invested with horrific import ('the sound of an aspen leaf shall shake him'); but I am not talking of the noises made by birds trapped in chimneys, water dripping from eaves, squirrels, rats, mice or bats on their urgent and furtive missions. We know that timber contracts in cold and expands in heat, as also do metals, and that many a creak or crack, unwelcome in the small hours, can be put down to floorboards relaxing.

But there is a whole range of sounds incapable of logical explanation. Often they are heard separately. But sometimes they presage the appearance of an apparition. The following straightforward, but nevertheless descriptive account, was given to me by Mr. E. J. Harden, of Whitstable, Kent, who is a painter by profession:

'I was working in a detached house just off the main road at Whitstable. While I was painting at an upstairs room I heard some banging on the window ledge, or board, in the next room. I went to see who was there, but saw no one. The window ledge was bare, yet the sound was like a plumber's pipe spanner being put down on it. This was between three and five o'clock in the afternoon. The house was empty and there was no wind. I then heard four bangs on the ceiling, but thinking no more about it, I carried on with my work. I had nearly finished the ceiling when I heard another five bangs on it. I used my ladder to get into the loft, had a look round, but could see no one. I then went downstairs (all doors were left open to save time) and into the kitchen to mix some more paint. As the light was getting bad, I came out of the kitchen some time after five o'clock and saw a figure standing on the fourth step from the bottom of the stairs, in the form of a Quaker with a round hat, stockings and breeches. He was holding on to the banisters, then disappeared. With that, I took fright and went home.'

From Mr. Geoffrey Wilson, who informed me of the ghost at Mill Street, Bedford, I was interested to hear of a personal experience he had as a lad of ten years. It took place in the garden of his grandparents, Mr. and Mrs. Howell (Mr. Howell

was his step-grandfather) at 25 Montague Road, Cambridge. The
year was 1924.

It was a beautiful summer day, and he was playing in the
garden, at the bottom of which was a summer house. Suddenly he noticed 'a frail but quite beautiful young woman in
the summer house, reclining in a hammock. To me this seemed
nothing unusual, but I can remember the panic when I
returned to the house and asked who the lady was, giving a
description. The woman was my aunt (my father's youngest
sister) Stella Wilson, who had died in the summer house
earlier that summer of tuberculosis. You may remember that
outdoor treatment for TB was usual then. At that time, forty
years ago, I knew nothing of an aunt and was not told why
my grandparents were so upset. Certainly that ghost never
troubled me, nor as an adult have I had any personal brushes
with the occult; in fact, this was a case where I did not learn
until some years later that I had seen a ghost.'

In answer to further questions Mr. Wilson told me that the
ghost was not transparent but appeared to be substantial. It is
fortunate that his grandparents—although not able to dissemble
their own distress—did not tell him at the time what he had
seen, for he was a shy and nervous child and would certainly
have been terrified at the thought of a ghost. Not until he had
reached maturer years was he allowed to learn the truth.
'You could, I think, describe Stella's as a kindly ghost,' he told
me, 'as she made no attempt to frighten a timid boy.'

From Lieutenant-Colonel A. T. Shaen Mazan, C.M.G., whose
memory of a ghost he encountered half a century ago is—at the
age of eighty-five—still clear and lucid, I have the following
brief but vivid account:

'The event took place in Walton Hall, Warrington, the
beautiful ancient home of Mr. and Mrs. Ludington, who were
cousins of an aunt of my wife's. The month was June, 1915. I
was back on short leave from France, and my wife came over
from Ireland to meet me. It was a Sunday, a beautiful morning, bright sunshine and not a breath of wind; the time: 7 a.m.

Our bed faced the window. There was a door on the right
behind the bed leading out into the passage. The second door
was on the right leading into the dressing room. The third was
on the left and led into the lobby.

'I got up, pulled the curtains and opened the window, got
back into bed and we were yarning together when suddenly
the door on the left opened with a bang, stayed opened about
thirty seconds and then shut back with another bang. My wife

said, "What in the world did that? Get up and look!" I did so but the door was *locked and bolted*. After breakfast, my wife and a Miss Molly Pigott were out on the lawn and my wife said, "What a wonderful old house it is—it should be haunted." "Oh, but it is," Molly replied, "and what is more, you two are sleeping in the haunted room. Some 200 years ago there was an elderly lady who slept in that room. She used to have a bath in the lobby in a round tub. One morning she was found dead in her bath, and ever since, on certain mornings in the year, she tries to get back into her room ...'

Mrs. A. Coleman, of Ragland Avenue, Worthing, Sussex, told me that many years ago when her son, now aged thirty-two years, was a boy of six, he was very ill with bronchitis. Her husband was away on business and she was alone in the house, feeling depressed and worried. 'I had moved a bed into my son's room to be with him at night-time, and my mother, who had died about twelve years ago, suddenly appeared to me. She seemed to be fully clothed and wore her hair in the familiar way I knew. It was so unexpected—I had not even been thinking of her. She just stood there, and then turned her head to look down at my son, who of course she had never seen. She smiled gently and after a moment, disappeared ...'

It was on November 20, 1947, the wedding day of the Queen and (as he was then) Prince Philip that Mrs. Kay Candy, of Newbridge Road, Bath, encountered a ghost. 'It was in a house nearly 400 years old. I was with my small grandson, aged six and we were sitting in the dining-room (which had three steps leading into the hall) listening to the ceremony on the radio. The door was wide open, and I glanced up to see it very slowly closing. I took no notice of this, but four or five seconds after, I glanced up again and, standing on top of the stairs, was a most beautiful girl. Apparently a bride, she was dressed in a most beautiful crinoline and a veil, and in her hands she held a small posy of flowers. The door continued to move until it was closed completely. I said nothing to my grandson, as I did not want to frighten him, but in the afternoon, as I was going to take him out, I took him upstairs to get him ready. Suddenly, he said: "Did you see that lovely lady standing on the stairs in a white dress and holding some flowers?" '

This phantasm, Mrs. Candy told me in response to further questioning, was substantial-looking and not transparent. The phenomena was not accompanied by any sort of noise. Mrs. Candy found the experience interesting but not frightening.

From Mrs. Minerva Simpson of Howard, Rhode Island, U.S.A.,

I heard of a ghost which shows a polite solicitude for guests in a haunted house. She told me:

'A middle-aged widow I know fairly well asked me to drive her to her home in the late fall. Her husband, Walter, had passed away several years ago, in the kitchen, by gas asphyxiation, though it was never established whether by accident or suicide. Mrs. W ... has worked off and on, and goes over to the home to see if everything is all right, as she does not live there all the time. As it was a rather cool day, we wore coats.

'After we arrived, I removed my coat and sat down to peruse a magazine while Mrs. W ... made a survey of the rooms. She was in her bedroom and I was near by in the living-room when she called: "Put on your coat now, I think we'll be going." I put the magazine on the table, picked up my coat, and had one sleeve on when someone or thing helped me on with the rest of the coat. I said "Thank you" and turned round but couldn't see anybody. It was the most eerie sensation I have ever known. I told Mrs. W ... about it and she said: "That was Walter. He was always gallant, always helping people on with their coats or rubbers." She is a practical woman not given to seeing spooky things. She honestly believed "Walter" had returned to assist me.'

More in keeping with the common conception of a haunted house is Brynaber Hall in Montgomeryshire, Mid-Wales, where Miss Shuttleworth-Roberts of Bodfor Terrace, Aberdovy, North Wales, was brought up as a girl. Her father, the Rector of Penegoed, died on January 9, 1926, and since the Rectory had to be vacated for the incoming incumbent, the family moved to the old hall. The only place they could find at the time, it was a mansion at least 100 years old, with a bell dome, from which a peal was sounded as warning whenever there was a fire in the vicinity. The house was remote, and reached by a long drive flanked by very tall trees. In front was a terrace and at the back were trees and a small coppice wood.

The hall was of dark oak, panelled, and the staircase had a double banister. The front door had a large shutter which came up from the floor to cover a glass door and the two front sitting-rooms had wooden shutters which folded. There was also a back staircase.

The family took with them two dogs, a spaniel, and a retriever crossed with a sheep-dog. At first they were put to sleep in the dining-room, but one night both dogs refused to go anywhere near it, so they were given an old dressing-gown of

Mr. Shuttleworth-Roberts to sleep on, to give them the comfort of something personal to their late master. But as time went on the dogs refused to stay there alone, so the mother took the spaniel into her room and Miss Shuttleworth-Roberts took charge of the collie. But the collie was so restless that she and the dog went to her mother's room for the rest of the night.

One night Miss Roberts heard footsteps along the back landing and stairs, got out of bed, opened her door, and looked out, but there was no one there. Some time later, she was coming from the bathroom at night when she felt there was someone behind her, but again she could not see anybody. On another occasion, when her mother and younger sister were on holiday, she heard the shutters of the dining-room being opened and the window pulled down. In the morning she asked the maid if she had found the shutters open in the morning, but the maid had found them fastened as usual.

This strange sensation of a presence which could be sensed but not seen was not confined to Miss Shuttleworth-Roberts. Her brother had the firm conviction that there was somebody or something under his bed, even to the point of looking under it and striking matches to see what it could be.

'At about Christmas time,' she told me, 'I heard a noise such as chains might make if they were being dragged about on each side of the bed, and heard someone say, "It's him". At the same time, a picture in the room seemed for a brief second to become illuminated. I shot out of bed and went across the open landing to Mother's room, the dog following me.

'My younger sister then said that *she* would sleep in my bedroom and would speak to it! but she would not tell us what she heard until we moved to Chester. When we got there, she told me that the experience had so scared her that she could not speak—her heart was thumping so violently. On our last night there, before we moved to Chester, my uncle and the maid went to bed and Mother, the dog and myself walked from the dining-room and across the hall to the stairs. The dog was *quiet* by my side—the other spaniel had died—when the back door was given a *terrific* shaking. I said to Mother: "Do you hear that?" and she said: "Indeed I do!" So we crept upstairs and opened the bathroom window to see if anybody was by the back door, but there was not a soul there. I said to Mother: "Thank goodness it is our last night here!"

'It appears it was a haunted house, and had been left empty for forty years as no one would live there. A servant once fell over the landing banisters and was killed in the hall below ...'

That is an example of a haunted house of the sort peculiar in fiction—easy to read and write about, but decidedly unnerving to experience.

Another example of a haunted house was described to me by Mr. John Harper of Rose Brae, Mossley Hill, Liverpool. He writes:

'I give you the following account of my family's only experience of the apparently supernatural. This was my parents' experience rather than mine, as I was only four and a half years old at the time.

'The incidents occurred in September, 1938 on the occasion of our annual month's holiday. The place was a two-roomed holiday cottage, now ruined, half-way across the Castletown (Isle of Man) bay coast of the Langness Peninsula.

'One mile inland from the cottage, where the peninsula joins the main land, is the hamlet of Derbyhaven. A rough, narrow road follows the shore and joins Derbyhaven, the cottage and the lighthouse, which is a shore station at the tip of Langness half a mile from the cottage.

'Langness is a place of rugged rocks and turf. The rocks are outcrops of steeply inclined limestone beds, giving the area an unusual appearance. In fact when the sun is down some call it eerie. In the middle of the peninsula is an old watch-tower, cylindrical in shape and known as the Herring tower, as it was used as a look out for herring shoals and fishing boats during the last century—and possibly in this one too. There are some remains of an old lead mine shaft half a mile from the cottage and near to the lighthouse.

'The cottage itself is in a field on the landward side of the road, and is surrounded by a gravel path invaded by large patches of turf.

'The incidents began as follows: my mother, who is an imaginative but not a nervous woman, was in the house with myself and my sister (a baby of two and a half years of age) while my father was night-fishing by moonlight. This night was the first of our holiday. My mother was in bed, but awake, at about ten o'clock in the evening when suddenly she had an overpowering feeling of fear, followed by a sensation of being choked. She was too afraid to make even the smallest movement. When my father returned at about 11 p.m. he was very surprised to find my mother distressed, as she had never been concerned about being alone in any circumstances.

'The first incident does not seem to be related to what followed, and I tell it only because it happened. Being a very active person who had just finished a year's work, with the added burden of two young children, I lean to the view that she was overtired at the time. However, what followed prevented anyone else from being left alone to experience anything similar.

'During the same night, between midnight and dawn, a sound exactly resembling the wheeling of an iron-tyred wheelbarrow was heard by my father and mother. Both ignored it, and went back to sleep, because the head lightkeeper at the lighthouse, with whom my father had quickly made friends, had promised to bring some of his surplus coal during his night watch. However, in the morning no coal was there. My father, when he spoke to the head keeper, whose name was George McKenzie, mentioned the coal and said that he thought he had heard him bringing it. McKenzie asked my father why he imagined that. My father told him he had heard a wheelbarrow, whereupon McKenzie replied that he was welcome to all the coal he wanted, so long as he fetched it himself. McKenzie had never heard any stories of a ghostly nature relating to the peninsula, nor is there a tradition of any such in the communities round about.

'For the next month, while we lived at the cottage, we heard what my parents dubbed "the barrowman" almost every night between dusk and nine o'clock in the morning. His performances were lengthy and he often gave several per night. His route never varied, always travelling round and round the cottage on the gravel path. He would often carry on after dawn or even restart in bright sunshine.

'The sounds were always, as I have said, exactly like an iron-tyred barrow, and because of the easily-remembered patches of turf on the gravel path, we could tell exactly where the "barrowman" was at any time during his circuit. The wheel noise on the gravel came clearly and the silence as it crossed a patch of turf was anticipated by the listeners. I remember it perfectly, though I remember little else as, being so young, I was often asleep, and in any case my parents were anxious not to alarm me. On one occasion I awoke in the night and asked who was wheeling away my cart (there was a small handcart in an outhouse, with which I used to play).

'As for the daylight haunting—this was extraordinary. My parents would frequently fall asleep to the sound of the wheel as it passed round and round the house, always falling silent on the turf patches for the time it would take to cross them,

always travelling at the same speed. They would often awake
to the same noise next morning, regular and persistent enough
to be monotonous, were it not for its nature. Of course, on the
first, and on the many following daylight occasions of the manifestation, my father took the obvious action. He would slip
quietly out of bed and crawl across the floor to the open window, then wait until the wheel had traversed turf patches
silently and gravel patches grindingly, until it was on the gravel
exactly outside his window, no more than six or eight feet away
before thrusting his head quickly above the window-sill and out
into the full daylight. Whereupon the sound would stop instantly, and there was nothing there. My father would be astounded, having assumed until then that someone was playing
a prank. The same thing happened on every other occasion
when my father tried to surprise "the barrowman".

'Towards the end of September, when nights close in, "the
barrowman" became almost more than they could bear. On
one occasion my mother, who was kneeling at her prayers (a
lifelong habit), leaped into bed fully clothed when the wheel
noise suddenly became much louder. My father, a most un-
imaginative man (with regard to the supernatural) became apprehensive and, farmer-like, procured a pitchfork which he
kept in the bedroom as a tangible means of defence.

'My late grandfather, who was a founder-member of the
Kipling Society, and interested in all kinds of legend and story,
failed to find any explanation for, or even reference to, "the
barrowman", though he found records of one or two fatal acci-
dents at the old lead mine.'

The last chapter in this strange story occurred during and
after the Second World War. While Mr. Harper senior was
managing a limestone quarry in the Isle of Man, his office boy
mentioned that he was spending his annual holiday with some
friends in the south of England. Their names, which I will
not give, struck a bell with him. Surely, he thought, they were
the previous tenants of the haunted cottage? But of course,
interested as he was in what they might have experienced
whilst they were there, he realised that if he were to ask them,
he should do so in a way as not to put ideas into their heads.
So he simply asked the office boy to inquire from them what
they thought of the cottage.

On his return, the office boy said that the people (a childless
couple) had been forced to leave the cottage after three weeks,
as the husband suffered a nervous breakdown.

Mrs. Beatrice M. Conquest, of Iddesleigh Road, Bedford, had

an extraordinary experience in 1955. At that time she had
two young grandchildren staying with her for the week-end and
was then living in Barkers Lane, her family being the first
tenants in a new house. On this particular Sunday afternoon
she gave both children a bath before taking them home. Jenni-
fer was the first to get out of the bath and go to the bedroom
to get dressed. While Mrs. Conquest was giving Robin a rub
down someone gave him a slap on the arm. 'I heard the slap,'
she says, 'and the strange thing was that I knew the exact
spot where he was slapped. The child also knew, and felt it.
He turned round with his hand raised ready to spank his
sister, thinking she had slapped him. I shall never forget the
surprise on his face when he found the bathroom door closed
and nobody there. I have no explanation to give.'

It is interesting to compare this account of a 'slapping ghost'
—which can fairly be classed amongst the poltergeists—with
the ghost which was reported to have slapped children at the
house in Maryland, which I have described in the chapter on
poltergeists.

Sixty years ago, Mr. E. H. Faulkner, of Newland, Northampton, lived in a haunted house—since demolished—at 18
Horsemarket, Northampton. A three-storey building, he was
there with his father (who was a hairdresser), mother, sister and
brother.

'One morning at about 10 a.m.' he told me, 'I was mounting
the stairs on my way to my bedroom on the top floor. I had
just reached the third step of the last flight when I saw a lady
walking down. I stood still, I should think for about a minute.
The lady looked about thirty years old and was dressed in
the English style of about 100 years ago. She was putting a
glove on when she looked at me, then vanished.

'After the 1914 war I lived in London, coming back to 18
Horsemarket in 1941. I was married by then, with a daughter
and son. One night, my daughter ran upstairs to change as
she was going to a dance and when she entered the top bedroom, she saw the same lady. Although, like myself, she has
strong nerves, it gave her a shock. She was about eighteen
years old at the time.

'A week later another young lady stayed with my mother.
She also saw it and left the house at once.'

In response to further questions, Mr. Faulkner told me that
he saw this ghost in May 1906. It was unaccompanied by any
noise and was solid-looking and surrounded by 'a bright violet
light'. The woman was wearing a black bonnet and a black

shawl over her shoulders, and wore a bodice with white lace down the front. Her black dress was very full and flowing. She was wearing a black glove and looked at him in the act of putting on the other. His daughter saw the ghost on two occasions: in 1941 and 1942.

The next story concerns a hospital somewhere in the North of England, which I do not propose to identify, in case the patients should be alarmed or the staff inconvenienced. Similarly and for the same reasons I withhold the name of my informant, a pharmacy porter employed there.

Last year a cloudburst struck the district, and there was 'some danger and some damage'. The large laundry was put out of action and the fire brigade had to pump the flood water from the cellars. There was grave danger of the flood waters reaching the fire-boilers and electrical switch gear, but fortunately serious damage was averted by prompt action.

On the third morning after this downpour and flooding, the porter, after clocking-in at the hospital gates, walked towards the Porter's Lodge with the hospital barber, discussing the damage. As they approached to within a few yards of the Lodge, a lady, in dark blue overall and with black bobbed hair, approached in the opposite direction and at a tangent so that only her profile was visible. She carefully picked her way (for it is rather bad under foot at that particular spot) and preceded them down the steps into the Porter's Lodge. 'As it is the job of the women cleaners to keep the Lodge tidy, we did not mention her or take much notice. Only afterwards did I realise that 8.20 was not their usual time to be cleaning the place. In any case, because of the flood the cleaners were starting work a bit earlier each morning.'

'The Porter's Lodge consisted of two rooms, with one entrance serving also as an exit. There is also a door connecting the two rooms. The first room has a table in the centre, a wash-basin by the side of the door and metal lockers for changing purposes. As the barber and I changed into our overalls, I continued the conversation begun after clocking. The barber then cocked his head in a warning manner, which surprised me, as I was watching what I was saying because I knew the woman must be in the second room. I preceded my friend into the dining-room, but when I looked around, there was only one other porter present, to whom I said, "Good morning," dismissing the lady from my mind.

'There is a little cubby-hole between the two rooms containing buckets and other things and not believing in ghosts I assumed

she had left the cubby-hole by another door. It was only
when the barber demanded where she was, that I discovered,
after looking, that there was no other door there. It shook
my friend, the barber, but I'm afraid I was not convinced. I
therefore checked on all the women cleaners and discovered
that not one of them had black hair, or wore a dark blue
overall and it was impossible for the lady to have turned back
and retraced her steps for the half-dozen steps down to the
Porter's Lodge will take only two side by side and we would
have had to step aside to make way for her.

'Was the lady a ghost? She seemed very real to me, but when
I searched around I never found her.'

13

Beyond explanation

It is interesting to theorise about ghosts and hauntings. It is easiest of all for those whose lives have been untouched by any experience arcane, supernormal or supernatural—whatever term happens to be acceptable. For in dealing with the unexplainable, precise terms of measurement and description are elusive. Indeed, the popular over-simplification 'ghost-hunter' is deceptive. You cannot hunt ghosts. You can hunt an elephant or a fox, for so long as it exists somewhere it can be smelt out, surrounded, cornered, captured—but you can't do that with a ghost. The late Harry Price brought into use an impressive armoury of gadgetry for recording drops in temperature, fingerprints, footprints, sounds and so on. But how do you measure terror, or the paralytic conviction that an invisible presence is at hand? Drink, says the layman, or shattered nerves. The uneasy subconscious says the doctor or psychiatrist. A breakdown in the optical valves or synapses, says the optician. But the percipient, or person actually experiencing this particular sensation, lacks any adequate means to describe it, and certainly has none to prove it.

I am all for corroboration and, where possible, seek it, but I do not discredit or reject stories simply because an experience has not been shared. I acknowledge the scientific limitations of a single experience, but individually they can be interesting and cumulatively significant—the common factor, such as the habit of ghosts of walking along the level traversed during lifetime, irrespective of level changes in floors and roads, or the destruction of buildings, staircases and doors, is a case in point. So, too, does the interesting fact emerge that ghostly lights tend to be (though not always) a kind of electric or steel blue.

However, there are places so consistently 'haunted' that there is ample corroboration. Take, for example, Amwellbury House, the home of Mr. and Mrs. Peter Ffrench-Hodges. Mr. Hodges tells me:

'Amwellbury House is situated on a wooded rise off the A.10 Cambridge Road, one mile from Ware, on land which once belonged to the Monks of Westminster. The present house, now much reduced in size, was once a substantial Georgian mansion, with considerable Victorian additions. I lived there during the early part of my childhood and two of my cousins, Lawrence and Helen, were frequent visitors.

'It seems that on their visits one or the other would sleep in a bedroom at the end of the house facing the drive, and it was in this room that the monks would appear, chanting as they marched past the bed. Helen always went under the bed-clothes, but Lawrence, a little braver, was once shaken by the shoulder as he slept, to awake to the sound of chanting and marching feet as the dim procession passed through the room. The children never told anyone of their experiences at the time, believing them to be some kind of nightmare.

'One morning, Lawrence appeared so shaken at breakfast that my grandmother saw to it that he slept in a different room that night, but the matter was never discussed. She herself had once slept in the room when ill and had asked that she might be moved to another part of the house, so it is probable that she, too, saw the monks. There was always snow on the ground the morning after the monks appeared.

'During the war, Amwellbury House was used as a school and afterwards, the greater part of the house was pulled down, including the bedroom where the monks walked.

'Nothing was seen in or around the smaller house until just before the Christmas of 1964 when once or twice when I was in my bedroom and happened to pass the window, I caught glimpses of a figure moving down the drive, who, on closer examination, disappeared. But I didn't attach much significance to these "mirages", as I imagined them to be, until the day when I looked out and saw quite clearly the cowled figure of a monk passing down the drive . . .'

In St. Monance, Fife in Scotland I traced a man who believes he owes his life to a ghost. That his experience happened over fifty years ago in no way detracts from its interest, for the factors operating do not change from century to century. Mr. Kemp was living at the time in the town of Forres, and his strange experience happened when he and a pal were looking for a farm about ten miles east of Elgin.

It was late autumn. Ted and his pal left together at about 7 p.m. on their push bikes—without lamps! After travelling many miles of this lonely country road 'we still had not found the farm we were seeking and, as it was now pitch dark, decided to return. On our way back we came to the top of a steeply descending road and, fearing a collision between us, I asked my friend to stay back for at least five minutes.

'I then went on alone, and was half-way down when a light suddenly appeared at the left-hand side of the road. I jumped off my bike and stared at this unexpected phenomenon. It was a thin column of light about six feet in height. While I stood there wondering the light flickered for a few seconds and then vanished as mysteriously as it had appeared.

'A few minutes later I heard my friend approaching and shouted to him to dismount. When he did so I explained my reason for stopping and standing there half-way down when he would naturally have expected to find me at the foot of the hill. We then searched around for some time but found no natural explanation to account for this light. There were only green fields on both sides of the road and no animals, no dwellings within miles and no marshes where "marsh lights" might appear. After our fruitless search I suggested that we walk down the remainder of the steep road, and it was a lucky thing that we did so. When we reached the bottom of the road we found a small stone bridge at right angles to the road. But for that warning light we must both have crashed over the bridge and sustained serious, if not fatal, injuries.'

An eerie and unaccountable story was recounted to me by Mrs. H ... of Southwick, Sussex:

'The events described did not include the actual appearance of a ghost, but I think they were certainly beyond normal explanation.

'In 1947 my brother and I took over the tenancy of a house in a poor district near here called Fishergate, and as the achievement of any kind of accommodation in those days was an occasion for rejoicing, to celebrate this good fortune we each invited a friend to stay with us for a week or two.

'We were all ex-service, recently demobilised. My husband was still with the R.E. in Germany. The house was very sparsely furnished but we were young and used to "roughing it" with camp beds and army blankets, and we looked forward to an enjoyable house-warming party.

'We didn't learn the history of the house until much later —after the disturbing events were well under way. Apparently it had originated as a bungalow erected by a small jobbing builder who later built on some upper rooms, divided the result, let the right-hand part to an elderly lady and her daughter and lived in the remaining part himself. He then built another place for himself and let the left-hand half to us.

'It was agreed that I should occupy the largest room upstairs, the others sleeping downstairs, and we moved in happily, but I soon found I could not sleep properly and kept waking with a start to the strong sensation of someone else being present, despite the proof when switching on the light, that there wasn't. I began to experience an inexplicable fear but was too ashamed to mention it to the others, and chided myself for the absurd fancies.

'But the disturbance grew worse: one night I woke with a violent start and the room was jangling with echoes as after a fearful scream. I lay paralysed with funk and sweating profusely but finally managed to get out of bed and downstairs where I woke the others and complained of a nightmare. I noticed a loud clicking sound as I fled down the stairs, and this was heard on the subsequent occasions of disturbance. We thought it must be due to something wrong with the gas and electricity meters under the stairs.

'Strategy led to my change of room to one downstairs as being more convenient for getting the early tea, etc. and my brother gladly installed himself in the "best" room, only to suggest a few days later that it would be more appropriate for our male guest to use it, so there was a further change round. Subsequently, I observed the guest's strained expression with secret disquiet but little dreaming what appalling event was about to break, exactly a fortnight after the beginning of his stay with us. With very little warning he went completely and violently insane to the accompaniment of screams so blood-curdling and terrible as to bring a large audience of neighbours crowding outside. The doctor, police and Relieving Officer soon took charge and our poor friend was taken away in an ambulance to a mental hospital where he was to spend a year. The friend I'd invited fainted and I was fully occupied with looking after her and the shattered household. The girl never properly recovered from the shock, attempted suicide some months later and was taken to a mental hospital for a long stay. My brother, standing badly shaken and white-faced in the bathroom confided, "You'll think it absolutely crazy, but there's something wrong with that room he was in—I had to get out of it— kept waking up thinking I'd heard someone screaming and I got the impression of a ghastly cat thing in there."

'It was too late to wish I'd spoken in the first place—I'm sure they'd have laughed and "ribbed" me had I done so.

Victim No. 3 was myself, some weeks later—not, mercifully, insanity but ill health and a spell of amnesia.

'I know little or nothing of ghostly matters, but thought the following discovery might bear on the foregoing events. The daughter of the lady next door had investigated spiritualism with great enthusiasm and, just before our coming into the house, had become No. 1 candidate for the mental hospital. Did she, I wonder, start the whole ball rolling, so to speak? Had she made some sort of contact with things better left alone and left us to reap developments?'

A very unusual ghost was seen by a lady in Darlington, when she was a small child.

One night she saw the figure of a man standing in her bedroom door, water dripping from his shoulders downwards. The next day she heard her mother telling a neighbour that it was so many years ago that her brother was drowned—when H.M.S. *Eurydice* foundered in a terrible squall off the Isle of Wight on March 24, 1878, with the loss of over 300 lives. At the very day and hour that it foundered, the Rev. W. Aitken was preaching to seamen in Southsea, quoting from the Psalms: 'Thy rowers have brought thee into great waters, the east wind hath broken thee in the midst of the seas.'

The *Eurydice* was a twenty-six gun frigate launched in 1843 and commissioned as a training ship in 1877. She sailed for a cruise to the West Indies, left Bermuda on March 6th and was making her way to Spithead with only one more headland, Dunnose, to round. She had passed Ventnor, and was off Luccombe Chine, only two and a half miles from land, in twelve fathoms of water, and under the lee of a shore which rose in a cliff of 500 feet and which would hide the first signs of a change of weather on the horizon.

She was going about ten knots on the port tack. The captain had given orders to shorten sail, but before his order could be complied with the wind veered, a howling gale swept against the billowing canvas, a driving snowstorm caught the vessel from the north and she heeled over 'lying over so completely that her keel was in sight. The men were all swept to the lee side of the vessel, not only rendering action impossible, but greatly increasing the weight.' The pressure of water on her sides, which would have tended to upright her again, was neutralised by the water which poured like an avalanche through the open ports on the main deck. The storm increased and, hidden from land by the blinding snowstorm, the *Eurydice* went down with awful suddenness, bow first. Only two survived.

The ghost whom my informant saw was that of James Turner, a twenty-four-year-old marine. His correspondence, which I have read, shows him to have been an adventurous but disciplined, pleasant and upright lad. His letters are written, in the fashion of the time, on ship's notepaper surmounted by vigorous and detailed steel engravings of the ship on which he happened to be serving at the time of writing, such as H.M.S. *Minotaur* ('Ironclad, 28 guns'). Another letter shows a frigate in full sail and underneath the sentimental verse:

SWEET REMEMBRANCE

Urged by love's ever conquering spell
My trembling pen in truth would tell
How dearly prized art thou to me
How my soul's hopes are fixed on thee.

The poor lad—his photograph shows a youth open of countenance—was a bachelor and those nearest and dearest to him were his own family. His mother had died when he was a youngster, and he received very little education. There is immense pathos in his appearance at his sister's house after his death. Did her reference to him summon up this vision in some strange way?

Sudden death is so often associated with the appearance of phantasms—sometimes, as I have described in the chapter concerned with death visitants, before the disaster. Such a case, and again an unusual one in many respects, has been described to me by Mr. Joe Campbell of Kilkeel, Newry, County Down, Northern Ireland.

Mr. Campbell believes that a ghost which he and a friend saw was in some strange way connected with a tragedy which occurred in his family a few weeks later. His experience is interesting because of an unusual feature: a normally inanimate object, such as a post, became illuminated as though glowing with fire. Furthermore, to both percipients it appeared larger than usual and nearer than normal:

'The last part of my story concerns the death of my eldest son aged fifteen years on Easter Sunday. He was an exceptionally good-looking lad, quiet and obliging ... Some five weeks prior to Easter Sunday, 1964, I went to visit a friend's house and when it was time to go my friend escorted me to the road which is the main Newry to Kilkeel highway. As we stood talking I noticed a lady coming towards us. I said, "There is my mother; I will wait for her." But the woman came along the straight part of the road to a gate leading into my friend's field, and disappeared.

'Now, to get into this field she would have had to climb the gate as it was chained. And there would have been no point in her going into the field anyway, as it did not lead to any house. We both noticed her disappearance and thought it peculiar, as there were street lights on the side where she disappeared, which light up a part of the field. I stood on the ditch and looked but could see no one. We both then walked down to the gate and I got into the field and searched around, but there was no trace of her. I went home and told my wife what had happened.

'Easter Sunday dawned—a feast day for children when they all go to the fields and partake of eggs, lemondade and cakes. My daughters went with their friends. My son left to meet up with his pals. Some time around five o'clock I experienced an awful restlessness. I went in and out of the room where my wife was confined with a fractured leg, and back and forth to the front door. Earlier I had prepared pencil and paper to go up and make a sketch of the mountains, having selected a certain field from which there was a magnificent view. The day was nice, but I could not go out of the house; something kept me back ...'

Mr. Campbell's daughters returned at about 5.45 p.m. The family had tea, and still John had not returned, but this gave no cause for alarm as it was presumed that John was making the most of the fine day. On looking out of his window however, Mr. Campbell saw some of his neighbours going up the road, and something prompted him to go and find out what it was about. He saw a crowd congregating in a lane and instinct told him his son was in dire trouble, so he ran down it, through a gate and across the field where he had intended to paint. At the bottom of the field, suspended on the high tension wires, was his son, electrocuted. A report of the inquest on the boy appeared in the *Belfast Telegraph*.

Later Mr. Campbell compared notes with the friend who, with him, had seen the phantasm of the woman who disappeared into the field. The friend's name was Hugh O'Hagen of Dunavan Kilkeel. Both were agreed on the following strange points:

1. The gate post by which the woman disappeared was about fifty yards from where they had been standing at the time.

2. There was absolutely no explanation of where the woman could have gone to.

3. The stone post became luminous and appeared *to be about eighteen* feet from where they were standing. But in the day-time the top of this post, which is about five feet high, is barely visible from the spot where the men were standing.

Some years ago a man was killed near the same gate.

A curious and a sad story. The connection between the occur-rence of the disappearing woman and the tragic death of Mr. Campbell's son may be imagination; but connected or not, both things happened as stated.

It is possible for a vision to be very plain indeed to one person, yet entirely invisible to another who is present at the same time. One day, Mrs. E. M. Scott of Grove Street, Leaming-ton Spa, Warwickshire, was sitting in the lounge of her home with her husband, and ... 'I opened the door to come out of the lounge and there stood a ghost. It was a man in a check coat, a cap, scarf and grey flannel trousers. I was really fright-ened. I called my husband, but the ghost had gone. I went into our bedroom and the same man was there, but my husband did not see it. If I had been alone in the house I would not have dared to stay.'

In reply to questions, Mrs. Scott said that the ghost was 'solid-looking'. When she screamed on finding the 'man' in the bed-room her husband raced to see what was the matter, but saw nothing. The phantasm bore some resemblance to a friend of hers in Canada.

Mr. A. E. C. Morgan, M.A., of Llalsadwrn, Anglesey, is an ex-clergyman who has had many extraordinary encounters with ghosts. He saw his first spectre when he was a very young child —scarcely more than four at the time:

'It was about 1884 or 1885 and I lived in Tidmarsh Rectory near Pangbourne, Berkshire. One clear June evening, when there was a full moon, I was looking at the stream 100 yards away, while my nurse was putting me to bed. It may have been eight o'clock or earlier. There was a light mist about the stream, perhaps about a foot high or less. A figure seemed to rise and stand on the bank ... and then disappear ... not walk away. My nurse said "a ghost" and my mother came in. When she was told, she said there was a story that a Pangbourne boy had been drowned in the pool there.'

Some people are more prone to such experiences than others. Mr. Morgan met his next ghost—or should one say, heard it— when he was a curate of the Parish Church in Doncaster. He shared the very old clergy house (then over 200 years old) with another curate named Rutter. Mr. Morgan's room, a small one,

faced the church on its north side. It was simply furnished with
a truckle bed, a cupboard to the right and a chair. A window
faced his bed, while to the left was a fireplace. Past his room
a set of ten or twelve shallow oaken stairs, very old, led up to
the attics. The lower part of the stairs led to other bedrooms.

One evening, Mr. Morgan was alone. His supper had been
laid for him downstairs, but his fellow curate had evidently gone
away for the night while a further search of the kitchen showed
that the old housekeeper and her daughter had also disappeared. However, he did not worry overmuch. He ate his
supper and retired to bed.

During the night he was awakened by what he describes as
'a terrific gurgling noise' close to his bed and towards the
(unused) fireplace. He struck a match and got out of bed,
wondering angrily who on earth it could be. But there was
nothing under the bed, and no indication that the noise could
have come from the chimney.

In the morning, when he met the housekeeper and her
daughter, he asked them where they had got to the previous
night. 'Oh,' said the housekeeper, 'I couldn't stay in the house
since the day that poor man killed himself in your bedroom.'
The story was that a young man had proposed to one of the
daughters of an Archdeacon and, being refused, went back to
his room—the one in which Mr. Morgan was to find himself
sleeping—and killed himself.

It was, Mr. Morgan told me, a very strange house. In due
course the other curate left for another job and the housekeeper also left. After their departure, Mr. Morgan stayed in
the house alone, contenting himself with the services of a daily
help.

The house had a narrow paved path running to the roadway
and was bordered by a very low wall adjoining the churchyard.
A friend of his, a Mr. Bazin, who worked at a carriage works
in Doncaster, was sitting on this wall one May evening in 1916
when he suddenly said to Mr. Morgan (who was standing in
the doorway of the clergy house) 'Who is in the house behind
you?' 'Why, no one,' Mr. Morgan replied, greatly surprised. But
his friend spoke with such conviction that he went over to him
and sat on the wall too. He could see nothing unusual, but
there was a distinct sound of talking to be heard coming from
inside the house. Mr. Morgan immediately searched the house
but could find nothing to account for the sounds. 'My nerves
were very strong,' he said, 'and I was furious at anyone daring
to invade the house.'

Then Mr. Morgan pointed to a tomb in the churchyard. 'Look at that skull,' he said. 'I have put it back under its big, square tombstone three times and covered it with soil, but it always comes out again.' But if the tombstone itself didn't shift, I asked, how did the skull reappear? 'The skull,' he told me, 'had been pushed in underneath and finally blocked with a goodish piece of stone, so that no rat could move it.'

The same tomb—that from which the skull continually appeared—was the scene of a fantastic occurrence, also during the First World War. Early one May morning Mr. Morgan was awakened by a tremendous hammering at the front door. He opened it to see a soldier, excited and bewildered. 'What is the other side of yon wall?' he demanded. 'I saw a man get up from under that big tombstone and run up the wall. I challenged him; I'd have shot him, but he dropped down the other side.' The soldier explained that he was on sentry duty around the church.

The figure had been seen to emerge and run from the tombstone under which the skull was buried. Mr. Morgan unlocked the garden gate, and showed the soldier that there was a drop of about eighteen feet into a school-yard below from the top of the wall.

Mr. Morgan was not afraid of ghosts. An ex-Oxford heavyweight boxer, Yorkshire cricketer and a member of the British Rugby team which visited Australia and New Zealand, he felt equal to any emergency—even when, lying in bed in the otherwise deserted Clergy House, he was awakened by the steady thump of footsteps going slowly up the oaken stairs that led to the attic, for he jumped out of bed and lit his candle, and went to investigate, but although the steps were thick with dust, there were no footmarks above his doorway. The next day he unlocked the attic, a long one running the entire length of the house, and which no one had entered for years. Once again Mr. Morgan heard the ghostly footsteps.

In due course the Clergy House was demolished. No one would live in it—and if Mr. Morgan's experiences were the usual lot of the residents there, no wonder!

Numerous churches are reputed to be haunted, while ghosts are often seen in churches and cathedrals which have no such reputation at all.

A lady in Bedford, who wishes me to keep her name and address private tells me of a strange experience she had in Newnham Avenue Methodist Church about five years ago. The church is quite small and was built about fifteen years ago.

Newnham Avenue stretches between Godlington Road and the river, and about twenty-six years ago was 'a lovely lovers' lane, all winding, with very big trees on both sides.'

The Minister, she remembers, was the Rev. Stanley Dixon. My informant went to church on Christmas Day with her sister. 'During the sermon,' she told me, 'I saw a tall, very smart man walk across the church in front of the vicar. He was walking on his toes as though to keep quiet and was wearing plain black trousers and a light tweed top coat. I couldn't help smiling to myself at the way he tiptoed along, and through watching his feet I did not look up to his face. I just thought it was a member of the congregation going out through the door—but he did not. He went through the wall, and left a trail of white smoke after him for quite a second before the wall went flat again. I was surprised that nobody saw him but myself; but everyone was sitting quietly listening to the sermon . . .'

The wall 'going flat again' is a curious part of the story. One hears of ghosts going through walls often enough, and of locked doors opening and shutting although, on inspection afterwards, their bolts are still in place and the locks secure, but one seldom hears of walls moving.

Mr. Edward R. Hart, Head Verger of Exeter Cathedral for seventeen years—he is now retired—has described his experiences in a brochure: *After Seventeen Years*. On the night of 3rd-4th May 1943, when bombs were falling fast and a 1,000 pounder struck the cathedral, he was in the cloisters with the Master Mason, Mr. George Down, everyone else being scattered into the various spiral stairways, and 'very clearly felt the presence of the builder Bishops and the great host who have served and loved our Cathedral'.

'At different times,' he says, 'many others have told me what they have seen and felt, and I well recollect one of my staff whose duty it was to ring the curfew at 8 p.m., absolutely refusing to enter the building unless I allowed him to have every light full on.'

One evening a lady living in the cloisters saw clearly the figure of a nun emerge from the wall of the south side of the nave and disappear into the wall of Church House, on the other side of the Cloister Hearth. The time was 7 p.m. and the evening very clear, in the month of July.

An intelligent young boy in a near-by house was once playing the piano—or at any rate, since it was a grand piano and he only an amateur, picking out a few simple tunes, when his mother, coming suddenly into the room just after he had stopped playing, found him shocked and distressed. He said he had seen somebody enter the room through the wall, and the drawing he made of it afterwards corresponded to the figure of a monk. In Saxon times there were monasteries on the site of the old cloisters.

On one occasion, Mr. Hart and his wife were astonished, one morning, to be greeted by their immediate neighbour with the remark, 'You were having a very merry evening!' On giving an assurance that both had gone to bed early and slept soundly they were informed that their neighbour had heard their visitors running about the house laughing heartily and enjoying themselves!

It is not unknown for the appearance of an apparition to cause an argument. This happened in the case of the Nab Lane Apparition, described in *Stories of Samlesbury* compiled by Robert Eaton. Samlesbury Hall is a medieval manor house near Blackburn, Lancashire.

Near the old hall is a well-used road which leads to Blackburn Corporation sewage disposal works and a little farther on arrives at the Nabs Head Inn. About half-way to the Nabs Head is a house called Sorbrose House, the home of Mr. Hubberstey. It is rather secluded. A little farther down is a general store run by a married couple. One night, when the couple were having a stroll with their dog, they passed Sorbrose House and were turning the bend in the road, with the dog prowling in the shallow gutter *well away from them*, on a taut lead, when a woman in a light coat came towards them. She brushed past them closely and was gone before both remarked how silent she had been—no footsteps and ... and ... they suddenly remembered that *she should have tripped on the dog lead*, as it was above ground level, not trailing on the ground. How then could she have passed through it? It was too dark for the lady, even if she had been observed doing so, which she was not, to have noticed the lead and stepped over it.

The next evening the couple read in a local newspaper of an argument which had ensued between a Ribble bus driver and his conductor. It appears that the bus driver stopped at a bus stop near Samlesbury Old Hall to pick up a woman dressed in a light coloured overcoat. The conductor then looked out and, seeing that there was no passenger waiting there, asked the driver why he had stopped, as they were already behind schedule. Then the argument followed! The apparition, it is believed locally, was that of Lady Dorothy, a daughter of the Southworths of Samlesbury, who lived about 360 years ago.

There is absolutely no explanation for the fact that a place may be haunted to one person and not to another (although there are, of course, numerous theories). Mrs. Dora Kendall of Bosville Drive, Sevenoaks, has vivid recollections of what she described to me as 'two horrible years' in a council house in Bromley where she met her first and, she hopes, her last 'ghost'.

The year was 1930, and she was in her late teens. She was one of a large, happy family and the atmosphere was made extra cheerful by the arrival of a new baby to her father and his second wife.

Dora Mundy, as she was then, slept in a very small room and after a holiday came back feeling fit and happy; but awakening one night she saw, in a mirror which faced the door, a man 'to my mind an American type' wearing a large, broad-brimmed black trilby and—what was comparatively rare in those days—dark glasses. He 'just stood there in the doorway and, so far as could be possible through the dark glasses, our eyes met.' This became a regular nightly occurrence. At first she kept the experience to herself, but eventually told her father, who advised her to shut the door. But 'he' was there just the same, even when, in response to her appeal, her step-sister came to live with her. Her parents agreed to her having a night light—and thereafter the 'ghost' did not appear.

Incidentally, Mrs. Kendal wrote to the Housing Officer of the Borough of Bromley asking him if the house had any sort of history and whether he had received any complaints about it or any other information which might throw light on her experience. The reply she received was that the present tenant had been in occupation of the same premises since 1935 and had made no complaint. So the man in glasses, whatever may have brought him to that comfortable but prosaic-loking council house, has taken himself off somewhere else.

An encounter with a ghost by Mr. Clifford C. White of St. Keyna Road, Keynsham, Bristol has all the traditional details associated with phenomena.

In the hamlet of Hanham Abbots (near Bristol in Gloucestershire) there is a church in the grounds of Hanham Court many centuries old and probably, before the Reformation, forming part of the Catholic Bishopric of Keynsham.

'I lived,' says Mr. White, 'about half a mile away, and was returning from the doctor's house at Bitton one night at about midnight, my journey being necessary at that hour because I had to collect some medicine for my little girl, who was very sick. I was then about 40 years of age and was certainly not a nervous character. I cycled along the road which led past Hanham Court and the church when I suddenly observed a cold and clammy atmosphere. Then I saw an apparition—a woman in white.

'I fell off my cycle, but when I picked myself, up, the apparition had disappeared. I hastened home and told my wife what I had seen. However, she was more concerned with the illness of my daughter, so the incident was soon forgotten. Two or three years later I learned from an article in the *Bristol Evening Times and Echo* that the ghost of a nun was a regular visitant at Hanham Abbots.'

A story entirely without explanation—and one which he has kept to himself for thirty years—was told to me by the Marquis of Ely.

In 1933 he visited a friend whose house was in Bryanston Square in the West End of London. It was a handsome home, and photography being a hobby of his, he took with him his 35 mm. Leica camera. One of the pictures he took was of his friend's wife who posed by the handsome marble fireplace.

When the film was developed the Marquis was astonished to find, in the right-hand corner of the film, the distinct outline of a ghostly figure in Elizabethan dress. She has an elaborate coiffure and there is a delicate, Dresden-china touch about her small ear. Her bearing is proud and upright, her chin finely-chiselled and graceful and her neck finely proportioned. A powerful magnifying glass shows that she is wearing a pearl choker. The dress appears to be made of satin or silk and has puffed sleeves reaching to the wrist. The frame of the picture cuts through her, omitting one arm, and the rest of her features.

The figure is shadowy; that is, darker than the rest of the photograph, as though in a half light. 'No one,' the Marquis of Ely told me, 'saw or noticed anything unusual at the time the picture was taken.' In reply to questions as to the technical arrangements under which the interior photograph was taken, he said that two photoflood lamps were used, one behind the sitter and 'one on the front right which should be shining straight on the ghost, but she does not seem to be illuminated by this lamp at all. I had an assistant with me who saw nothing unusual'. The house had no reputation of being haunted, nor had its occupants ever seen anything unusual. To avoid frightening the occupants, he said nothing about it at the time, but the mystery puzzles him still.

A less satisfactory ghost photograph is in the possession of the present Lord Combermere, descendant of the Lord Combermere who sealed and later opened and inspected, the haunted vault at Barbados.

The photograph was taken at Combermere Abbey on December 5, 1891, in the Abbey library, by Sybell R. Corbet, who was staying with her sister, Lady Sutton. At the time the exposure was made, the remains of Wellington Henry, Viscount Combermere, were being buried at the family vault at Wrenbury, three miles distant.

Lord Combermere has allowed me to inspect the original photograph. The figure, which could be thought to be that of an old man with a beard, is rather vague, but the extraordinary thing is that the 'ghost' sitting in a chair has no legs.

The picture was the cause of some controversy in 1926, when Sir Arthur Conan Doyle, creator of Sherlock Holmes, and a noted spiritualist, described the photograph as a 'spirit' photograph. Mr. A. A. Campbell Swinton, F.R.S., a nephew of the late Lord Combermere, challenged Sir Arthur to have the much-discussed photograph reproduced side by side with an authentic photograph of the dead peer. Mr. Swinton then sent the 'spirit' photograph to the *Daily Sketch* (the *Morning Post* having declined to print it on the grounds that it would not reproduce) which published it.

The Proceedings of the Society for Psychical Research, No. CXXIV, Volume VII contain an interesting critical analysis of the circumstances in which the picture was taken. In 1895, photography was in its infancy. The exposure of the plate took over an hour, and as the photographer did not stay in the library all that time, the possibility cannot be excluded that somebody, perhaps a butler, came and sat in that chair—moving perhaps, thus explaining the missing legs—and caused a double exposure. But, as the SPR Journal made clear, the lady who took the photograph, Miss Corbett 'was from the first fully alive to the inconclusive nature of the evidence of any supernormal agency being concerned'.

Miss Corbett was sure that the plate had not been exposed before—it was one of a parcel of dry Ilford plates. Although she did not attend throughout the exposure of the plate, and did not lock the door, the only men in the house at the time were her brother, the butler and two footmen, and all four were young *and beardless*. In answer to inquiries, Miss Corbett stated that the servants would not have been at all likely to have entered the room, while even if one of the four men had entered the room for a practical joke, it would hardly explain the superimposition of a figure which some relatives maintained was very like Lord Combermere, and which was quite unlike anybody living in the house.

Miss Corbett said that her sister had thought the 'ghost' so like the late Lord Combermere that she begged her to look in her photographic record book to discover at what time it was taken—and so it was revealed from the records that the photograph was taken at the exact time of the funeral. On the question of the possibility of the plate having been used before, Miss Corbet assured the SPR that she had never taken a photograph of a human figure except as a minute detail of a landscape. Incidentally, Professor Barrett experimented, with the aid of Mr. Gordon Salt, on the effects which could be produced by the transitory introduction of a figure during a long exposure on a plate. The result thus obtained of a person coming into the room, sitting on a chair and moving his legs, proved so much like the reputed 'ghost' picture as to remove all further necessity for argument.

14

Soldiering on

Soldiers include every variety of temperament, but in general they are practical men of action. They have to assess facts and take realistic decisions on the basis of those facts. They have to follow orders exactly. Precision and realism are their business.

Yet army history is full of ghost stories. Soldiers have been scared by ghosts, and have themselves become ghosts. There was the court-martial of the sentry at the Tower of London who fainted with horror in 1864 after putting his bayonet through a huge phantasmagoric figure and who was supported in his story by two independent witnesses, and acquitted. And a former Constable of the Tower, Colonel Carkeet-James, once told how 'a certain Guards officer' in the pink of condition and stone sober (he was training for the British Olympic Games) was aware, as he reached the Bloody Tower Archway in Water Lane of 'a most queer and utterly distasteful atmosphere'. His desperate wish was to be away from it; his hair stood on end. The next moment he found himself on the mess steps, 300 yards away, bathed in perspiration and panting heavily. He remembered nothing of his sprint.

At Woodmanton, in Wiltshire, the tramping of feet and the spectacle of headless horses, on the site where a battle was once fought between the Romans and Britains, have often been reported in the course of the last two centuries. And Wellington Barracks in London was once reputed to be haunted. Early in the last century, a Coldstream Guardsman murdered his wife and tipped her headless body into a near-by canal, and as her ghost was subsequently reported to have been seen quite frequently, an official inquiry was held at which some sentries gave evidence on oath that they heard a ghostly voice say 'Bring me a light!' while another swore that the ghost of a headless woman had risen up from the ground in front of his sentry-box! Even the bravest sentry is not expected to face that sort of thing.

Following publication of an article I wrote in 1961 for *Soldier*, the British Army magazine, on the subject of military ghosts, many readers wrote in, describing their experiences. One of the most remarkable accounts came from Lieutenant-Colonel The O'Doneven of Gold Mead, Lymington, Hampshire. He had, he said, once played billiards with a ghost and beaten him 100 up! He describes his experience in these words:

'It happened after I had taken two batteries up to the Midlands in 1943. We were billeted in a lovely old house, surrounded by park lands. All the furniture and pictures were covered with dust-covers, and two old retainers of the family, one of whom was the butler, had been left in charge for the duration. I formed a small mess and retained the services of the butler to help us out and to emphasise that we were guests and not just intruders. Our frugal dinner was timed at 7.45 p.m. each evening.

'One cold night my watch must have gone wrong for, as I turned down the stairs into the hall where we dined, I saw by the clock that it was only 6.45 p.m. I was on the point of sitting in front of the fire when I heard the sound of billiard-balls being clicked about.

'I pushed open a door and found myself in a longish room. At the table was a youngish man, in a sort of Kitchener Army Blues knocking the balls about. He was humpbacked. He said nothing, but smiled when I asked "Want a game?"

'So we began. We were ninety-eight-all when I heard my officers moving about in the hall. The shot was mine—a sure pot at his ball or the gentlemanly cannon shot off red to white. As I took my shot, he quietly put his cue back in the rack, gave me a smile and quietly walked through another door, into what I afterwards discovered was a bathroom.

'Halfway through dinner, I asked "Any of you seen the little chap in blues?" but none of my officers had and I was on the point of letting the matter drop, when I added, "A nice lad, with a hump. I've just beaten him at billiards."

'The butler, on the point of handing me some apple tart, froze and went pale. "You've seen Master Willie, Sir," he said.

'I waited, sensing, as a Celt, what I already knew. The butler went on: "Master Willie, sir, was her Ladyship's brother. He had managed to join Kitchener's Army, in 1915, but the authorities threw him out on discovering that he was deformed. He came back here, Christmas, 1916. He played a good game of billiards and shot himself in the room where he loved to play. We see him, sometimes . . ." '

Colonel O'Doneven prefers not to name the house, but recalls (with what I suspect is satisfaction) that a newly-rich tenant who pooh-poohed the idea of a ghost couldn't get out quickly enough after a very short stay there.

The room in which the billiard table was placed was, he tells me, a very large room, comfortably accommodating a full-sized billiard table with cue racks along the walls. It was almost the normal club billiard room for one table only, which is still found in some old inns. I asked the Colonel how near he came to the ghost. He hardly noticed this, 'as it was all so natural. We just went on playing our shots as they came.' Beyond his invitation to have a game, to which the ghost gave only a smile by way of reply, if reply it was, no further words were exchanged—normal enough, as Colonel O'Doneven does not generally speak when playing. I asked who else had seen the man in blue. 'A few nights later,' he told me, 'two of my subalterns, coming down the stairs, spotted the wee figure walking away from the fire. Instead of following, they rushed back upstairs to collect the other subalterns and possibly more courage, and all tumbled down stairs again to check. There was a light switched on over the billiard table: two lights in fact, but no player. I feel my officers missed a chance.'

Ex-Sergeant S. Leake, formerly of the Grenadier Guards and now living in Wetherby, Yorkshire, tells me of the extraordinary experience he had, as a young guardsman of eighteen in the year 1927 of finding himself on sentry-go with a ghost.

It was the custom for the guard at Windsor Castle to be augmented sometimes by recruits from the depot. One such was a young man of melancholy aspect whose name, to avoid pain to any relatives he might have had, I will omit. He was a solitary type. He had not long been in the battalion before he was detailed for duty at the castle, and was assigned to sentry duty on the Long Walk—an eerie enough place at the best of times, where the moonlight seems to the apprehensive to animate the marble statuary, where the wind whines mournfully through the leaves and branches of the trees, and where the ghost of Hearn the Hunter is reputed to stalk.

One night, whilst on duty, the young guardsman shot himself.

A few weeks later Leake was detailed for the Long Walk post. It was a bright moonlight night and his two hours passed uneventfully. Hearing the 2 a.m. relief on its way, he decided to create an impression of alertness by continuing to patrol the beat until the relief turned the corner. Consequently he marched towards the terrace, turned smartly and began the march back to his box.

As he did so, ex-Sergeant Leake saw marching towards him the figure of a guardsman. Surprised at this, he looked at the features below the man's bearskin cap, and saw the face of the guardsman who had shot himself! But the dead man's features did not have their usual mournful, lost expression; they were happy and smiling. As the relief turned the corner the phantom guardsman vanished.

Leake, remembering the agitation of the guard he had relieved, now thought he knew the reason for it. Back in his quarters he aroused his friend. 'Why were you in such a hurry to get off when I came on duty to relieve you?' he asked. 'I was glad when you came, kid,' the other guard replied, 'because a ghost did double sentry with me!' Both men had had an identical experience.

Ex-Sergeant Leake is still very clear in his recollections of all the details relevant to what occurred. It happened, he told me, during the summer months, when they were in tunic order. The dead man was about his age at the time—eighteen years. He estimated the duration of the appearance of the phantom as having been about ten seconds. The spectre was solid-looking and in colour—not monotone. He could not say where he could hear the footsteps of the ghost, because of course, he heard the footsteps of the oncoming relief. I rather liked Mr. Leake's answer to my query as to whether he was scared when he saw the ghost: 'My hair stood on end. It still does when I think about it and that's after forty years.' He and his fellow-guardsman, whose name was Morrell, told the whole Guard about it, but were laughed at 'though some laughed apprehensively. Naturally some of the Guard told other people, and we received a certain amount of leg-pulling afterwards. At the age of eighteen I was somewhat sensitive and did not "plug" the story.'

Does the 'spirit' or ghost of a living person project itself in times of great emotion? The numberless accounts of telepathy and phantasms of the living imply that this can happen. I have already quoted numerous specific instances, but, by courtesy of *Soldier* magazine, let me recount the extraordinary story which concerns James Simms of Brighton who, on the night of September 17, 1944, was parachuted into Holland with the 2nd Battalion, Parachute Regiment, and who fought bitterly towards the main bridge in the centre of Arnhem. This particular battle was one in which the invading party had to cope with an alerted enemy—a traitor in London had betrayed the whole plan to the Nazis—but at any rate, Simms and his mates

fought on until, on the 19th, he was badly wounded and bleed-
ing so profusely that his death seemed very probable. And as he
lay in a comfortless cellar on September 29th an officer and
another man on each side of him died of their wounds.

When at last, manifestly weaker but at least healed of his
wounds, Simms returned to England, he called on a lady he had
known since boyhood, and learned from her that on September
19, 1944, as he lay between life and death in Arnhem,
she had been sitting in her front parlour thinking of him when
she had the distinct feeling that there was somebody there. She
looked up and was astonished to see the outline of his figure,
luminous, through the thick folds of the heavy curtains in front
of the window. She described accurately his dress at the time:
the webbing, the smock, the helmet—even the field dressing on
his thigh. He appeared to be utterly exhausted, holding the
curtains as though depending on them for support, and contemplating stepping into the room. It was a terrible and a
poignant moment. The friend, torn between fear and pity and
overcome by a feeling of impending tragedy, spoke words of
comfort: 'It's all right, Jim. It's all right,' she said, gently,
kindly. The tense hold of the curtains was seen to be relaxed;
slowly the vision faded.

Our next ghost was encountered by a group of hard-fighting
soldiers during the Normandy campaign in the last war. The
thousands of military vehicles had churned up the dust to such
an extent that it had settled on the verges and hedges, and everywhere there were notices: DRIVE SLOWLY—DUST BRINGS SHELLS
AND SHELLS BRING DEATH!

In the Falaise Gap, hundreds of thousands of Germans were
caught in a pocket. Into that pocket the Allies poured bombs,
shells and bullets. The roads were strewn with dead and dying
men and horses, and fat, dead cattle lying on their backs, their
legs pointing stiffly to the sky.

My informant and his mates were trying to get from the
Falaise Gap to Argentan to link up with others of the Regiment
who were bisecting the pocket from a different direction. Their
rendezvous was a large field just outside the small, deserted and
largely destroyed town of Trun.

The unit, reaching its rendezvous before darkness fell, had a
wholly unexpected, and domestic problem awaiting it. A troop
sergeant had got drunk at a local café and in an access of al-
coholic generosity had given his Sten gun and eight magazines
of bullets to his drinking companion. So somewhere, a drunken
civilian was lurching around with his lethal load, a menace to

himself and everyone within range. Their troop officer could have wasted time with recriminations—loss of weapons, especially when in action, is a most serious offence which in extreme cases can be punishable by death and in any case merits a court martial. But the first and essential thing was to catch up with the man who had carried away the Sten gun and ammunition.

He called for volunteers and seven men, including the officer, piled into a 'half-track' (a vehicle with wheels at the front and tracks at the back). Weighing about 12 tons and armed with a 50 calibre Browning machine gun, the machine lurched down the old Norman lanes, aided in its course by the light of a full moon.

They called at the inn, long locked and shuttered, and persuaded a reluctant and only vaguely comprehending innkeeper to describe the man who had the gun who proved to be a local butcher living in a village about three miles away. Still muttering irritably into his beard, the innkeeper joined them and directed them. He sat in the centre seat at the front of the truck with the officer on his right and the driver, Tommy, on the left. My informant stood on the little platform behind and above the officer, his head poking through the 'Scarf' ring on which the heavy Browning was mounted. The four others squatted in the back, their heads well down behind the protection of the half-track's steel sides.

As they got under way there were sporadic bursts of firing in the near distance. Nobody—least of all the French innkeeper —was particularly happy about the assignment, occasioned only by the thoughtlessness of one drunken soldier.

The winding lanes and tall hedges reminiscent of Devonshire afforded a comparative shelter; but now they left the lanes and moved along the main road to the butcher's village. It was a typically French road, broad, straight, cobbled in the centre with packed earth shoulders and a deep ditch on either side. Behind the ditch lay a thick hedge and tall trees. Further up the road, an untidy assortment of farm buildings were etched in sharp silhouette against the night sky.

Suddenly, as the party were about thirty or forty yards from the entrance to a driveway which appeared to lead towards the buildings, the little Frenchman started shouting BOCHES! BOCHES! BOCHES! and at a fast gallop there emerged from this driveway a farm cart drawn by two horses. On the flap of the wagon immediately behind the horses, which were harnessed abreast, were two men. At that distance, and by moonlight, the party couldn't make out whether they were Germans, or whether they were Frenchmen who thought the party in the approaching truck were Germans. They pulled out on to the road in front of the soldiers, the driver whipping up his team frantically. Of course, the army truck was making such a row with its tracks, that nobody heard any noise from the farm cart and its horses.

The officer spoke, sharply: 'Give 'em a burst over their heads!' My friend settled down behind the Browning and, not wishing to actually kill anybody, sighted the gun roughly. Suddenly he realised that there was nothing—nothing—to shoot at, anyway. The cart, the horses and their men had vanished before their eyes, and in the instant they did so the truck stopped dead in its tracks as though braked by an invisible hand, causing the gunner to fall off his perch and the lads to pile up at the back.

It all seemed too absurd for belief. The officer jumped out of the truck and ordered four of the men to come with him and investigate. The driver stayed at the wheel and the Frenchman, wishing perdition to Boche and Anglais alike, sat gibbering on his seat. The gunner kept them covered, watching the swirls of dust set up by their feet as they walked away. The searchers walked well beyond the part where the cart had vanished, looked around carefully examining their immediate surroundings, then turned back and retraced their steps to the truck. Then, with no signal but by synchronous intuition, all broke into a run and bolted back to the truck as though all the devils in hell were after them. The driver banged the starter button and shoved a gear in. With much straining and tugging he somehow managed to turn the unwieldy vehicle round in one go; and as the last of the lads had climbed on to the tailboard, with the gunner spinning the gun round to face the rear, they roared away.

On the homeward journey, the officer and his men described what they had found. They had walked up the road looking in the ditches for concealed openings, but there wasn't a clue as to where the cart could have gone. Most uncanny of all, there were neither wheel marks nor hoof marks in the fine, thick dust —only their own footprints.

The following experience of an encounter with a ghost was recounted to me by Mr. William Porter of Island Street, Belfast. It happened in 1920 when he was stationed in a fort at Multan in the Punjab. 'The ghost was that of a soldier with shirt-sleeves rolled up. I saw him twice, but the first time I assumed he was one of my own battery out for a cool, and thought no more of it. I saw him the second time at the top of some steps leading to the flat roof of the barracks. There was only one set of steps on to the roof, and that was how I discovered he was a ghost, for I went up thinking that it was one of my pals, and then realised that one doesn't jump from roofs two stories high, for there was not a thing to be seen on the roof, and no one had come down. I discovered afterwards that I was not the only soldier or non-soldier to have seen the ghost. One of our Indian cooks told me that what I had seen was the ghost of a soldier who had cut his throat at the top of the steps many years before I was born.'

In the First World War, in 1915, Canadian soldiers billeted at Cheriton Grange, near Folkestone refused to stay in it after a ghost had wandered in and out of rooms. No disciplinary action was taken against the men, for the disturbances were so chronic and so alarming—and furthermore were attested by so many of the men—that it was pointless to argue. The house was pulled down in 1918 but even than a local man saw a woman wandering amongst the debris. When he called out to her that it wasn't safe, she vanished into thin air.

In the last war, when the Allied Military Mission commandeered a house in Iserlohn, one of the secretaries found herself persistently hurled out of bed. There was nothing wrong with the strong lock on the bedroom door; nevertheless, despite the door being locked it would open of its own accord and then slam back with a terrific bang. It was discovered that a murder had taken place in that room a few years earlier.

A few years ago the police training centre at Ipoh in what was then Central Malaya was plagued by the legless ghost of a Ghurka soldier who had been shot one moonlit night about seven years previously. The two thousand trainees were terrified at the sight, and one policeman died from the after-effects of fright. Eventually the authorities, concerned at the increasing reluctance of the men to go on jungle patrols, called on medicine men to placate the departed spirit with offers of saffron rice and mutton. But the men claimed that nothing would satisfy the outraged spirit but to disinter his corpse from his grave near the centre, cremate it and send the ashes back to his native Nepal. I have not investigated this particular story, which had wide currency at the time.

Malaysia has a fair share of military ghosts. Mr. D. C. Horton, broadcasting in the Home Service in 1959, described how, on being posted to Kuala Selangor he found himself in an historic place, notorious for what were called 'presences' which lived on Kuala Selangor Hill. The houses on the hill had been occupied during the war, and the wife of a police officer had a terrifying experience:

'She was sitting in her bungalow one evening, waiting for her husband to return from work, when she heard steps coming up the hill path. Coming nearer and nearer, they sounded as though they were being made by heavy boots. She thought at first that it was one of the constables coming up with a message. Then the steps came to the house and on to the veranda but when she looked up, there was nothing there. The steps came slowly past her down the veranda, across the dining-room and into the kitchen, where they stopped. For a while she dared not move, then plucking up her courage she went over to the kitchen, but there was no sign of anyone. The only explanation was that a Japanese officer had lived there in the occupation and had been accustomed to climb that path at about that time.'

In 1961 sixteen RAOC reservists in training packed their bags and got out of Hut 106 during the summer camp at Arncott, near Bicester, Oxon. Two rather sceptical officers, Captain N. Waterhouse and Lieutenant Gurney were sent to the hut to investigate. They spread powder on the floor and waited for results. During the night there was—as the previous occupants had all the time insisted—an eerie pattern of footsteps within the hut. But there was no imprint whatever in the powder.

Many men have objected to sentry duty at St. Mary's Barracks, Chatham, because of the haunting of the ramparts during the middle watch, from midnight to 4 a.m. There were persistent reports of mysterious footsteps and a tap-tap as though of a walking stick being used by its owner to feel his way. Once a sentry flew to the guardroom in a panic, claiming that he had seen the ghost of an old-time sailor hobbling along on a crutch, and his description tallied with the uniform worn by sailors in Nelson's time. But the authorities take a more prosaic view, for the pacings of sentries echo through the underground passages, giving a man the feeling that he is being followed.

From Mr. Arthur Holmes who was a trooper serving with the Royal Army Veterinary Corps remounts unit during the last war, I heard of what he describes as 'a very strange happening' which he witnessed while stationed at Rossington Hall in the course of his army service. Here is his story, in his own words:

'Rossington Hall, a very old mansion standing between Doncaster and Bawtry, was taken over by the army authorities. The troops were accommodated in huts dotted about in the woods facing the stable yard of the hall. The archway entrance to the yard had been built for the use of horse-drawn carriages, and on passing through the archway there were about twenty loose stable boxes arranged in a circular manner. Any person using this entrance could be clearly seen, whether by day or night.

'During the night a soldier was constantly on duty as stable guard. He would, from time to time, walk round with a storm lantern, attending to the animals under his care.

'I had often heard men talk of seeing the old man who walked with two sticks passing through the stable yard at night. I took very little notice of this, but some time later I got out of bed one night to use the toilets situated near the entrance of the yard.

'As I approached, the guard on duty was standing inside the archway smoking a cigarette, and at that moment I saw a very old man walk from the hall towards the archway entrance. He was dressed in an old fashioned top hat and frock coat, and walked with great difficulty, aided by two walking sticks.

'The guard on duty then commenced his round of the stables, and I clearly saw the old man walk behind him, almost on his heels. I stood for a short time and watched them both. Then feeling something was wrong, I ran into the yard. The guard was astonished to see me and wished to know why I had come in to the yard at such an hour, the time being 1.30 a.m. He assured me, on hearing my story, that he had been alone all night and had not seen or heard anyone. We searched the entire stables but could find no trace of anyone.

'The following day I mentioned this to Mr. Thomas Jenkinson, proprietor of the Mount Pleasant Hotel on the Bawtry Road. "That was the old man who owned the estate before the First World War," he said. Apparently, he often walked round during the night to see if his horses and property were safe.'

In reply to further questions, Mr. Holmes could not recall the name of the guard on duty, but he did say that he was a trooper serving with the Northumberland Hussars. Mr. Jenkinson died several years ago. But as to the reality of what he saw, Mr. Holmes is quite unshaken; and the corroboration of Mr. Jenkinson, when he reported the matter, does make his experience extremely interesting.

The phenomena of people getting, so to speak, outside of

themselves and observing themselves is not so unusual as one
might imagine. The scientific explanation of such a thing is
quite another matter, but there is no reason to doubt the testimony of those who have experienced such a thing, because the
sensations of those who have had no contact one with another
are strangely similar.

The following is a case from the *Journal of the Society for
Psychical Research*, Volume XXXIV, pp. 206-11:

'I was stationed in Aden in 1913 and was seriously ill with
dysentery. I got to the stage of having to be lifted from side to
side, as I was too weak to move myself in bed. From the instructions I heard the M.O. give the orderlies (we had no nurses in
Aden then) I gathered that a collapse was expected and that in
the event of the occurrence I was to be given a saline injection
via the rectum.

'Shortly afterwards, I found myself lying parallel to the bed,
about three or four feet above it and face downwards. Below me
I saw my body and witnessed the giving of the rectal injection.
I listened to all the conversations of the two orderlies and of a
strange M.O. who was directing affairs and was indeed an
interested spectator of the whole business. I remember well
that the saline came from an enamel kind of vessel which was
connected to a rubber tube—the vessel being held up at arm's
length by an orderly.

'I found myself next back in bed, feeling much better. I told
my story to the orderlies, who were quite sceptical. I particularly inquired about the strange M.O. I found there had been
one; he was *en route* for Bombay, I think, and had called at the
hospital in time to help. I never saw him again.

'I have always been convinced that my spirit (or soul if you
will) had actually left my body but returned as a result of the
injection. When kindred subjects have cropped up I have told
friends of my experience. They have listened in a tolerant
fashion, but I have always felt that my story was really being
received "with nods and becks and wreathed smiles". You can
imagine then how delighted I was to hear you relate an almost
similar experience.'

One can understand the feeling of incredulity when stories
are told by people who believe that they have left their bodies,
and returned. Yet in the case of this particular man, he observed something which could not have been revealed to him
except in unconsciousness—that there was a strange Medical
Officer on the job. He himself had never seen him. He was unconscious before, during and for some time after the operation.

Such incidents point strongly to the survival of some form of consciousness after death.

Another example of somebody 'looking down on themselves' was told to me by Mr. J. S. Dinsdale of Maghull, Liverpool:

'I had been working overtime one evening on stock-taking—a tiring and dirty job, as goods and fixtures were disturbed which had hardly been touched for twelve months. At the end of the day, when I was feeling anything but my best, I boarded the ferry boat to cross the river to Seacombe (an area of Wallasey).

'I was sitting in the saloon of the ferry boat, which had commenced the journey, when I had a vague and peculiar sensation of not being quite present on the seat. Instead of viewing the other few passengers and the saloon from the normal position on a seat, I appeared to be near the roof looking down at everyone and everything, and I saw myself sitting on a seat on the floor of the saloon. This sensation lasted about five seconds at the least, and probably nearer to ten seconds. In reviewing the occurrence at the time I was sure I had not fallen asleep and I remember even now the sensation I had of something momentous happening. During the incident I appeared to have no control over my body, which sat limply on the seat without movement.' At that time Mr. Dinsdale was a twenty-five-year-old student apprentice in a weaving factory at Fife.

I have mentioned before that the Battle of Edgehill was re-fought by ghostly hordes over three hundred years ago, but in more recent times a case quite as remarkable was reported to the Society for Psychical Research. The Society made intensive investigations into the matter and the result of their report is as follows:

In August, 1952, Mrs. Dorothy Norton, aged thirty-two and her two young children, in company with her sister-in-law Miss Agnes Lawton went for a holiday in Dieppe, the small fishing port which took such a battering during the war and which was the centre of the Dieppe raid, mounted from Britain, on August 19, 1942. Although not a spectacular holiday resort, the one-time lair of Norman pirates, with its old fortified castle and ancient churches, has a quiet charm of its own—and there is the sea and the homely activities of a port. Plenty to enable the two women to relax and for the children to explore and enjoy. The Nortons wanted a quiet holiday, but for reasons beyond all explanation—so far, at least—they didn't get it.

They chose as their pension a pleasant three-storied house facing the sea at Puys, a mile east of the town. It was supposed to have been used by German troops as a headquarters during the war. Dorothy and Agnes Norton shared a bedroom on the second floor, and the children shared a room two doors away. The beach, of which they had such a fine view, had been the scene of bitter and bloody fighting by British and Canadian troops, in a gallant exploit which was a reconnaissance in force designed to obtain information and experience as a prelude to a general offensive later on. Of a total raiding force of over 4,000 about 2,500 were killed, wounded or captured. Heavy casualties were expected as it was known that the operations were against a well-fortified and strongly-held coastline.

But for a mishap, the hoped-for element of surprise would have succeeded but at 3.30 a.m., the landing craft carrying No. 3 Commando ran into a number of armed enemy vessels which were protecting a tanker. The mere fact that the tanker was moving in those quarters was a sign that the enemy did not expect an attack. However, the minor naval engagement that ensued thoroughly alerted the German forces on coastal defence and as a result a large number of No. 3 Commando could not land in the Berneval area as planned, though a small detachment of this unit did.

At Varengeville, about five miles west of Dieppe, No. 4 Commando landed according to plan, storming the enemy battery, taking prisoners and destroying their guns and ammunition dumps.

At the same time as these assaults, Canadian troops were to land at Pourville and at Puys—the hamlet which the Nortons were to choose for their holiday nine years later. The task of troops landed at Puys was to secure the headland east of Dieppe, from which the enemy would otherwise menace the landing on the beach at Dieppe, but as the enemy had been alerted, this meant that the attack on the beach at Puys, delivered by the Royal Regiment of Canada, commanded by Lieutenant-Colonel D. E. Catto, had to be slightly delayed. This unit was to have landed at 4.50 a.m., when meteorologists had reckoned they would be partially protected by the enveloping darkness, but turning from their course at the time of the naval engagement, they landed twenty minutes late—in broad daylight. They were met with formidable defences and mown down with a deadly cross-fire from machine guns and mortars, and because this headland could not be cleared and held as hoped, the landings on the beaches elsewhere were in great jeopardy. Despite these hopeless odds the Canadians fought with the utmost gallantry.

These facts are worth restating in the light of what happened to the Nortons.

Their holiday was drawing to a close. It had been pleasant and uneventful. But at 4.20 a.m. on the morning of Saturday, August 4th, Agnes got out of bed, went out of the room and returned to say to Dorothy: 'Did you hear that noise.' Dorothy did, indeed, hear it—both the women, without saying anything to each other, had heard 'the noise' for the last twenty minutes, and both had been wondering that on earth it was all about. They could hear the rattle of machine-gun fire, cries, shouts, words of command. Together they went out on to the balcony and listened. Above the hubbub could be heard the crash of guns and the whine of dive-bombers.

It seemed extraordinary that the children had not been similarly awakened—indeed, why hadn't the other hotel guests been awakened from their sleep, and come to see what all the racket was about?

Then, at 4.50 a.m. (they looked at their watches) there was a lull in the noise. But at 5.5 a.m. it started up again, louder than ever. There was a lull again at 5.40, but more noise burst forth at 5.50, the sound of aeroplanes being expecially noticeable. By 6.20 the sounds seemed of the same character, but more distant.

Fortunately, the Nortons made a note of the times of these extraordinary noises, and it was later possible to confirm that these coincided with the sequence of events at the time of the Dieppe raid in 1942. For it was at 3.47 a.m. that the approaching vessels and landing craft ran foul of German vessels and the coastal defenders were thereby alerted. The time scheduled for landing, 4.50 a.m. was, in fact, a period of comparative silence because of the delay in landing caused by the naval engagement. It was at 5.7 a.m. that the landing was really effected and all hell broke loose; the bombardment of Dieppe by destroyers began at 5.12 a.m.; three minutes later Hurricanes swooped on the coastal buildings; at 5.20 a.m. the main Dieppe force, under intense cross-fire, began their heroic attack; at 5.40 there was a pause in the naval bombardment and at 5.50 forty-eight R.A.F. aircraft arrived from England to do battle in the air.

Mr. Guy W. Lambert, C.B., a former president of the Society for Psychical Research, spent months investigating the Nortons' story. Apart from the coincidence of the times, showing an analogy between the noises of the original Dieppe raid and those heard by the sisters, the obvious explanation of what they

had heard could be ruled out. For instance, they could not
have been listening to wind-borne noises of some war films
being shown in a cinema—there was no cinema in Puys, nor
was any radio programme of such a character being broadcast.

Could the Nortons have read up the times of the various
attacks and landings in some official account, and recounted
them afterwards? The answer is 'no, they could not have done'
for the official account of the Dieppe Raid was not published
until five months *after* their experience.

From Major G. N. Hampden Morris of Bacchus Cottage, Til-
ford, Surrey, I heard an account of 'the ghostly runner of
Waterloo'.

This ghost has been running ever since 1815!

Two and a half miles west of Aldershot Town and Barracks
lies a lane known as Alma Lane. To its north is the wild
country of Caesar's Camp, which, as its name implies, was
a spot where Romans were once stationed. Their barrows
remain but whether Caesar himself ever encamped there is
unknown.

When the news of the victory at Waterloo came over the hill
tops to Caesar's Camp an orderly was despatched to Aldershot
to bring the good news. Down the track that later became
Alma Lane he ran. It was wild country, and on his urgent
mission he was set upon and done to death. Alma Lane now
has a narrow pavement on one side which passes the strip
of garden of a cottage which Major Hampden Morris rented
after the Second World War. The lane was still a lonely place
at night.

'Twice,' Major Morris told me, 'I was puzzled between eleven
and midnight to hear the running steps of heavy boots. On a
third occasion I dropped my book and was out of the front
door as quickly as I could move. The lane was visible in the
moonlight to the bend 150 yards away, but there was not a soul
in sight, nor was there by now any sounds of footsteps, walking
or running. They had ceased as I got to the door.

'A hundred yards down the lane towards Aldershot and on
the opposite side is the Alma, a humble pub then kept by Mr.
Rob Adams. After hearing the ghost I went into the Alma for
my pint, and mentioned the curious "runner". Rob looked at
me, his eyes clear and genuine. "So *you've* heard the running
soldier, have you? You haven't seen him, though, now have
you?" He had heard the ghostly footsteps himself, and knew
many others who had as well.'

Major Morris stayed in that house—Known as Beam Cottage—in Alma Lane from 1946 to 1949. Both he and his wife heard the running on no less than three occasions, all within a fortnight during the winter of 1948.

15

Nautical ghosts

It is not so surprising that sailors as a class are both religious and superstitious. Free of the numberless distractions of city turmoil, the man at sea is near to nature and the tremendous forces, seen and unseen, which are generally held in balance and check. I remember a mate on the deep sea tug *Turmoil*— which is frequently at sea for weeks on end, and in rough waters, for it is a salvage vessel—saying to me on a trip we shared: 'Believe me, one never feels so near to God as when there's a storm blowing.' He did not mean this in the sense that he felt fear; what he experienced was a feeling of awe.

The innumerable stories told of ghosts at sea must be weighed against this fact. Monotony of routine, the fact that the spume of waves can swirl and coalesce and form fantastic shapes, that an incipient flash of moonlight, lasting perhaps a fraction of a second before the pale rays of light are obscured once more by a cloud, can produce a visual image—all these, I agree, are factors which the rational investigator of the occult and arcane should bear in mind.

But there are plenty of occurrences not so easily dismissed.

In response to an appeal which I wrote for original nautical ghost stories, kindly published by the *Shields Gazette*, I received from Mr. H. Davison of South Shields an account of the appearance of a ghost at sea:

'I am an ex-sea-going engineer. I first went to sea at twenty-one years of age and followed the sea for eleven years until I took up a shore appointment in 1947.

'In 1938 I was fourth Engineering Officer on board the S.S. *Brookwood* belonging to the Constantine Steamship Company of Middlesborough. We left the River Tyne on August 30th for Archangel to load timber for Durban, and after leaving Archangel in late September we sailed round the North Cape into the North Sea. Being fourth engineer I was on the eight to twelve watch and was on sole duty in the engine room. During the evening watch, at about 10.30 p.m., I was standing near the engine controls when I noticed a figure in a white boiler suit standing with his back towards me near the propeller shaft tunnel entrance. He stooped, and stepped through the open watertight door into the tunnel.

'Thinking that it was the Chief Engineer who occasionally came down to the engine room on a tour of inspection, I stood by the tunnel entrance waiting for the Chief to come out.

'I think here I should explain that the shaft tunnel was only wide enough to allow one man to walk alongside the shaft, and as was the practice with ships built before the war, an emergency escape up to the main deck was not provided and this meant that you had to come out by the same way as you entered.

'After waiting for some time I went into the tunnel to see what had detained the Chief but I went the whole length of the tunnel right up to the stern gland without seeing anyone.

'At breakfast next morning the Chief informed me that he had not been in the engine room the previous night, and was very concerned when I told him of my experience. He then told me that I was the third person to have had this experience in the engine room.

'He went on to tell me that his predecessor, while serving as Chief Engineer in the same ship had met a violent death while the ship was at Archangel on a previous voyage. It appears that the unfortunate man, being rather deaf, had not heard the Russian sentry's order to halt when walking through the docks, and had been shot dead.

'It may have been coincidence, but we had an engine break-down twenty-four hours later.

'The S.S. *Brookwood* was later lost by enemy action during the war.'

The *Flying Dutchman*, described by Sir Walter Scott, the Scottish novelist and poet, as a harbinger of doom, refers to a phantom ship alleged to have been seen near the Cape of Good Hope, easily identified because it bears a press of sail when all others fail to show an inch of canvas. The legend is that she was originally a treasure ship and that she was boarded by pirates who, after an orgy of murder and loot, were repaid for their wickedness by a frightful plague. In desperation they attempted vainly to put in at port after port, but so great was the fear of contagion that they were never allowed to anchor. They drifted until all died—and so the shade of the ship looms up at unexpected moments, to strike terror and apprehension into the heart of the toughest sailor.

Cornish tradition tells of a spectre ship to the westward of

St. Ive's Head, which appeared in the eighteenth century. One night a gig's crew was called to go to the rescue of a ship—thought from appearance to be a foreign trader—in distress. She was a schooner-rigged vessel and had a light over her bows. The men rowed with a will until the helmsman yelled 'stand by to board her!' The sailor rowing the bow oar slipped it out of the row-lock and prepared to spring aboard. The ship was so close that its crew could clearly be seen, and at the right moment the oarsman made a grasp at the bulwarks. But his hand grasped at air, despite what his eyes told him and he fell back into the boat telling his mates that there was simply nothing there. The ship and lights towards which they had rowed, and which they had held constantly in sight until they were next to it, just disappeared. The next morning the *Neptune*, whose Captain was Richard Grant, was wrecked at Gwithian with the loss of all hands.

In that story, the phantom ship appears to have fulfilled the same role as the 'death visitant' whose appearance presages a tragedy of some kind.

Sir Walter Scott, in his *Demonology and Witchcraft* tells the story of how an elderly member of the crew of a slave ship from Liverpool was shot in a fit of temper by the captain, whose agreeable disposition could become tyrannical and cruel under provocation.

This elderly man, Bill Jones, had incurred the captain's wrath by giving him an unsubordinate answer. As he lay dying he looked fixedly into the captain's eyes and said: 'Sir, you have done for me, *but I will never leave you.*' The captain cursed and abused the dying man, telling him he would have him thrown into the slave-kettle (in which food for the Negroes was prepared). The dead man was actually thrown into the slave-kettle. Thereafter the ghost of the dead sailor was seen frequently by members of the crew, who dared not mention it to the captain for fear of his wrath. But one day the captain told his mate: 'He told me he would never leave me, *and he has kept his word.* At this very moment I see him.' In desperation the captain hurled himself overboard and, as he was drowning, shouted to the mate: 'He is with me now!'

Blackwood's Magazine for 1840 contains a letter from a reader who saw a ghost at sea:

'The *Hawk* being on her passage from the Cape of Good Hope, towards the Island of Java, and myself having the charge of the middle watch, between one and two in the morning I was taken suddenly ill, which obliged me to send for the officer next in turn. I then went down on the gun-deck, and sent my boy for a light. In the meantime I sat down on a chest in the steerage, under the after-grating, when I felt a gentle squeeze by a very cold hand. I started and saw a figure in white. It stood and gazed at me a short time, stooped its head to get a more perfect view, sighed aloud, repeated the exclamation "Oh!" three times and instantly vanished. The night was fine, though the moon afforded through the gratings but a weak light, so that little of feature could be seen, only a figure rather tall than otherwise, and white-clad.

'My boy returning now with a light, I sent him to the cabins of all the officers, when he brought me word that not one of them had been stirring. Coming afterwards to St. Helena, home-ward-bound, hearing of my sister's death, and finding the time so nearly coinciding, it added much to my painful concern; and I have only to thank God that when I saw what I verily believe to have been her apparition (my sister Ann) I did not then know the melancholy occasion of it.'

This reminds me forcibly of a story which the late Captain Dod Orsborne, skipper of the *Girl Pat* during the Spanish Civil War, told me just after the last war. Orsborne, to recap a little, looked like a twentieth-century buccaneer—which, in effect, he was. His sun-tanned, lean face, intensely penetrating and deep-set eyes and goatee beard were a fair guide to his character. He was absolutely indifferent to danger and to authority, and had got into hot water by gun-running for the Republicans. As he has written his own memoirs, I will not attempt to catalogue his many other adventures. Suffice it to say he was a man of iron nerve and not the sort of man who 'sees things'. However, this is what he told me.

While on a particularly lonely watch in the North Sea, the spectre of the second mate who had served with him on the previous voyage (and had unaccountably not rejoined the ship) suddenly appeared on the bridge with him. Around the spectre, which was unmistakably that of his friend, was the suffusing, sweet smell of death, coupled with a feeling of intense cold and a kind of humming vibration.

'I have never been so terrified in my life,' Captain Orsborne told me, 'and was not ashamed to fly to my cabin and slam the door. But—and this is the most dreadful thing of all—the figure materialised at my bedside and actually spoke to me. I remember the words, which he repeated twice before he vanished: "Come and get me, Dod."

'Later we discovered that he had been attacked and robbed,

while about to join his ship, and had slipped into the water and been drowned. His body was discovered after we had set sail.'

Dod Orsborne's story has a sad and sinister sequel. He himself was attacked and murdered—sandbagged—on the docks at Marseilles. I have always regretted that I did not ask him at the time to fill in more details of his story, but at that time it was not in my mind to write a book on the subject of ghosts or indeed any book at all.

In the last century there were frequent reports of the appearance at Cap d'Espoir, in the Gulf of St. Lawrence, of the ghostly flagship of a fleet sent by Queen Anne to attack the forts and which was wrecked there. The phantom ship, laden with soldiers, carried lights. On the bowsprit stood an officer, pointing towards the shore, while a woman stood at his side. Then there would be a scream, the lights would go out, and the vessel would sink.

Bassett, in *Legends and Superstitions of the Sea,* tells of a phantom which saved a ship and its crew from shipwreck. The *Society,* bound for Virginia from England in 1664, was heading for the Capes, believed to be about three hundred miles ahead, when a vision appeared to Captain Rogers, R.N., who was in command. It told him to turn about and look around carefully. He did as bidden, but the phantom appeared again and told him to heave the lead. On doing this he was aghast to discover that the reading was only seven fathoms. He tacked ship, and when dawn rose saw that instead of being far out at sea he was actually under the Capes.

The *Chicago Times* of March, 1885 reported that following the death of two members of a lake vessel—the men had fallen from the top of the mast—the ship was thought to be a 'Jonah' by its crew who, on being paid off at Buffalo, were reluctant to rejoin it. A member of the crew continues the story:

'On its arrival at Buffalo, the men went on shore as soon as they were paid off. They said the ship had lost her luck. While we were discharging at the elevator, the story got round, and some of the grain-trimmers refused to work on her. Even the mate was affected by it. At last we got ready to sail for Cleveland, where we were to load coal.

'The captain managed to get a crew by going to a crimp, who ran them in, fresh from salt water. They came on board two-thirds drunk, and the mate was steering them into the forecastle when one of them stopped and said, pointing aloft: "What have you got a figurehead on the mast for?" The mate looked up and then turned pale. "It's Bill!" he said, and with that the whole lot jumped on to the dock. I didn't see anything, but the mate told the captain to look for another officer. The captain was so much affected that he put me on another schooner and then shipped a new crew, and sailed for Cleveland. They never got there. They were sunk by a steamer off Dunkirk.'

Mr. Frank D. Gardner of Derby Road, Southampton related to me the following story of how he encountered a ghost on a ship at sea. It appears to be an example of a death visitant—a ghost seen at sea but of somebody who was at that time dying on land, far away:

'Towards the end of the last war I served in the supply ship *Harrogate* as Stores Superintendent for the Ministry of Transport.

'With the capture of Southern Italy tension was easing and regulations relaxing. Thus it was that early in April, 1945, we were able to celebrate in Taranto Harbour by having a party of WRENS and WAAFS on board one night, and early into the next morning. They were, however, all safely ashore before we sailed at 0600.

'That same afternoon, as I was crossing through an alleyway that led completely from port to starboard of the forward accommodation, I saw a lady in one of the fore-side cabins—the door being open and just the door curtain hanging at one side.

'Very startled and surprised, and not wishing to intrude, I walked on and out by the starboard side on to the deck. There I saw the Chief Officer (a Mr. White) and called him.

' "Who's the dame in the spare cabin?" I asked excitedly.

'He looked blankly at me, then replied, "Dame! Dame! There's no dame aboard this hooker, I'll swear."

' "But are you sure," I asked, "that none of those girls from the party didn't stow away? There'll be a hell of a row about this unless we can smuggle her ashore in Ancona."

'I stepped into the alleyway again. The Chief Officer followed me. We went straight to the spare cabin and I peeped in furtively, but there was no one there. Quickly I passed on to the other cabins. The doors were all open but there was no one inside. Then to the Chief Steward's cabin, where the door was closed. I knocked. He opened. "Is there a woman in here?" I gasped. The Steward eyed me up and down. "Wish there was!" he retaliated.

'I turned to the Chief Officer again. "Was the ship inspected before we left port?" I queried.

'Impatiently he replied: "Of course! I made the rounds in

the usual way, and with the second and third Mates on the job as well."

'My mind was now in a whirl. I went to the spare cabin again. What had I seen? was the thought agitating me. I studied the room. Though only a fleeting glance, the woman I had seen was so vivid. I shook the curtain, trying to make a similar reflection in the Compactum mirror. I tried the port glass at all angles. I did all I could think of to simulate, from the contents of the cabin, something which I *could* have mistaken for a black dress, lace trimmings, brown hair and fair face. I felt a complete fool. The Chief Officer and the Chief Steward accepted my apologies with a grin—and a wink at each other.

'It was the end of 1945 before I reached home again. My wife and I were discussing the contents of various letters which had passed between us. Among other things she mentioned the illness and death of an Aunt Katie (not a real aunt but a lady whom, due to her fondness for our children, we had got into the habit of calling "Aunt").

'To my astonishment, I had not heard of this. Not all letters, chasing ships around, arrived at their correct addresses. So she told me again of Aunt Katie's illness, and her sister chimed in: "And do you know that her last words were 'If only Frank had been here.'"

' "When did she die?" I asked.

' "April the fourth!"

'My thoughts went back to the appearance of the figure on the ship for it was about that time that I had had the hallucination. So I told my wife and her sister of my experience, and when I had finished they said, almost together: "That was just the way that Aunt Katie used to dress." '

Aunt Katie was Mrs. Girdlestone. Mr. Gardner assures me that on the day he saw the vision she had not been in his mind at all. 'Neither,' he says, 'can I say that the woman I saw even suggested Aunt Katie to me. Indeed, Aunt Katie as I knew her was deeper in complexion and her hair was a little gingerish. The woman I saw was very pale and her hair, high on her head, was very fair. I had never seen Aunt Katie dressed in black, though my wife says she dressed in black after the death of her husband about a year before. The black dress of the woman I saw was the most impressive part, relieved only by the lace cuffs and collar. Yet I wondered myself afterwards how I saw so much in just a passing glance.'

None of the ladies who had been guests on board fitted Mr. Gardner's description of the vision he saw, and after a thorough search was made of the vessel no unauthorised person was found on board, so Mr. Gardner's experience must remain a mystery.

A century ago the Admiralty had a surveying vessel, H.M.S. *Asp*, which had such a persistent reputation for being haunted that crews were constantly refusing to serve in it. Its Commander, Captain Alldridge, R.N., said later in life that when the ship was entrusted to him in 1850 it was already said to be unlucky, and he was warned that he might have difficulty in getting men to serve in it. The shipwrights engaged in repairs to her came to him as a group and begged him to have nothing to do with the ship.

The Captain had not long been in command when these prophecies began to be fulfilled. It was the Captain's pleasure to get an officer to read aloud to him in his cabin in the evening, and he noted that the reading was often interrupted by unexplainable noises such as a drunken man might make when reeling about and banging into things. The noises seemed to come from the after, or Ladies' cabin, which was separated from the Captain's cabin by a companion ladder. From his cabin, the Captain could see anyone ascend or descend the ladder, and could see through the windows of the door opposite, because the cabin doors faced each other. Shortly after they set sail, for the River Dee, when the din from that near-by cabin was intolerable, he shouted 'Don't make such a noise, Steward!' and, this warning being ignored, he seized a candle and rushed into the cabin, to find it empty.

One evening he and his friend returned to the ship at about 10 p.m. from a visit to a house in Chester, and while they were descending the companion ladder they distinctly heard somebody rush from the after cabin into the fore cabin. He immediately went to his cabin, took the sword which hung over his bed, placed it in the officer's hand and told him to allow no one to pass. He then returned to his cabin and searched every inch of it, but found no sign of anyone.

Often, lying in his cabin alone, he would hear drawers open and shut, banging near his bed and a sense of some presence near him. One night, when the vessel was at anchor in Martyn Roads, he was awakened by a panic-stricken quartermaster, who maintained that he had seen the ghostly figure of a woman in the paddle-box, her finger pointed to the sky. This particular apparition was frequently seen by others. One Sunday afternoon, when the captain and the steward were the only men on board (the vessel was lying at anchor in the Haverfordwest river) the steward, while descending the companion ladder, was spoken to by an invisible presence. He collapsed with fright and, sick with abject terror, begged the captain to give him a discharge immediately—he could not even face the prospect of another night on board. The Captain, on the basis of his own eerie experiences, agreed.

It says much for the Captain's stubborn spirit that he continued his command. According to his account, he was once, while asleep in his bed, awakened by a ghostly hand touching his leg outside the bed-clothes. He made a grab for it, but found nothing. On another occasion, when he was not even asleep, he felt a cold, clammy hand touch his forehead.

The phantom of the *Asp* seems, by all accounts, to have been extraordinarily persistent in its manifestations. In 1857, when the ship docked at Pembroke for repairs, a sentry stationed near the ship saw the phantasm of a lady in white mount the paddle-box and with her hand outstretched towards the sky, step ashore and come along the path towards him. The sentry brought his musket to the ready and issued a challenge, which the ghost ignored by coming towards and *through* him. Being human, as well as a sentry, he dropped his weapon in terror and raced for the guard-house, while another sentry who had seen it all fired his gun to alert the guard. The figure glided past a third sentry towards the ruins of Pater Old Church; moved towards a grave in the churchyard and, finger still pointing to the sky, vanished.

The men told their incredible story to the sergeant of the guard, and so frightened and unanimous were they that no question of indiscipline or cowardice could arise. After that, so long as H.M.S. *Asp* was in dock, the sentries would not do duty singly, and their experiences were duly reported in the 'Report of the Guard'.

What no one had told the Captain, and what he was left to discover for himself in due course, is that prior to his taking the vessel over for survey work, it had been the scene of a peculiarly horrible and wholly unexplained murder or suicide. The *Asp* had at one time been used as a mail packet between Port Patrick and Donaghadee. At the conclusion of one voyage, when it was thought that all passengers had disembarked, a stewardess on entering the ladies' cabin found a young and lovely girl, dead with terrible throat wounds. Nobody ever discovered who she was, how she came to be on the vessel nor who was responsible for her death.

This haunting is of particular interest because at the time there were so many witnesses to it. Superstitious apprehension might explain some hysteria—but many witnesses, such as the sentries, were unaware of the ship's reputation.

In response to my appeal in the *Nautical Magazine* for nautical ghost stories I received from Mr. J. C. Davies of Porth, Rhondda, Glamorganshire, a strange story of how the ghost of a dead seaman came to him, although he did not actually *see* it.

It was in June, 1946, that a shipmate of his, John Gooding, an ordinary seaman of eighteen years who came from Cardiff, stumbled on the accommodation ladder on entering the living quarters at about 7 p.m. in the evening. In falling he received a severe blow in the abdomen, which proved fatal. The ship was the *Ocean Volunteer*.

When Mr. Davies was taking watch on the forecastle head, on the night his friend had died, he became conscious of his friend's presence, and this distinct feeling that 'something' was there lasted a long time—from half to three-quarters of an hour. Although there was no appearance, Mr. Davies told me that accompanying the sensation of there being an invisible presence was 'a most profound stillness and a sense of deep, deep, solitude prevailed'. This happened while the coal-burning tramp steamer was on its usual run from the Bristol Channel to Trois Rivieres, St. Lawrence. It was taking coal on its outward journey. In reply to further questions, Mr. Davies informed me that he has never had a similar experience since—nor had he known anything like it before.

I am well aware of the difficulty of conveying the intensity of an experience of this kind, which some might think subjective. But 'ghosts' which are sensed but neither seen nor heard, are not unknown.

16

Haunted furniture

Some years ago a series of poltergeist disturbances at the thirteenth-century Stanbury manor caused suspicion to centre upon a sinister-looking chest. Its shape was reminiscent of a coffin and on the outside were carved figures, including one of a woman holding a corpse.

Pictures and shotguns would fall from the walls and so many things happened that the 'presence' was nicknamed 'Old George' by Mr. T. A. Ley, the owner of the manor.

Mr. Ley noted that the disturbances dated from the time that he bought the chest from an antique shop and brought it into his home. He appealed to the local vicar, the Rev. K. Rees, to investigate the matter, and one of the first things the vicar discovered was that the arm of the carved figure holding the corpse was actually blood-stained. There was another blood-stain on the carved body of a headless man.

The chest would have made a hiding place for a corpse. The blood-stains suggested that it might have been so used centuries ago.

Furniture which becomes a focal point for unexplained disturbances is often reported from various parts of the world. One interesting story which came to my attention, originally by the good offices of Mr. Bernard Kelly of the *Denver Post,* concerns a haunted clock owned by Miss Helen Verba, a member of that newspaper's staff. The clock has been in her family for five generations, and on several occasions has stopped at the minute that a member of her family has died.

It stopped at the hour and minute of the death of her great-great-grandfather, Charles Spelman, then, when it became the property of Helen Verba's great uncle, Emerson Spelman, it stopped again when he died—at the very moment of his death. From Emerson Spelman the clock passed to Helen's grandfather, R. J. Spelman, and, sure enough, when *he* died it stopped at the hour and minute of his death.

When Miss Verba's father inherited the clock, he was in no

great mood to have it on display at all. There's something disturbing about having a clock which seems to have a prescience of death. So he put it away and out of sight.

Eventually, Miss Verba decided that she would try and sell it—when people die in the family one knows all about it without requiring confirmation from an old clock—so she took it to Richard's Antiques, 600 Ogden Street, Denver, Colorado. Some time after that the proprietor, Richard Vaughn, went to look at it and could scarcely believe his eyes for the dial of the clock had turned upside down! The XII was where the VI should be, and vice versa. It was not to be explained by the vibrations of passing traffic or some accidental jolt: the dial was fastened on.

There was a further sequel when Orin A. Sealy, a photographer, arrived to take a picture of the clock and its inverted dial. Although some of the works had been removed, while Sealy was adjusting his camera the clock suddenly started to run.

Miss Verba told me: 'After father and mother died (he on February 22, 1954, she on April 11, 1957) I found the clock in the basement of our home wrapped in a blanket and hidden, or forgotten, in an old trunk. I didn't think it a very pretty clock so made no attempt to resurrect it. I just kept it, storing it away in an out-of-the-way place as I moved from apartment to apartment. Upon my last move, since it was a burdensome item, I turned it over to an antique dealer on a consignment basis. I still own it. Although the clock has brought considerable traffic into his shop, out of curiosity I suspect, it hasn't been sold.

'I remember my father saying the clock originally had wooden wheels and wooden pegs instead of nails. However, when my antique dealer and I removed the back recently we found large brass wheels and the back attached with screws. If my memory hasn't played tricks on me and if my father was talking about this same clock, I can only deduce that the works were replaced at some time or other during the years.

'I've searched and searched through old papers but can find no mention of who was the first to own the clock. But I must admit I was somewhat bewildered when I ran across a notation my father had made on a paper containing dates of when he took various degrees in the Masonic Lodge, which read: "Clock arrived at Denver, Colorado, Tuesday, March 23, 1909 at 8 o'clock—morning." I can't help but wonder why of all the things which were shipped from Massachusetts to Denver, the clock was of such importance to him that he made a note of it.'

The haunted clock has a date on it—either May 10, 1850 or 1859 (the last figure is hard to read). It strikes on the hour and half-hour and has an unusually pretty tone. This puzzles Miss Verba because her parents were the sort who never threw anything away. The clock is black iron inlaid with mother-of-pearl. It weighs 12½ pounds and is 17 inches high and 9 inches wide. An instruction paper on the inside of the back board is barely legible and most of the instructions are covered with the clock's works (another reason for me to believe the original works have been replaced). The advertisement at the bottom can just be deciphered with the help of a magnifying glass. It says: 'Plain, Ornamental, Inlaid Pearl and Fancy Eight Day and One Day Brass Clocks and Marine Time Pieces. Manufactured and sold by Upson Brothers, Marion, Conn.'

A remarkable example of a haunted chair came to my notice many years ago when I was collecting material on ghosts. It came from Mrs. Barbara L. Barnes of Waterside, Barton-on-Humber:

'I have always longed for an antique chair. Last year my husband bought one at a sale in Retford and although it was without any covering I liked it very much as soon as I saw it.

'Unfortunately, my husband was away and unable to re-upholster it, so we put it in the children's playroom—and there it stayed until the two little ones, Vicky Rose and Piers, were taken ill with tonsilitis when we had to move the chair out of the playroom into the kitchen so that we could have their beds downstairs for convenience of nursing them.

'We put the chair at the end of the long kitchen table facing the hall door, and with its back to the scullery door. As I went through the kitchen with a tray—facing the chair—I gave a shout, for someone was sitting in the chair watching me. Yet when I looked again it had gone. Telling myself how silly I was I turned to have another look (on my return journey from the scullery)—and there it was again: the impression of an old man with dark hair and white narrow trousers, looked at me with a most kind and benign expression. Then it vanished, and feeling very shaken, but determined not to see things, I went on attending to the two children which kept my mind occupied, to say nothing of my hands. Several times on going through I saw the same thing, till I stood still and said "What is it you want?"

'To be within call, I had my lunch at the opposite end of the table facing the chair, and propped a newspaper up in front of me with my thoughts occupied, when "he" was there again, quietly watching me, then vanished. The rest of the afternoon was spent with the invalids. Later, the other three girls returned from school and took their tea in the kitchen, but I carefully refrained from mentioning the ghost I had seen to any of them. The two older girls (fourteen and eleven) went out to their Guides and choir practice leaving Jo'ella (aged nine) alone. I then left the kitchen to wash the little ones for the night. When I returned, Jo said: "Mummy, do you know, it is silly, but I went up to that chair and I thought Anne was sitting there, and I said 'Oh, Anne, do come and play' and when I looked it wasn't Anne at all but an old man with dark hair and a real thin white face. And while I was looking there wasn't anybody there at all."

'This is an *exact* account. The child must have seen something because she hadn't known I'd seen it too. Also, she came up *behind* the chair and looked over the wings when she saw what she thought was Anne's dark hair.'

I went to Barton-on-Humber to inspect the chair. When purchased it had been upholstered in plain canvas, and there had been no stuffing coming through, which by an optical delusion might have given children the idea that they were looking at the hair of a person sitting in the chair. The canvas was left on when the chair was upholstered in brocade, being used as a basis. The ghost did not appear after the chair was upholstered, at least not in the chair; but one evening the door of Mrs. Barnes' bedroom opened unaccountably and 'quite frankly I was so petrified that it was half an hour before I could get up and close it.'

Before the last war, to be precise, on the evening of March 7, 1929, a little girl called Lucie was lying ill on a small iron bed in a house in Charlottenburg, a suburb of Berlin. There had been reports that since her uncle died persistent disturbances had broken out in the house, and seemed in some strange way to be centred around the child.

Five doctors, one of whom, Dr. Hermann Neugarten, wrote a detailed account of the proceedings, gathered round her bed and all heard a succession of bumps, thuds, knockings and rappings for which no rational explanation such as subterranean disturbances, vibrations transmitted by passing traffic, minor earth movements, practical joking and other fakery could be found. But the wierdest manifestation of all, which gave even the doctors the creeps, was *the doll that danced*. The child's doll, about six inches high, jigged up and down as though propelled by an invisible hand. Furthermore, when Lucie's brother played his accordion, the doll danced to the tempo of the music, changing as the music changed, faster and faster, or slower and slower. When Lucie spoke to the 'presence' of her dead uncle and asked him to make the doll dance, the doll would immediately begin to move.

Stories of haunted furniture are fairly numerous but accounts of haunted toys are on the whole uncommon. Toys or models associated with magical rituals, or used for symbolic purposes in religious ceremonies, sometimes appear to have 'something' about them. In 1958, for example, there was the odd case of a salesman, Richard Crocker who, seeing in Sotheby's famous auction rooms in London a box containing some dolls once used in ancient Egypt in connection with funeral rites, felt impelled to touch one for curiosity. The little figures, known as Ushtabi Dolls, lay like miniature mummies in their decorative box. In the instant that Crocker touched the doll his infant daughter at home five miles away had, for no known reason, a fit. Exactly a year later, by a coincidence, Crocker happened to spot, in the window of an antique shop, another Egyptian Ushtabi doll. At the moment the object attracted his glance his daughter again succumbed to a fit. Coincidence?

Mrs. Barnes' haunted chair has a companion somewhere in America. The facts, according to my informant, Miss Stella Metchling of Woodlaw Avenue, Ashville, N.C., U.S.A., are these:

Some years ago Miss Metchling was living in an apartment house in Starnes Avenue, Asheville. The owner of the house was an invalid and an atheist, who lived in a wheel chair whose rumbling and squeaking perpetually announced the lady's movements. At last she was taken more seriously ill, and when she was dying the local minister called expecting that his kind offices would make her last hours peaceful and more bearable. But she rejected his offer with scorn, saying that she had lived long enough whout prayer and did not propose to pay lip-service to something in which she did not believe, simply because she was dying.

On the night she lay dying, 'the door which connected the attic with the hall flew open and a big bulky object which she couldn't see came through the hall and out of the front door. Everyone in the apartment house heard it. The next day she passed away.'

Her body was taken to the mortuary. The rug which was in

her room was taken away by relatives, but her wheel chair was left in the room. The windows and doors were locked and sealed after a formaldehyde candle had been burned to disinfect the room.

That same night, at about ten o'clock, the dead woman's wheel chair began to move noisily about the room, as if being used by somebody angrily trying to get out. The chair rolled around the bare floor, occasionally banging with much force against the inside of the door. Terrified, Miss Metchling and another lodger listened, and they were too scared to go to bed. Sometimes the door of the bathroom would open and shut with a bang. The racket went on all night.

The same thing happened to a rocking-chair which had belonged to the deceased. It was an antique rocker, and Miss Metchling bought it and moved it to Charlotte, N.C., with some other furniture.

One night Miss Metchling was reading in bed when the rocker began to rock. It would rock for a few seconds, then stop suddenly as though pulled up with a jerk. There was absolutely no draught in the room. Of the chair's present activities, I have no direct information. 'I gave it to a cousin' Miss Metchling informs me, 'who has such a large family that it doesn't have a chance to rock as there is always someone in it'.

Hampton, one of the great post-Revolution mansions of America, is said to have haunted chandeliers. But first a word about this huge house, built between 1783 and 1790 in Maryland, and serving for 158 years as the home of the Ridgely family, whose roots go deep in Maryland history. The Ridgelys came from England to St. Mary's County. The third Ridgely known as 'Charles the Merchant' moved to Baltimore County and acquired 'Northampton', a 1,500-acre tract laid out in the wilderness half a century before. This was the beginning of a vast estate and palatial home, for within five years it had extended to 7,000 acres and, iron ore deposits being found, the 'Northampton Works' were founded (it supplied military stores, including cannon and shot, to the patriot forces during the Revolution). The home became grander as the family became richer and more distinguished, and one of its striking features was and is the splendid collection of chandeliers which add grace and opulence to the mansion.

And therein lies a story. For many generations, according to legend, a terrible crash of falling glass—an utterly shattering noise as though one of the chandeliers has fallen, followed by a few odd tinklings as though scraps of displaced glass are coming to rest—has been heard by everyone in the house. Inevitably everyone rushes to the scene of the noise, expecting to find chaos and destruction and, just as inevitably, they find—nothing. But within a day or at the very most two days, the head of the maternal side of the family dies.

It has happened many times. It presaged the death of Mrs. Ridgely, the fifth Lady of Hampton. It was an Easter Monday, while Mrs. Ridgely was sitting with her daughters, that a tremendous crash and splintering of glass was heard. Her daughters and Lena Bevan, the housekeeper, rushed to the spot from which the noise came. Nothing was to be seen there, nor anywhere else in the house. Mrs. Ridgely died within a day.

But Mrs. Pauline McPherson, the Resident Curator of Hampton National Historic Site says that although 'there are numerous persons who claim they have seen and heard these ghosts' (for there are numerous ghosts at Hampton besides the ghostly sounds I have just mentioned) she herself has had no experience of them during her seven years' residence in the house. However, she does believe in extra-sensory perception.

From my friend Mr. Simeon Edmunds, a member of the Society for Psychical Research and a noted hypnotist, I heard a remarkable story concerning an African ju-ju stick now in his possession. A few years ago a Mrs. Sarah Mollet of Trinity, Jersey, who was at that time eighty years old and has since died, wrote to ask if he would be interested in a strange carved stick which was in her possession and which she would like to give away.

Giving it away had hitherto proved a little difficult. She had bought her house about thirty years before, the previous owner having returned to Africa, where he died in mysterious circumstances. One day she found in the loft this stick which, as a curiosity, she gave to her brother. He took it with him to Canada, but bad luck pursued him to such an extent in all his ventures that, suspecting the stick to be the cause in some strange way, he asked an expert on African witchcraft about it. The expert said unhesitatingly that the stick was a malignant influence and should be returned without further ado to whoever had given it to him, adding that on no account must it be destroyed, since this would bring death to the perpetrator of such an act. With this dire warning ringing in his ears, the brother forthwith returned the stick to his sister, who then endured a run of bad luck.

Mr. Edmunds, who has investigated many psychic phenomena, quite willingly took custody of the stick. 'It doesn't worry me,' he told me, 'but some visitors react very strongly to it. I once had a patient who positively refused to stay in the same room with it, so powerful an emanation of menace it implied to him.'

Are there haunted pictures?

Many years before the war I came to know Austin Osman Spare, an artist who lived in Walworth and who claimed to be one of the founders of surrealism. A superb portraitist, he also produced a great number of fantasies in which nymphs, dryads, fawns and vaguely demoniac creatures disported themselves in an unreal and, at times, strange and terrifying world. He was, all his life, keenly interested in the occult—even as a youth—and exhibited at the Royal Academy at the age of sixteen. He wrote several illustrated books on the occult which may be seen in the British Museum. Nobody can doubt, seeing those strange illustrations with their obscure symbolism, that they have about them a brooding melancholy, perhaps even a sense of menace.

Spare maintained a staggering output of work, holding his exhibitions at first in West End art galleries but latterly, having become a virtual hermit in a house in South London, in public houses. He despised money and wrote long treatises on magic and the occult. Towards the end of his life he drew what he described as 'Magical Stelle', in which he incorporated invocations drawn in a code of his own. After his death I gave one of these as a gift to a friend on a magazine, only to receive an urgent request some weeks later that I take it back! I suggested it might save her time if it were left at a club near by, and somehow it got lost. I cannot, therefore, say who the present owner is or whether it can have affected their fortunes for good or ill. But recently I wrote to my friend, who is now in America and posed the simple question: 'Why did you want to get rid of it?' The answer was as straightforward as my query—that from the moment of taking possession of it, it seemed, in some strange way, that literally everything went wrong. The thing seemed to have a baleful influence. The run of bad luck ceased immediately she parted with it.

It could, of course, have been association of ideas. Although so engrossed in the occult, Spare was in private life a kindly man with a wide circle of friends, and greatly liked by the costermongers and barrow-boys whose company he enjoyed so much. Artists such as Frank Brangwyn and collectors such as

Lord Howard de Walden were amongst the fervent admirers of
his art. But, as George Bernard Shaw once remarked, 'Spare's
work is too strong a meat for the normal'. Perhaps Shaw was
right.

17

Ghostly animals

Since phantasms were first seen, there have been reports of ghostly animals. So far as folk-lore is concerned. I do not doubt that many of the stories told are vestigial remnants of old religious or superstitious beliefs, based on the belief that gods and human beings could assume the form of animals. Hunt, in *Popular Romances of the West of England* says that in the last century the belief was still current in Cornwall that a woman seduced and betrayed, and who died forsaken and broken-hearted, would return to haunt her deceiver in the form of a white hare. Such a phantom hare would be invisible to all except the false lover whom it was intended to punish and persecute. In *Shropshire Folklore* one reads of a woman who at her request was buried with her jewels when she died. A clerk rifled the grave, and the outraged spirit of the woman assumed the form of a colt, known locally as Obrick's Colt, from the name of the thief, who was driven to despair and the exposure of his misdeeds by the persistent attentions of the ghostly colt.

Ghost dogs are connected with many sinister happenings of the past. A strange story once attached to the village of Dean Combe, Devon. A prosperous weaver, having died, was found after death to be hard at work, as usual, at his loom and shuttle. His family invoked the aid of the local parson, who in a commanding voice told the weaver, Knowles, to leave his shuttle and come down at once. This the weaver declined to do until he had worked out his quill, but in response to further commands, he came down to the parson, who straightway threw in his face a handful of consecrated earth from the churchyard. At this the ghost became immediately transformed into a black hound.

A correspondent of the *Book of Days*, published last century, described how in Tring, Hertford, an old woman was drowned in 1751 for alleged witchcraft, while the chimney-sweeper who murdered her was himself hanged in chains near the scene of his crime. Thereafter, it was said, a large black spectral dog haunted the spot:

'I was returning home late at night in a gig with the person who was driving. When we came near the spot, where a portion of the gibbet had lately stood, he saw on the bank of the road-side a flame of fire as large as a man's hat. "What's that?" I exclaimed. "Hush!" said my companion, and suddenly pulling in his horse, came to a dead stop. I then saw an immense black dog just in front of our horse, the strangest looking creature I ever beheld. He was as big as a Newfoundland, but very gaunt, shaggy, with long ears and tail, eyes like balls of fire, and large, long teeth, for he opened his mouth and seemed to grin at us. In a few minutes the dog disappeared, seeming to vanish like a shadow, or to sink into the earth, and we drove on over the spot where he had lain.'

Around Leeds there used to be frequent reports of a ghostly donkey 'with shaggy hair and eyes like saucers' known locally as 'Padfoot', supposed to run on two or three legs. To see it was considered a sure indication of approaching death. It is told in Henderson's *Folklore of Northern Counties* that on one occasion a man going home by Jenkin saw a white, spectral dog in a hedge and, lunging at it with his stick, was appalled to note that his stick went right through it. He raced home in terror, and died shortly afterwards of fright.

There are similar legends in many counties: the Boggart of Lancashire—a large black dog with luminous, malevolent eyes —was supposed to be a harbinger of death, while ghostly dogs, to see which was an invariable presage of misfortune, were once said to haunt the locality of Throstlenest, between Darlington and Houghton, and between Wreghorn and Headingly Hill, near Leeds.

During the Peninsular War the Duke of Wellington, whose men had dug in behind the lines of Torres Vedras, had a pack of foxhounds sent out from England so that his men could relieve the tedium of waiting with a good, vigorous fox-hunt. A famous sportsman of the time, Crane, took them out hunting, since then the local inhabitants have often claimed to see a ghostly pack, led by a spectral huntsman, in hot and noisy pursuit.

J. C. Couch, in *Folklore of a Cornish Village* describes a ghostly pack encountered by 'a poor herdsman journeying home-ward across the moors one windy night, when he heard at a distance among the Tors the baying of hounds, which he soon recognised as the dismal chorus of the dandy-dogs. It was three or four miles to his house and, very much alarmed, he hurried onward as fast as the treacherous nature of the soil and the uncertainty of the path would allow; but, alas! the melancholy yelping of the hounds and the dismal holloa of the hunter, came nearer and nearer. After a considerable run they had so gained upon him that on looking back—oh, horror!—he could distinctly see hunter and dogs. The former was terrible to look at, and had the usual complement of *saucer eyes,* horns, and tail, accorded by common consent to the legendary devil. He was black, of course, and carried in his hand a long hunting pole. The dogs, breathing fire and yelping mournfully, were about to descend upon him when in a moment of desperation and inspiration he fell on his knees and prayed. The pack drew off from him and continued their ghostly pursuit in another direction.

A ghostly dog was often seen in her childhood by Mrs. Patricia Bick of Redland, Bristol, who told me:

'I was born and lived in a haunted house, called Holly Bank House, Arvagh Cavan, Ireland. Passing the gatekeeper's lodge you had to go up a long drive to the house. Half-way up a large black dog appeared, or a lady in white. No rider on horseback could ride past this spot mounted—the horse stopped dead, or reared and went backwards. The dog always went through a window at garden level and the lady also. My people had all seen this strange apparition and I personally saw the black dog. It was said by local people that a man had shot himself there. However, we left there soon after—having sold the house and the ghost.'

In reply to further questions, Mrs. Bick told me that Holly Bank was 'a rather small, ornate house with a lodge containing, usually, a gardener and a handyman who opened the gates for my mother and father as they rode in on horseback. Holly Bank was known as a haunted house; no tenant ever stayed long in it.'

From an old miner, Mr. T. Gibbon, of Kepier House Hostel, Gilesgate Moor, Durham, I have the following very clear recollection of his encounter with a ghostly pit pony in a disused mine working:

'This experience is true in every detail. The year was 1919 and it was my job to descend the pit every night to relieve a man at the electric pumps. This particular incident took place in a worked-out coal seam in which no one was employed but the pumpman. On New Year's Eve I went to work as usual at about 9.30 p.m. Before descending the pit I looked in at the turbine house and bid my pal "good night". He said "I will

ring you up on the telephone and let you hear the colliery
buzzer hooting the old year out between 11.58 and 12.2 a.m."

'I got my gunnie (lamp) and went down. From the bottom
of the shaft to the pumps the distance was 500 yards or so. When
I got to the pump house I sat down for a breather, but I had
only sat down for a few seconds when I saw a large moth flying
around. I had a good look at it and discovered it to be a Death's-
Head Moth. I tried to knock it down with my cloth cap, and
missed it, and after chasing it for about five yards I got tired of
it and sat down to get my wind.

'I was at the cross road, and directly in front of me the road
turned to the right and inclined. On my right a manhole (recess)
was cut from the coal face. As I sat in solitude and deathly
silence I heard the distinct clatter of a pony's hooves and har-
ness and chains approaching. The row stopped and an arm
lunged out of the manhole and grabbed at the pony, which
turned around and went back into the mine. The pony and arm
shone fairly clearly. Believe me, chum, I was in a hell of a
pickle. I then examined my lamp flame for any signs of gas
and then made my way back to the pump house. Just as I got
in, the phone rang (about 11.55 p.m.) My pal at bank (surface)
said "Are you all right, Tom?" I replied "Yes, Joe." He said
"You had better come to bank for half an hour or so, as I have
a bottle of beer." When I entered the turbine house, Joe said to
me "Hell! One would think you had seen a ghost!" So I told
him of my experience and we agreed to say nothing to anyone.
Three months after this I asked our enginewright whether there
was any occasion when someone was hurt or killed in the disused mine seam. He gave me a keen look and replied, "A
laddie was killed there one New Year's Eve, by a runaway
pony." But that is only half the story. Years afterwards I
happened to be in a miners' home at Leamside. I was mending
a man's wireless for him and while I was doing this I told him
of my experience. While I was talking he never said a word until
I finished. He then said "Aye lad, that's reet, ah was there at
the time and helped to carry him out." As he said this, a picture
fell from the wall. The glass and string were not broken, nor
was the nail out of the wall . . .'

In reply to further queries, Mr. Gibbon filled in a few further
details. The mine in which he saw the ghost was Littleburn
Colliery, County Durham. His pal in the turbine house was
Joe Hope. The colour of the Death's-Head Moth was 'grey to
buff' and in chasing it he had no wish to kill, but simply to
examine it. The enginewright who told him about the lad

being killed was David Pearson, who died about fifteen years ago. The name of the man whose wireless he was helping to mend, and who helped to carry out the dead lad, was Mr. Robson. I asked Mr. Gibbon: 'When you say that the pony and arm shone fairly clearly, do you mean that they shone by the electric light in the working, or by your lamp?' His answer to this was, 'There was no light other than my oil safety lamp. The pony and arm appeared to be luminous and phosphorescent.'

The reference made by my informant, Mr. Gibbon to the Death's-Head Moth is interesting, because there is in Yorkshire a long-standing belief that night-flying moths are the souls of the departed. Bulgarians used to believe that at death the soul assumed the form of a butterfly.

There are many stories of haunted mines. In the last century a mine at Wheal Vor was said to be haunted and a watcher reported that he heard a sound 'like the emptying of a cartload of rubbish' in front of the account house where he was staying. *The Times* of September 21, 1874 reported that men employed in some of the Bedworth collieries refused to descend because of a ghost. And the apparition of a woman was once supposed to haunt Polbreen Mines, Cornwall.

Shropshire folk-lore includes a legend (I call it legend in the absence of acceptable written records, although for generations it was recounted as a fact) of a ghostly bull at Bagbury. It was the ghost of a wicked man who, in the form of a phantom bull, terrified the neighbourhood before being run to earth by twelve parsons in Hyssington Church, with bell, book and candle. But ghostly bulls, it would seem, are no more docile than the real variety and, indignant if not contemptuous of all this ecclesiastical showmanship, it charged the wall of the church and cracked it from top to bottom!

Cobham, Surrey has amongst its numerous ghosts, a blue donkey, which a party of bell-ringers claimed to have seen near St. Andrew's Church.

One author (Mr. Pierre Van Paasen) has described in a book *Day of our Years* an almost incredible story of a ghostly dog which he met in France. A big black dog brushed past him one evening, producing as it did so the same 'creepy' and chilling feeling one associates with the proximity of ghosts. On looking for the animal—in a house where windows and doors were closed and there was absolutely no other exit—it was simply not to be found. He saw the black dog several times thereafter, and mindful that people might think he was going off his head if he related his experience with no other corroboration, he asked a friend and his sturdy son to come and keep watch with him. This they did, and the dog not only appeared to all of them, but wagged its tail when they whistled to it. But as they approached closer, it faded into thin air. Two police dogs brought in to keep watch not only bristled with terror at the sight of the spectre dog, but one of them fought as with an invisible foe and then dropped dead.

A most peculiar feature of this haunting was that it appeared to be associated with the presence in the house of a girl in a state of puberty for when she left the house, the disturbances ceased. It has often been noted that psychic disturbances frequently coincide with the presence of children in puberty. No one, whether doctors or scientists or psychiatrists or any other class of person who might be expected to be assisted by their professional knowledge, has ever been able to explain satisfactorily why this should be.

In an earlier chapter I referred to the ghost of a bear seen in the Tower of London. The authority for this is Edmund Lenthal Swifte, Keeper of the Crown Jewels in the Tower of London from 1814 onwards. In an article in *Notes and Queries* in 1860 he wrote at some length of the many strange occurrences in the Tower, including this one. A sentry was alarmed by a figure of a bear rising up from underneath the Jewel Room door. When he attacked it with his bayonet and observed it to go through the 'beast' harmlessly, he fainted. Mr. Swifte took not only the testimony of this sentry, but of another, who maintained that his friend had been his usual cheerful, quiet and efficient self. The stricken guard died of fright.

In a work with the agreeable title *Satan's Invisible World Discovered*, by George Sinclair, there is a reference to a ghostly dog which haunted a house in St. Mary's Close, Edinburgh. The wife of the occupant (Mr. Thomas Coltheart), was reading at home one day when she was astounded to see, floating in the air, the apparition of the head of an old man. One night she and her husband both saw the head, together with the head of a child, and a pale, ghostly, disembodied arm reaching menacingly towards the two heads. Later the family was plagued by a ghostly black dog, which would jump in a chair and then vanish.

It is not part of my self-imposed mandate to get lost in the labyrinth of witchcraft, magic and mysticism, but it can at least be remembered, in considering accounts of ghostly animals that there are broadly three theories. Some maintain that animals become ghosts just as human beings are alleged to do; others consider that the ghost of a human being can assume the form of an animal while students or adepts of the occult consider that spectral animals are the 'familiars' of the sorcerer.

Whatever the explanation, it is a fact that reports of the appearances of ghostly animals are far too numerous, and too well corroborated, to be discounted.

18

Can dreams come true?

Although this is a book about ghosts and hauntings, some mention of dreams must be made. For where these appear to have a telepathic effect or origin, or where they prove actually prophetic, not in any vague way such as the fortune-teller often foretells, but in terms of tangible fact, we have evidence of a secret source of mental energy.

The only explanation we have for ghosts, even if we allow for the defects of human observation, the credulity of many people and the hysteria of others, is that in terms of vision or sound or feeling, thoughts are 'projected' or registered, being picked up by others either at the time or later, perhaps generations or centuries later.

The existence of dreams proves that within the human mind much happens which is beyond the scope of the most skilled psychiatrist or scientist to explain.

Freud believed that the most fantastic dreams make sense; that truths are disguised as symbols. 'A dream,' he said, 'never deals with trifles.' The late J. W. Dunne, the scientist who came nearer to proving immortality by scientific argument than any other man of this century, told me that in dreams the mind moved backwards and forwards along the dimension of time at will, with the result that different periods of time become jumbled together in one mental picture.

Before the last war, an old Malayan came into the office of Mr. Sydney Bond, manager of the Milnerton Turf Club totalisator and asked to see the following Saturday's racing programme and the lists of runners. Mr. Bond produced the papers. The Malay glanced idly down them and within seconds had ticked off seven of the horses. 'Those horses will win,' he said, 'I dreamed about them last night.'

A likely story, thought Mr. Bond. The world is full of people who have a certainty until the race is run.

The Malayan, convinced because of the vividness and exactitude of his dream, went frantically from friend to friend trying to raise enough money to back his sevenfold fancy. His pals, understandably, did not consider dreams a good investment, and in the event he turned up at Milnerton racecourse on the Saturday with only two shillings to speculate.

By the time the afternoon was ended he had turned his two shillings into £1,000—which included £700 for the double tote, paid by a cheque which the once-sceptical Mr. Bond had to make out!

Consider the following authentic example of a dream re-uniting a father and son. In March, 1914 the fourteen-year-old son of a man living in Saarbruecken crossed the French frontier and was never heard of again. The father never ceased in his inquiries and 'missing person' notices were sent by the German police all over the world. But in 1938, twenty-four years after the boy's disappearance, the father, by now living in Heiden-heim, dreamed that his son, accompanied by a lady who appeared to be his wife, and two children, stepped from the Paris express on to the platform at Stuttgart.

The dream was so vivid that the father reasoned that if his son were alive and *had* married, he would need to have obtained the necessary birth certificate and similar documents from the authorities at his birthplace, Schiltigheim (Alsace). He wrote to the Mayor of that town and was told that the papers had been sent to his son at the village of Bizots in the department of Soane-et-Loire. The father thereupon wrote to the Mayor of Bizots, and learned from him that his son had moved to the village of Monceaux-les-Mines. At last the father was able to write directly to his son, and contact was established. When the son sent his father a photograph of the family, he at once recognised the woman and the two children he had seen in his dream.

That is a quite extraordinary example of telepathy. The son was constantly in his father's thoughts and somehow an image of the son's family reached him.

It was in Lamport, Northants, that a strange dream tragedy was enacted in 1908, when a young gardener employed at Lam-port Hall was found hanging from a beam in a dingy outhouse.

The Rector of Lamport, the Rev. Walter Pitchford, once had a cook whose behaviour he suspected to be unsatisfactory. To pursue his suspicions, he changed her room, and he himself slept in what had been until then her room. At night he heard the window being raised and a male intruder about to enter by stealth, so the Vicar jammed the window down upon the man, gave him a stiff talking to, and sent him on his way.

Prior to this experience the Rector had found a young gardener, employed at the hall, waiting around for the cook. The lad was clearly in love with her, and when the woman left for another job, he cycled over to see her, until he suffered the shock of discovering that his affections were not returned. He disappeared, and although it was feared that he might have committed suicide, he tried, instead, to join the Navy. The Rector, in supplying a reference to the recruiting office at Bedfoed, gave the lad a first-class character, but the lad was too emotionally disturbed to settle, and disappeared once more. A few days later his body was found hanging in the outhouse.

That had happened in January, but six months later the lad's mother called at the rectory and said that she had had a vivid dream in which her son appeared to her and told her that his jacket, which was missing when his body was found, was hidden in the outhouse, and contained a message for her. Together the Rector and the mother went to the outhouse and, tucked away above one end of the beam they found, not a jacket, but a cap. Inside it was the boy's last message to his mother, describing his unhappy and unrequited love.

Abraham Lincoln, the sixteenth President of the United States, dreamed of his own assassination, the details of which were very close indeed to the fatal scene in the theatre.

The death in 1927 of Isadora Duncan, the beautiful and inspired dancer was attended by two examples of premonition (which could be called a kind of waking dream). A friend of hers, Baron Charles de Richter, and his wife, were travelling by train to Nice to spend a few days with Isadora. Sitting back against the upholstery, half dozing under the almost hypnotic rhythm of the jogging of the wheels, the Baron found a strange and unaccountable sentence going persistently through his mind, keeping in unison with the turning wheels ... *I have a rendezvous with death*. It was a morbid and unacceptable thought at such a time, and as the train drew into Nice he tried to throw off the feeling of gloom. But at the station a friend was waiting to give him the tragic news that, while trying out a new car, Isadora's flowing Spanish shawl had caught up with one of the wheels and strangled her.

Incidentally, Miss Desti, who accompanied Isadora Duncan, had so strong a premonition about the fatal accident that she begged Isadora not to go.

It is far from easy to group experiences into what might broadly be called 'psychic' and manifestations which are paranormal. We are not dealing with a subject in which standards

have been or can be set, although I do not say that this will
never be possible. It is a scientific fact that the working of the
brain involves electrical energy, but it is less generally known,
although established scientifically, that ordinary muscular movements involve the generation of electricity. We just do not
know whether anything that is human is transient, so far as
thought and activity are concerned. They seem to be, but we
are not sure. Religions, superstitions, cults and philosophies
(and they often merge) offer a thousand conflicting dogmatisms,
but the real answer has yet to be found.

What is one to make of the claim of Frank Etchers of Car-
narvonshire that he always smells flowers when passing a house
in which death is about to take place? It is a rather negative
and unsatisfying faculty, but there it is. What of Mr. Aynsley
of Darvel, Ayrshire, who tells me that on a fishing expedition
'all movement and sound stopped', that the heavens appeared to
open and in place of the normal sounds, music and singing
could be heard 'loud and clear'? Why should Miss Edith Wilson,
of Swindon, Wilts, have read *in a dream* a letter which her
father at that moment was in the process of writing in Ireland.
The letter said: 'I am sorry to tell you that poor Aunt Caroline
died last night'. Miss Wilson recorded her dream at the time
and in due course the letter arrived and confirmed every detail
of her dream—even the mistake which her father had made, for
he had written 'Aunt Caroline' when he meant—as his daughter
realised in her dream, because the address related to someone
else—Aunt *Agnes*.

'In my dream,' Miss Wilson told me, 'I knew from the address
whom he meant, because my Aunt Caroline was living in England. In my dream I did not read the first page of the letter;
I turned over and read at the top of the next page.' The link
between Miss Wilson and her father was obviously very close,
because on the night before he died—January 7, 1944—a
phantasm of a woman wearing 'a blouse, bunchy long skirt and
black three-cornered fringe shawl' appeared at her bedside. This
was at her father's home, 'Ardmore', Armagh, Northern Ireland.
The ghost's expression was kindly and Miss Wilson was not
frightened. She just sat up in bed and said 'How extraordinary!'
The ghost was looking at her, but turned quickly away when
Miss Wilson opened her eyes, disappearing through a closed
door.

Stories about haunted theatres are very numerous, and certain theatres, such as Drury Lane, have been so often the scene
of an apparition that whatever the explanation, there must be

'something there'. Stanley Lupino the comedian described at a luncheon in 1923 how he saw the ghost of Dan Leno at Drury Lane Theatre. Having decided to sleep in his dressing room after the show (it was a very wet and stormy night) he had just dozed off when he had a feeling that he was not alone. He saw a shadowy form moving across the room and so positive was he that he went out of his dressing room to find the night watchman and question him. Reassured by the watchman he returned to his room—and there, awakened by a movement, he looked up and saw the face of Dan Leno. The following day his wife saw the same vision in the same room and, terrified, fainted outright.

On April 29, 1944 *The Star* carried a report that Miss Drusilla Wills, who was appearing in *Yellow Sands* saw the ghost of J. B. Buckstone, the actor-manager of the theatre, whose phantom had often been reported as having been seen. 'I was back-stage speaking to a friend,' she said, 'when an elderly man in an old-fashioned suit passed between us. I remarked about him to my friend—and discovered that he hadn't seen him.' Later, seeing a picture of Buckstone, she recognised him as the man whose phantom had passed so near to her. The actor, Victor Leslie, sometimes heard a voice declaiming in one of the Haymarket Theatre's dressing rooms. Once he returned to find a man sitting in his armchair. Alarmed, he rushed out, locking the door after him, but on returning with a fireman and unlocking the door again, the room was quite empty.

The Haymarket Threatre ghost is mentioned by Cyril Maude in his book *The Haymarket Theatre*. 'Personally,' he wrote, 'I have never seen it but two firemen ... declare positively that they have seen a face staring through a window. Our valued business-manager, Mr. Horace Watson, is also inclined to believe in the existence of the Haymarket Ghost, for he declares that he distinctly saw the door of his office open and shut, but upon looking about could find no trace of any human being who could have done it.'

In 1957 the Theatre Royal, Portsmouth, which has often been said to be haunted, was the scene of a strange occurrence. A chorus girl, returning to the Rutland Room on the third floor, found that it wouldn't open. Fireman broke in—but found that the door was unlocked!

I am often asked, because of my interest in ghosts and hauntings whether I 'believe in ghosts'. The question is an over-simplification. I do not doubt the testimony of hundreds of people over the centuries. I say 'hundreds' because that would be the minutest proportion of the many thousands who have testified to seeing phantasms and other extraordinary phenomena. The prevalence of such testimonies cannot in my view be dismissed as the product of disordered senses, the delusions of those predisposed to believe in such things, or illusions produced by abnormal atmospheric conditions. The persistence of certain types of haunting, the very great number of phantasms which have appeared at the moment of death, and the degree of corroboration which exists with many known hauntings, makes me say, if I am asked the usual question: 'Ghosts do exist, but don't ask me what they are or what conditions cause them to appear, or why some people see them and others don't. It is a mystery which may be solved one day, but there is a great deal yet to discover. In the meantime, laugh if you wish; I agree that there's nothing quite so funny as the idea of a ghost—until you happen to meet one.'

THE "GHOST'S" HOUSE IN COCK LANE.   (see page 97)